STAR GAZING
THROUGH
BINOCULARS
A COMPLETE GUIDE TO
BINOCULAR ASTRONOMY

D1716176

Dedicated to the Big Pootsk

STAR GAZING
THROUGH
BINOCULARS
A COMPLETE GUIDE TO
BINOCULAR ASTRONOMY

STEPHEN MENSING,
ILLUSTRATIONS BY ANNE SHEPPARD

TAB BOOKS Inc.
Blue Ridge Summit, PA 17214

Notices

Astromak is a trademark of Astro Works Corp.
Banner, Explorer II, Insta-Forcus, and Sportview
are registered trademarks of the Bushnell, Division of Bausch & Lomb.
Binolux is a registered trademark of Compass Instrument Co.
Celestron is a registered trademark of Celestron International.
Formica is a registered trademark of Formica Company.
Fujinon is a registered trademark of Fuji Optical Co.
Lumicon is a registered trademark of Lumicon.
Milco is a registered trademark of I. Miller Optical.
Mirador is a registered trademark of Mirador Optical Corporation.
Meade is a registered trademark of Meade Instruments Corporation.
Nikon is a registered trademark of Nikon Inc.
Olympus is a registered trademark of Olympus.
Pentax is a registered trademark of Pentax Inc.
Scope City is a registered trademark of Tomlin Industries.
Slik is a registered trademark of Berkey Marketing Co.
Solar-Skreen and Stereoocular are registered trademarks of Roger W. Tuthill, Inc.
Swift is a registered trademark of Swift Instruments Inc.
Tasco and Tasco Halley's Comet Series are registered trademarks of Tasco Sales Inc.
Teflon is a trademark of Du Pont de Nemours & Co.
Velbon is a registered trademark of Velbon International Corp.
Zeiss is a registered trademark of Carl Zeiss Inc.

FIRST EDITION
FIRST PRINTING

Copyright © 1986 by TAB BOOKS Inc.
Printed in the United States of America

Library of Congress Cataloging in Publication Data

Mensing, Stephen.
Star gazing through binoculars.

Includes index.
1. Astronomy—Observers' manuals. 2. Binoculars.
I. Title.
QB64.M36   1986   522   86-5848

ISBN 0-8306-2703-0 (pbk.)

Contents

Acknowledgments

I would like to offer my special thanks to the many people and organizations who assisted me in preparing *Star Gazing through Binoculars: A Complete Guide to Binocular Astronomy*. It is their book, too.

The outstanding astrophotography is from a number of professional observatories and some of America's top amateur astrophotographers, including: Dr. Jack B. Marling, Ron Potter, Jim Riffle, Lee C. Coombs, Dr. Steven Simmerman, John E. Westfall, Paul Maxson, John Stiles, Al Takeda, Paul Kandle and Dan Stosuy, who also contributed most of the binocular-related photographs.

The observatories and organizations contributing photographs are: The Lick Observatory; The National Solar Observatory; The Canada-France-Hawaii Telescope; The Kitt Peak National Observatory; The Cerro Tololo Inter-American Observatory; The United States Naval Observatories at Flagstaff, Arizona and at Washington, D.C.; Meade Instruments Corporation; JPL/NASA; The ALPO Solar Division; and The Space Environment Services Center/The Space Environment Laboratory.

I would also like to thank my illustrator, Anne Sheppard, and the following individuals and their organizations for their input, charts, forms, and valuable information:

Dr. Janet A. Mattei and the A.A.V.S.O., Dr. Milton Friedman and the Rittenhouse Astronomical Society, Dr. David D. Meisel and the American Meteor Society, Joy Crist and the Willingboro Astronomical Society, the University City New Moon Society, Irv Miller, Dr. Wolfgang Rao, Alan Daroff, Richard E. Hill, the Association of Lunar and Planetary Observers, the British Astronomical Association, the Minor Planet Center of the Smithsonian Astrophysical Observatory, Molly Sayvetz (a living dictionary), Lee Cain and his valuable papers and photographs, Roger Re, Barbara Mellman, Linda Waible, Joseph A. Gordon, W. Bruce Cavey, Del Hurd, Caroline Meline, Albert Miccio, Barry Proctor, Robert Henderson, Bruce K. Mercer, and James O'Connell.

I would like to thank the following commercial concerns for sending me photographs and information about their products: Celestron International; Bushnell, Division of Bausch & Lomb; Optical Guidance Systems; R.V.R. Optical; Fujinon; Swift Instruments; Lumicon; Roger W. Tuthill, Inc.; Pentax Corporation; I. Miller Optical; Steiner (Pioneer & Co.); Meade Instruments; Swarovski Optik; Jason/Empire; Tasco; Zeiss; Lichtenknecker Optics; and Astro-works.

Introduction

Binocular astronomy offers a multitude of pleasures and wonders: aesthetic views of rich star clusters, tinted double stars, and curiously shaped nebulae. The challenges of becoming a keen-eyed observer and becoming involved in a world remote from your daily living. The opportunity to monitor the week-by-week, month-by-month, and year-by-year variations in a star's luminosity. The visceral pleasure of looking back in time at light beginning its journey millions of years ago from some distant galaxy. The fun of shopping for that first astronomical binocular or of overcoming the difficulties inherent in assembling an instrument from surplus parts. The joy of learning firsthand about the science of astronomy, of discovering a comet or nova, of going outdoors and feeling a part of the universe as you look heavenward, of enjoying affiliation and friendships in an astronomy club, of taking lunar snapshots with a camera and binoculars, and of learning about yourself through meeting the challenges of a hobby.

Fellow amateur astronomer—whether you are a "casual" sky-watcher whose viewing is done briefly and only during warmer seasons or a "serious" observer who undertakes useful research—this hobby is aimed at you. The casual sky-watcher can find much in binocular astronomy to sate his curiosity, and surprisingly, the serious observer might employ only his naked eyes or hand-held binoculars and find enough research projects to fill a lifetime.

Many amateur astronomers labor under the belief that they must own large-aperture telescopes, filar micrometers, photoelectric photometers, Schmidt cameras, chilled emulsion cameras, H-alpha filters, blink microscopes, and other highly involved gadgetry to do serious amateur research. Not so! Common hand-held binoculars with objective lenses of 50mm or larger and often just your naked eyes will permit you to discover comets and novae, do lunar occultations, discover new meteor showers, attempt magnitude observations of the brighter asteroids, follow the changes in several types of variable stars, make magnitude studies of comets as well as measure their position angles and tail lengths, and make useful observations about a whole range of meteor activity.

If you are a casual sky-watcher who has no hankering after research, you will likely find a good many chapters to occupy your interest when you read this book. After being greeted by a mini-history of astronomical binoculars, the more casual peruser of the heavens will find information on the binoculars' characteristics, as well as how to shop for, test, use, care for, clean, and repair binoculars. Other topics touched upon will be building binoculars, observing artificial satellites, and choosing the right star atlas. Next the binocularist will meet up with our solar system, where he will find an observational guide to the Sun, our Moon, the planets, the asteroids, comets, and meteors. Further chapters cover how to employ binoculars in the observation of double stars, variable stars, and deep-sky objects, such as galaxies, nebulae, and open and globular clusters.

Lastly, a constellation-by-constellation guide to the heavens is included, containing copious lists and descriptions of deep-sky objects, multiple star systems, and variable stars within the grasp of binoculars. This guide can be used by observers dwelling in both Northern and Southern hemispheres.

In rugged economic times, the binocular might be considered the instrument of first choice for the novice amateur astronomer. Nowadays telescopes are expensive items. A good 6-inch Newtonian reflector with a decent mount and clock drive will cost in the vicinity of $500 to $600. Cheaper Dobsonian reflectors—those masters of the dark skies that look like circus cannons—run around $300 and up. Fine, long focal length, 3-inch refractors start at $500, and those increasingly popular Schmidt-Cassegrains begin at $1,000. Good 7 × 50 binoculars appear to be the best buy at its starting price of $80, and binoculars are more likely to be used by the beginner (and

the advanced fellow) because of the binoculars' portability and ease of use. On a very cold night, you will tend to look more favorably on lugging out a device weighing 38 ounces rather than something 60 pounds or more with a mirror not wishing to cool down.

You might bear in mind that some of us are dabblers who never stay too long with a hobby. If this later proves to be your situation, you will find it far easier to store binoculars than to closet a large and cumbersome telescope. With binoculars you will be left with an instrument capable of offering you excellent terrestrial views.

This book is aimed at both the rural and urban amateur astronomer. The city dweller, although suffering the disadvantages of light polluted skies, will still have many celestial delights from which to choose. Just about every sky phenomenon can be viewed through binoculars: nebulae, galaxies, comets, asteroids, planets, variable and multiple stars, clusters of all types, the Sun (when properly filtered), our Moon, Jupiter's moons, and telescopic meteors. A first-hand education of the heavens can be had for a minimum of expense. As long as the skies remain clear, you will have a highly pleasurable and absorbing hobby—and even when those skies are overcast I hope I have given you plenty to read. Uncase those binoculars and go enjoy yourself!

Chapter 1

A Short History of Binoculars

The history of binoculars commences with the invention of the telescope in 1608 by Hans Lippershey (Fig. 1-1), an obscure spectacle-maker from the Dutch city of Middleburg. One of the more accepted legends has it that after Lippershey left his shop one morning, a young apprentice amused himself with a pair of lenses. Holding the lenses in a straight line a short distance from each other, the apprentice directed them toward an open window and noticed that a far-off church spire appeared larger and much closer. When the master returned, the young apprentice demonstrated what occurred with the simple concave and convex lenses. Old Lippershey quickly recognized the telescope's economic possibilities and the need for a tube to contain the optical elements. He must have wondered how long someone would be willing to hold two lenses and keep them in steady alignment. A lacquered parchment roll served as the first tube.

Essentially a binocular's optics work on the same principles as a refracting telescope (Fig. 1-2). Light from a distant object passes through the objective lens and is bent or refracted, causing the beam to converge into an image some distance from the objective lens. At the beam's converging point, the image is magnified by a smaller lens or set of lenses called an *eyepiece*.

A short time after the telescope's discovery, Lipper-shey demonstrated the telescope—then called a *perspeculum*—to the States General, Prince Maurice of Nassau. Holland at that period was undergoing a war for independence against the armies of King Phillip II of Spain. The initial meeting between Lippershey and Prince Maurice led to the development of binoculars because a request was made for a telescope that might be used with both eyes at the same time. Prince Maurice believed binoculars might prove more suitable for military purposes than a single spyglass. Perhaps the States General fancied stereoscopic vision and the possibility that his military men might not have to face straining with one eye. In any event the first commercially made telescope was a pair of binoculars with rock crystal lenses (a difficult glass to select and work) and was sold to Holland for 900 florin. Binoculars remain as two refractor telescopes hinged side by side.

Nearly a half century would pass before the binocular system received its first major improvements. In the mid-1600s, the initial single-lens eyepiece got supplanted when the astronomer and famed Renaissance man Christiaan Huygens improved the eyepiece's field of view by using two widely separated lenses to form a compound negative eyepiece, or what we know today as the Huygenian eyepiece (Fig. 1-3). In the mid-1700s these lenses

Fig. 1-1. Hans Lippershey, the inventor of the telescope and binoculars (Drawing by Anne Sheppard).

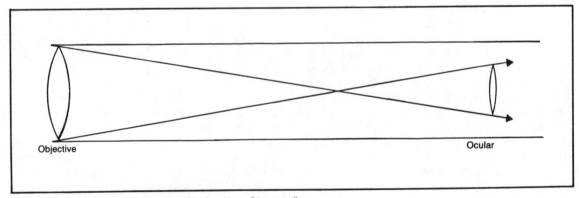

Objective

Ocular

Fig. 1-2. A refracting telescope (Drawing by Anne Sheppard).

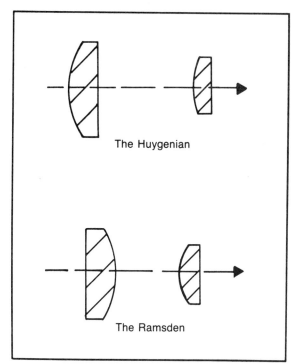

Fig. 1-3. Two early eyepieces: the Huygenian and the Ramsden.

were rearranged by an Englishman, Jesse Ramsden, so that two identical plano-convex lenses were mounted with their convex faces toward each other. The Ramsden eyepiece (Fig. 1-3) proved to have far less *spherical aberration* (a situation caused by the spherical form of a lens in which light rays fail to converge at a single point, but instead focus at a series of points whose distances vary) than the Huygenian eyepiece. Later these two designs gave way to the Kellner and the Erfle (Fig. 1-4) eyepieces which dominate today's binocular scene.

The objective lens end of the binocular underwent a dramatic change in the mid-1700s owing to the discovery of the achromatic principle in lenses by an Englishman named Chester Moor Hall. The early refracting telescopes and binoculars suffered from *chromatic aberration*, a problem caused by the differences in refraction of colored light rays. For example, red light is less *refracted*, or bent than blue light. False colors arise in an image viewed through a refractor telescope, creating a purple haze around bright astronomical objects such as Venus and Sirius.

Chester Moor Hall solved the problem of chromatic aberration by combining a concave flint glass lens with a properly shaped convex lens of crown glass. In the

mid-1750s, John Dolland, another Englishman, rediscovered the principle of the achromatic lens (Fig. 1-5). He began manufacturing achromatic objective lenses, in the process shortening the refracting telescope and solving chromatic aberration.

In 1851 an Italian, M. Porro, invented the first prismatic inverting system. Originally intended to shorten the tube length of the telescope, the Porro prism (Fig. 1-6) was marketed as *lunette á Napolean Troisieme*. Retaining the name *Porro prism*, the system consists of two identical prisms housed in the binocular barrel near the eyepiece. Almost like mirrors, these prisms reflect and reverse light off their steep sides. One of the duo's prisms reverts the image from left to right, while the second prism inverts the image from top to bottom, delivering an image erect and normal to your eyes.

Roof prisms (Fig. 1-7) employed in lightweight and more expensive, H-shaped binoculars, were invented shortly before 1900 in the optical workshops of Carl Zeiss at Jena, Germany by Ernst Abbe. A young physics professor at the University of Jena and the formulator of the mathematical laws for the paths of light through a microscope, Abbe, along with chemist Otto Schott, invented the first high-quality, reproducible optical glass. Using his own formulae and optical glass, Abbe also created powerful microscopes for Louis Pasteur.

The roof and Porro prisms have added immeasura-

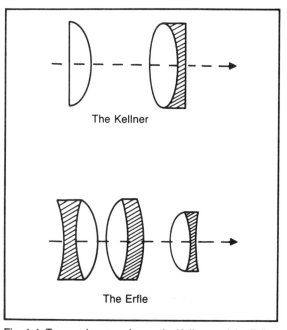

Fig. 1-4. Two modern eyepieces: the Kellner and the Erfle.

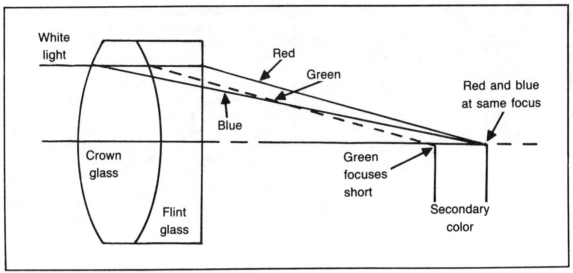

Fig. 1-5. An achromatic lens.

bly to the binoculars' usefulness. The prismatic systems increased the binoculars' *focal length* (the distance between the objective lens and the eyepiece), making it capable of higher magnification without employing longer barrels. There have also been some claims about the use of prisms increasing the distance between the binoculars'

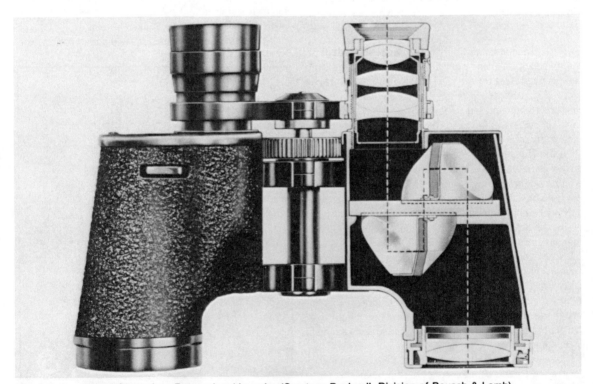

Fig. 1-6. A cutaway of a modern Porro prism binocular (Courtesy Bushnell, Division of Bausch & Lomb).

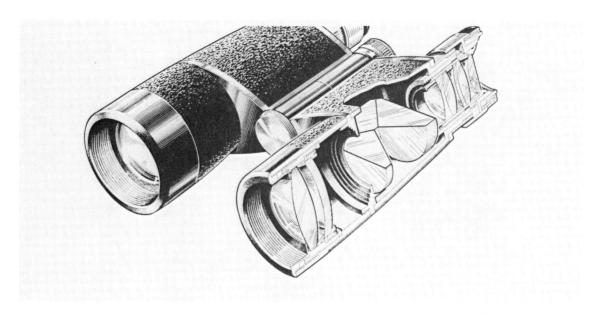

Fig. 1-7. A cutaway of a modern roof prism binocular (Courtesy Bushnell, Division of Bausch & Lomb).

Fig. 1-8. Some binoculars and field glasses from the first 45 years of this century at I. Miller Optical (Photograph by Dan Stosuy).

Fig. 1-9. The Celestron 10 × 50 Nova. All of the optical elements are fully coated with multicoatings (Courtesy Celestron International).

objectives and thus giving a widened perspective that enhances depth perception and stereoscopic vision, yet this does not hold up under scientific scrutiny.

This brief history of binoculars can not be concluded without rementioning the creators of today's modern eyepieces: Karl Kellner and Dr. Erfle. Both of their inventions added to the increased clarity and field of view we enjoy today when we observe the night sky.

The eyepiece invented by Karl Kellner, an optician from Wetzlar, Germany, is made with an overcorrected lens pair with its flint component facing the eye. The field lens, placed just within the anterior focal plane of the eye lens, is either bioconvex or plano-convex and produces a low magnification viewing field around 45 degrees.

The Erfle eyepiece, developed for wide-field and extra wide field binoculars, was introduced at the Zeiss works by Dr. Erfle at the turn of this century. This eyepiece provides a broad flat field and contains between five and eight lens elements. Most Erfle eyepieces found in binoculars possess five elements.

The last major innovation in binocular optics came during World War II when Bausch & Lomb developed hard coating for lenses for the improvement of light transmission. Prior to Bausch & Lomb's lens-coating process, binoculars required larger objective lenses to have adequate illumination (Fig. 1-8). Almost 4 percent of the light was lost due to the reflective properties of each optical surface. With nearly twelve optical surfaces per binocular barrel, only 50 percent of the available light reached the eye. With hard coating, however, a film of fluoride, generally magnesium fluoride, is vaporized onto the optics at high temperatures in a vacuum. The coatings get applied to every optical surface, be it a lens or a prism at the thickness of a quarter wavelength of light. Fully coated glasses (Fig. 1-9) reach 75 to 78 percent light efficiency and put a damper on the internal reflective haze that reduces image contrast and produces ghosts when the Moon, Venus, and bright stars are viewed.

Chapter 2

Binoculars

Essentially binoculars are two small refractor telescopes mounted side by side for comfortable viewing with both eyes (Fig. 2-1). An optical instrument enabling us to gather more light than the naked eye, binoculars also permit us to see more detail in distant objects. Each barrel contains a series of prisms—either Porro or roof style—arranged so the viewing image is normal, or correct, both from top to bottom and from left to right. From the purist's vantage, the modern-day binocular is a prism containing "glass" as opposed to the nonprism instrument, the field glass. Binoculars are optically superior and more compact than field glasses with their longer, straight-through, Galilean systems. A pair of binoculars might in rare instances be created out of dual Newtonian mirror systems (Fig. 2-2).

WHY BINOCULARS FOR ASTRONOMY?

Stacked against our naked eyes, binoculars offer both superior resolution and light grasp, making finer detail and dimmer objects more readily observable. The Moon will show more craters and mountains, and faint deep-sky objects such as galaxies (Fig. 2-3) and nebulae will be more accessible. Current studies report that binocular vision might give about a 40-percent gain in visibility to low-contrast objects such as galaxies and nebulae. Contrast is even more important than brightness in hunting out many deep-sky objects.

When compared with a telescope, binoculars deliver a wider field of view, less eye strain, a more realistic picture, and the ease of hand-held portability. The wider field of view, often called *rich field*, is more conducive to exploring starfields in the Milky Way (Fig. 2-4), galactic clusters, and areas where galaxies abound. Binoculars, owing to its dual eyepieces, offer a much more relaxed view than a telescope. Using both eyes at the same time is much less straining than squinting with one eye open at the telescope ocular. Our brain is habituated to looking through both eyes and comparing data from both eyes so that data is integrated into a single image. Binocular vision assists the brain in confirming a "real" image and disconfirming the impure messages sent from individual eyes as floaters. The hand-held portability of binoculars speaks for itself. There is no setting up.

When compared to the average "fast" reflector telescope, the binocular lens system offers superior image contrast—stars appear crisper and brighter against a darker sky. I don't want to be too harsh—telescopes are plenty of fun too! They also have certain advantages, but this is a book about binocular astronomy.

Fig. 2-1. A Zeiss 8 × 56 B Dialyt binocular (Courtesy Zeiss Optical Inc.).

BINOCULAR CHARACTERISTICS:
MAGNIFICATION

Magnification brings distant objects closer and makes them appear larger, thus increasing detail. Through 7 × binoculars, a target 700 feet away will appear 100 feet away. The magnification, or power, of a pair of binoculars can be found engraved on the barrel plate (Fig. 2-5) near the eyepiece. The magnification number is the first number in 7 × 50. Thus *7* is the magnification a *50* is the diameter in millimeters of the *objective lens*, the largest lens at the end of the binocular. In a pair of 11 × 80 giant binoculars (Fig. 2-6), *11* is the magnification and *80* is the objective lens's diameter.

Magnification is controlled by the optical design of the binoculars. The magnification of any such instrument can be found by dividing the *focal length* of the objective lens, which is the distance of the objective lens to the focal point, by the focal length of the eyepiece. Thus if the focal length of a 50mm objective lens is 210mm and the focal length of the eyepiece is 30mm, the magnification or power would be 7 × .

Problems travel with high mangification in binoculars. Image brightness falls off. The field of view becomes restricted. Hand-holding binoculars over 11 power becomes prohibitive because of vibration of the image. For this reason, the cutoff point for most hand-held glasses is somewhere between 8 and 11 power. Higher-powered binoculars also tend to be heavier owing to their larger objective lenses.

BINOCULAR CHARACTERISTICS:
RESOLUTION

Resolution, or clarity of image, is defined by the smallest pair of double lines that can be viewed through binoculars (Fig. 2-7). It is the quality of resolution that permits us to cleanly split double stars and make out the nightly shuttling of Jupiter's four brightest moons.

Resolution highly depends on how well the objective lenses have been corrected for the various aberrations. Binocular objectives are mostly cemented achromatic doublets. In fine astronomical binoculars, the highest-quality optical glass is chosen and on occasion the objective lenses will be air-spaced. In these expensive lenses there is very little striation. The figuring accuracy and polishing is first rate because light waves must pass through the objective with a minimum of distortion.

Hallmarks of a very good resolving pair of binoculars are that it seems to focus slowly and has a wide latitude for focusing. Image is resolved through the field of view, which is sharp to the center as well as the edges. Poor resolution forces the eye to strain and may cause headaches.

BINOCULAR CHARACTERISTICS:
FIELD OF VIEW

The *field of view* is the visible area of view afforded by stationary binoculars (Fig. 2-8). Field of view depends on the relationship between the diameter size of the eyepiece (the circular diaphram prior to the field lens) and the focal length of the objective lens. Field of view is expressed as width and is measured in feet of field you are observing at 1000 yards. Such measurements are engraved on the binocular barrel right below the magnification and objective size. Example: *378 feet at 1000 yards.* Often this measurement is expressed in meters on foreign binoculars.

Lower-powered binoculars tend to have larger fields

Fig. 2-2. A pair of Newtonian mirror-system binoculars: Lee Cain's Mammoth 13-inch Dobsonian (Courtesy Lee Cain).

Fig. 2-3. M81, an Sp spiral galaxy in Ursa Major, as photographed by the four-meter reflector at Kitt Peak (Courtesy National Optical Observatories).

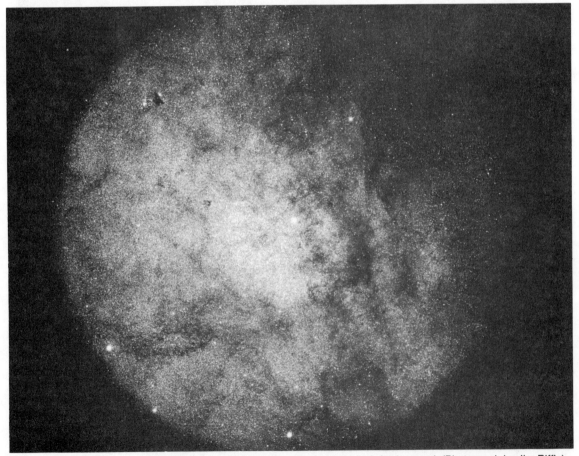

Fig. 2-4. The Milky Way in Sagittarius (Barnard 86); photographed with 12-inch f/5 Astromak (Photograph by Jim Riffle).

Fig. 2-5. The barrel plate of Swift 7×50 Mark II Commodore binoculars (Photograph by Dan Stosuy).

of view since field decreases as magnification increases. Wider fields give more panoramic views and an attendant feeling of expansiveness. Wide-field binoculars are the glasses of choice when it comes to comet hunting, nova searching, and scanning the rich and nebulous star fields of the Milky Way. Most wide-field binoculars use Erfle eyepieces with their corrected five elements and large-diameter field lenses (Fig. 2-9). Typical wide-angle glasses will be 10 degrees at 7×, 8.5 degrees at 8×, and 7 degrees at 10×. Extra wide angle glasses come as large as 10 and 12 degrees.

A full Moon subtends an angle of about 1/2 degree, so a field of view of 5 degrees would be ten full moons across. Since 1 degree is 52.5 feet at 1,000 yards, you can learn the degrees in the field of view by dividing the

footage expressed on the binocular barrel by 52.5 feet. If 377 feet were divided by 52.5, you would find that the binoculars would be 7 degrees at 1,000 yards.

Wide field glasses tend to be more expensive and stubby looking, and weigh more because they have larger prisms and five element oculars. Standard binoculars offer fields of view between 5 and 8 degrees, with generally sharper images at the field's edge.

Another fact should be mentioned; eyeglass wearers will find that fully extended eyecups will cut off some of the field of view.

Before this discussion of the field of view is concluded, I want to mention the problem of real field versus apparent field. *Apparent field* in binoculars is set by the angular diameter of the ocular field stop as seen through

Fig. 2-6. Celestron 11×80 binoculars (Courtesy Celestron International).

the ocular from the observer's eye. The *real field* is the angular diameter of the sky whose image is included in the apparent field.

BINOCULAR CHARACTERISTICS:
EYEPOINT, EYE RELIEF, AND EXIT PUPIL

The full field of view in binoculars is offered when the eye is at the correct distance from the ocular's outer lens and centered in the focused cone of light. This optimum position in the light cone is called the *eyepoint*. The distance of the eyepoint behind the eye lens is known as *eye relief* and is highly important to the eyeglass wearer and those binocular astronomers who desire comfortable viewing. Insufficient eye relief occurs when the observer is forced to hold the binoculars too close to his eyes and thus

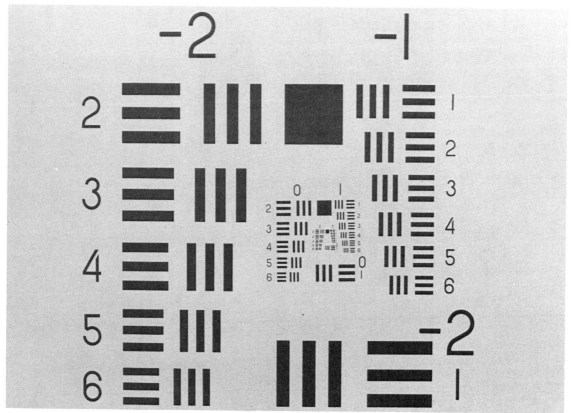

Fig. 2-7. A resolution chart for testing optics at I. Miller Optical. Note that this chart has been reduced slightly (Photograph by Dan Stosuy).

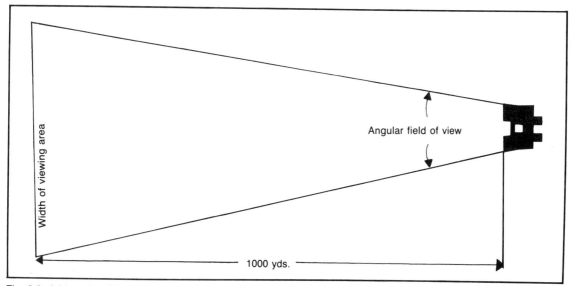

Fig. 2-8. A binoculars' field of view at 1,000 yards (Drawing by Anne Sheppard).

Fig. 2-9. A wide-field 7 × 50: the Swift Mark II Commodore with a 10-degree field (Photograph by Dan Stosuy).

pressure his eye sockets. Eyeglass wearers often need to fold down the binoculars' eyecups in order to attain a full field of view.

The exit pupil, or *Ramsden disk*, is that bright circle of light leaving the eyepiece. Its total area is a measure of light transmission. The exit pupil can be seen when the glass is held facing a bright light source. It is found mathematically by dividing the objective lens size by the magnification. For astronomical purposes, the exit pupil should correspond to the eye pupil. Under dark-sky conditions, the human eye pupil will be approximately 7mm

in diameter. If the exit pupil of the binocular is larger than the eye pupil, the difference will cause light to fall unused on the iris.

BINOCULAR CHARACTERISTICS: RELATIVE BRIGHTNESS

Because adequate light is required to see dim objects and to gauge color in stars, the term *relative brightness* has special meaning to the binocular astronomer. The binoculars must be able to gather and transmit enough available light to produce a bright image and good definition.

Fig. 2-10. A comparison of objective lens size between 80mm and 50mm binoculars (Photograph by Dan Stosuy).

Four major factors govern image brightness in a pair of binoculars. The first, and likely the most important, figures to be an objective lens's size (Fig. 2-10). The more lens area, the more light gathered and sent back to the ocular. The second major factor in the image brightness of binoculars is the intensity of light from the source or object viewed. A bright planet such as Jupiter or Venus will offer more light than a dim galaxy. The third factor is the eyepiece's magnification applied to the image. The fourth and final factor is light loss due to the absorption and reflection by the glass elements in the optical system (prisms and lenses). This factor can be offset by the use of optical coatings.

Relative brightness is a comparative measure of the image brightness of one coated glass against another coated glass or of one uncoated glass against another uncoated glass. Coated binoculars can never be compared to uncoated binoculars in measuring the image brightness of a binocular.

Relative brightness can be calculated as follows:

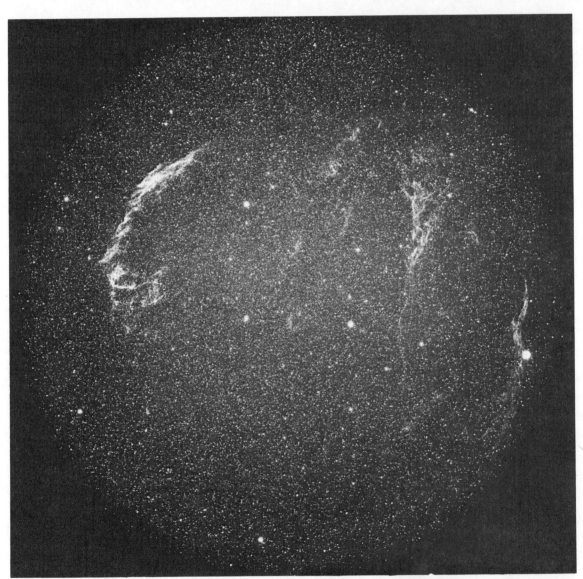

Fig. 2-11. The Veil Nebula in Cygnus; photographed with 12-inch f/5 Astromak (Photograph by Jim Riffle).

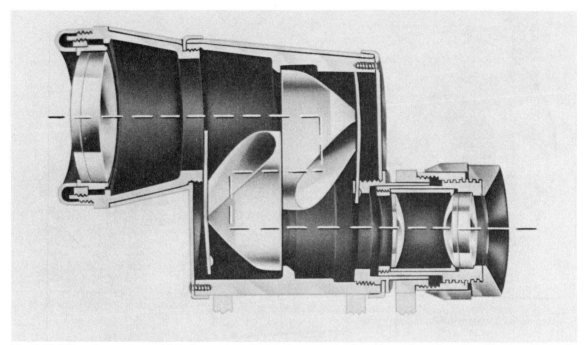

Fig. 2-12. This cutaway view exhibits the many optical surfaces encountered in modern binoculars (Courtesy Bushnell, Division of Bausch & Lomb).

$$Relative\ Brightness = Exit\ Pupil^2$$

BINOCULAR CHARACTERISTICS: TWILIGHT FACTOR

Twilight factor is the measurement of viewing efficiency and image detail under twilight conditions. The larger this factor, the more efficient the dim-light performance. Twilight factor is calculated by taking the square root of the product of both the magnification and the objective lens's diameter in millimeters. Like relative brightness, twilight factor is one more valuable gauge for the binocular astronomer in his hunt for the dim stuff of the night skies: comets, galaxies, and nebulae (Fig. 2-11).

BINOCULAR CHARACTERISTICS: RELATIVE LIGHT EFFICIENCY

Relative light efficiency (R.L.E.) is the increased light transmission produced by coated lenses and prisms. R.L.E., a term coined by the Riecharts of the Mirakel Optical Company, is computed by doubling the relative brightness figure and multiplying it by the percentage of light transmitted.

Relative light efficiency can be increased by the use

of barium crown prisms (10 to 15 percent in the average binoculars) and the use of multicoating (multiple layers of coating on a single surface). Most coatings are dielectric coatings (magnesium fluoride) and get vaporized on optics at high temperatures in a vacuum. The transparent film of magnesium fluoride is a few millionths of an inch thick. Coatings on all optical surfaces can increase the light efficiency of binoculars by as much as 50 percent.

A binocular (Fig. 2-12) may contain from 10 to 16 glass surfaces. Some 4 to 5 percent of the light per surface may be lost through reflection. Coating, because of its antireflection properties, may save as much as 3 percent of the light per optical surface.

Light efficiency is further affected by the light absorbed by the glass and any film or dirt on the glass's surface. Uncoated optics can further hurt the viewing ability by the binoculars by producing ghosting and internal hazing that can severely retard image contrast. Ghosting is caused by bright objects such as bright planets and first-magnitude stars.

Coatings can be examined by pointing the objective lenses at a fluorescent light and looking at the multiple light reflections. All reflections should have a uniform purple-violet cast. Blue and amber might be apparent depending on the coating's thickness. Any white reflections

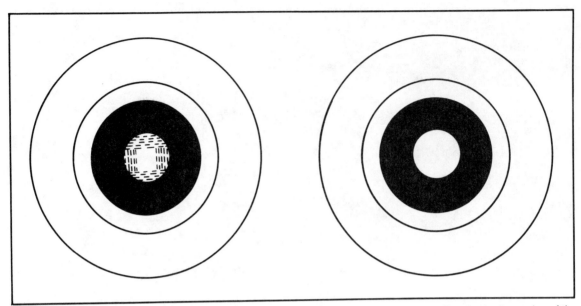

Fig. 2-13. A comparison of the effects of premium and cheaper grades of prisms, showing dimming and squaring of the eyepoint edges (Drawing by Anne Sheppard).

Fig. 2-14. American-style binoculars, from left to right: the Swift 7 × 50 MK II Commodore, an Orion 10 × 70, and a Swift 11 × 80 Observer (Photograph by Dan Stosuy).

will mean uncoated surfaces exist within the binoculars. Many inexpensive glasses only have their objective lenses coated.

In examining the problem of relative brightness, optical glass must be considered. Ordinary crown glass, used in inexpensive binoculars, can reduce the uniformity of brightness. Premium binoculars show uniform bright eyepoints or Ramsden disks. Cheaper prisms show dimming of the circle's four edges, making the circle appear square (Fig. 2-13).

BINOCULAR CHARACTERISTICS:
SHAPE

There are three prevalent shapes in binoculars: the American, the German, and more recently the H shape. The American style, pioneered by Bausch & Lomb, has one-piece bodies with heavy prism holders and separate unit prism plates (Fig. 2-14). Streamlined in appearance, the American style is known to hold its alignment better. The German or Zeiss type is of two pieces with its

Fig. 2-15. The German or Zeiss type binoculars: a Pentax 7×50 ZCF (Courtesy Pentax Corporation).

Fig. 2-16. The H, or roof prism style of binoculars. From left to right: the Swift 7×50 Trylite and the Swift 8×56 Trylite at I. Miller Optical (Photograph by Dan Stosuy).

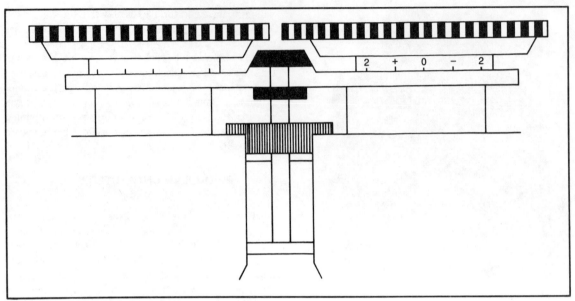

Fig. 2-17. A center focus (Drawing by Anne Sheppard).

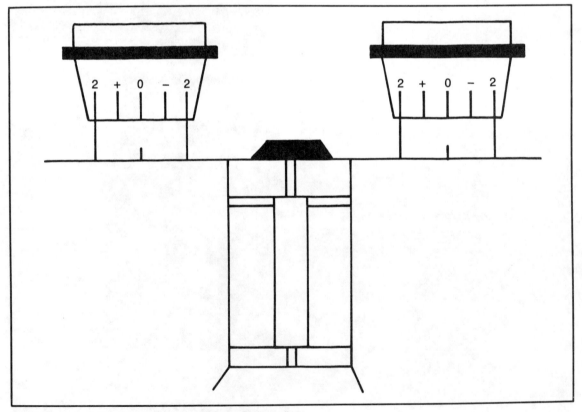

Fig. 2-18. An individual focus (Drawing by Anne Sheppard).

Fig. 2-19. A lever action focus on a Bushnell 10 × 50 Sportview (Photograph by Dan Stosuy).

eyepieces screwing into one end and its objectives screwing into the other (Fig. 2-15). Prism plates are integral parts of the body casting. H, or roof prism, binoculars are lightweight and generally of superior optical quality (Fig. 2-16).

BINOCULAR CHARACTERISTICS: FOCUSING

Focusing comes in three styles: center focus, individual focus, and lever focus (often known as insta-focus). In *center focus*, a focusing wheel is mounted on the center hinge and the right eyepiece is calibrated (Fig. 2-17). The left eyepiece does not adjust. In *individual focus*, two calibrated eyepieces focus separately (Fig. 2-18). In *lever focus*, a fairly recent innovation, a swift lever-type mechanism has replaced the screw-advance center-focus knob (Fig. 2-19).

Although lever focus is the quickest style of focusing, it often does not hold its focus well. The center focus style, even though it focuses fairly rapidly and holds its focus well, has a screw left open to moisture and dust. The individual focus style takes longest to adjust and is now almost extinct among commercial binoculars. However, the individual focus style is sealed from dust and the elements, and it is for this reason that so many military binoculars remain individual focus.

Chapter 3

Shopping
for Astro-Binoculars

The major criterion in choosing astronomical binoculars is the size of the binoculars' objective lenses. For hand-held binoculars, a 50mm objective is the lower limit while 70mm to 80mm rate as the upper limit. Tripod-mounted battleship glasses, possessing 100mm to 150mm objectives, are often seen in comet and nova hunting (Fig. 3-1). Like telescopes, these glasses require heavy support and are extremely expensive. *Standard* sizes are 7×50, 10×50, and 8×56 (Fig. 3-2). *Big* or *giant* binoculars are considered 10×60, 10×70, 11×80, and 20×80 (Fig. 3-3). *Battleship* binoculars come in 16×100, 20×120, and 25×150 sizes. *Mammoth* binoculars are those hulking Dobsonian Newtonian binoculars.

High magnification is not sought after in astro-binoculars. High magnification interferes with the light-gathering capability of the objective lens and makes for a trembling image when the binoculars are hand-held. Again I stress that for hand-held binoculars, the magnification should range from $7 \times$ to the maximum upper limit of $10 \times$ or $11 \times$. Astro-binoculars are basically used as a low-power, rich-field instrument for wide-field aesthetic views, for observing faint nebulous objects, for judging stellar variability, and for comet and nova hunting. Astro-binoculars are also a suitable instrument for learning first hand about the heavens.

When you are shopping for binoculars for astronomical purposes, it would be wise to choose an instrument capable of giving a 7mm exit pupil. Binoculars such as the 7×50, 8×56 (Fig. 3-4), 10×70, and 11×80 will supply a 7mm exit pupil. This size exit pupil is best for dark country skies. Arguments are alive for binoculars with a 5mm exit pupil, such as the common 10×50 (Fig. 3-5). The 10×50 may be used in an area where strong light pollution exits. In an urban environment, with its sky glow, the pupil will shrink to around 5mm or less, so the light of a 7mm exit pupil will be wasted. However, many binocularists will visit the country or the shore where they will want a 7mm exit pupil. My advice is to choose binoculars that can be held in relative comfort, such as the 7×50, 10×50, 8×56, or perhaps the 10×70 if you have a strong and steady grip. The 11×80 is a wonderful glass, but it demands a steady hold. For some of us, the 11×80 might make a solid choice for a second pair of binoculars. Bracing them is a must.

I find a center-focus style to be quite adequate for binocular astronomy. It is less likely to lose focus than lever focus, and it is easier and faster to use than individual focus. Center focus is especially desirable when several people are sharing the same instrument.

Standard field (Fig. 3-6) is recommended over wide

Fig. 3-1. 20×120 armored Battleship binoculars at I. Miller Optical (Photograph by Dan Stosuy).

field and extra wide field because standard field employs smaller prisms and less complex oculars, hence they are lighter. Extra wide field glasses, if they are not extremely well made, might suffer from chomatic aberration on the edge of the field. All lenses and prisms must be fully coated for adequate light transmission. *Note:* stay away from zoom binoculars. Because of their high power, they are difficult to hand-hold without seeing a jumpy image. Zooms also suffer from optical problems because of their sliding Barlow lenses. Sharpness is lacking at the edge of the zoom field and the field is narrow as a result of high magnification.

PURCHASING ASTRONOMICAL BINOCULARS

In 1985, a decent 7×50 pair of astro-binoculars cost around $85 or so. Bargains might be had but I caution you to learn the instrument's list price. Brochures, catalogs, and price lists can be obtained by writing the following recommended manufacturers and importers: Barr

Fig. 3-2. Standard field binoculars: the Bausch & Lomb Discoverer Center Focus (Courtesy Bushnell, Division of Bausch & Lomb).

23

Fig. 3-3. An Orion 10×70 (Photograph by Dan Stosuy).

& Stroud, Bausch & Lomb, Bushnell, Celestron, Zeiss, Meade, Lumicon (Newtonian binoculars), Sky Instruments, Fujinon, Goerz, Hertel & Reuss, Jaegers, Jason/Empire, Kowa, Milco, Mirakel, Nikon, Orion, Pentax, Binolux, Steiner, Swarovski, Parks, Tasco, University, and Swift. Most of these addresses are in Appendix E of this book, or check the advertising sections of astronomy, nature, and photography magazines. Some of the many fine retailers of these instruments are: Scope City, Ad-Libs, I. Miller, Star-tracker, Orion, R.V.R., and Edmund Scientific. Others are listed in Appendix F.

When you are hunting for binoculars, look only at grade B—sometimes called Banner (Fig. 3-7)—and premium grades. Never order directly from the manufacturer because they will charge you list price. Mail-order houses by and large offer the best discounts. Purchase your binoculars with an eye on many years of service (they should last several lifetimes). Look for a 10-year or bet-

ter warranty against defects. A well-made pair of binoculars will have first-rate machining and optics. It will never have loose prisms. Fine binoculars are also less likely to become misaligned after a solid bump. I will further detail these qualities in the coming sections.

Most binoculars nowadays are manufactured in Japan and sold under a wide variety of brand names, as you will quickly learn when you examine glasses and find the familiar little gold tag of the Japan Telescope Institute. American-made binoculars are rare—most American instrument companies import Japanese binoculars and place American brand names on them. Occasionally you will find some excellent glasses made in Hong Kong and Korea. The labor costs are cheap in those countries, but their optical standards are on a par with Japan. England, Germany, and Switzerland turn out some of the finest glasses in the world.

Likely the finest binoculars are manufactured by

Fig. 3-4. Swarovski 8 × 56 binoculars (Courtesy Swarovski Optik).

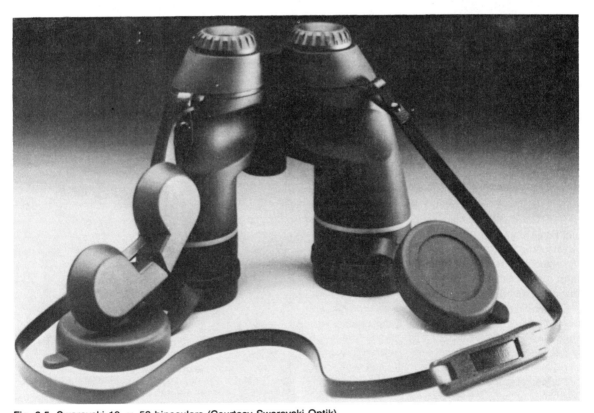

Fig. 3-5. Swarovski 10 × 50 binoculars (Courtesy Swarovski Optik).

25

Fig. 3-6. Standard field binoculars: the Steiner 7 × 50G (Courtesy Pioneer & Co.).

Bausch & Lomb, Barr & Stroud, Celestron, Fujinon, Kowa, Nikon, Ross, Steiner, Swarovski, and Zeiss. You will pay plenty for these first-rate instruments.

If you live in a large urban area, you might have a store specializing in binoculars and telescopes (Fig. 3-8). Check your yellow pages. Advantages exist in buying your binoculars from a local merchant. You will be able to test them and bring them back if they are not up to snuff, and you won't have the additional hassles of paying shipping charges on returns. When you are purchasing binoculars, buy them only conditionally. Binoculars must pass the Star test. Deal only with mail-order houses that allow returns.

Often bargains can be found in trade newspapers and pawn shops, at flea markets and porch and garage sales, from members of your astronomy club, and from swap and sell ads in some of the astronomy magazines. Remember that used glasses have no warranty and sometimes prove no bargain because of optical defects and previous bad handling. However, I have heard of many fine

Fig. 3-7. An example of Grade B, or banner grade, binoculars: Bushnell Banner Insta-Focus binoculars (Courtesy Bushnell, Division of Bausch & Lomb).

Fig. 3-8. The counter at I. Miller Optical (Photograph by Dan Stosuy).

glasses being purchased second hand. Check them thoroughly against the criteria described later in this book.

USING BINOCULARS

A quick lesson in binocular use will benefit the neophyte about to test his first purchase. Using binoculars is a simple enough affair. The initial step will be the adjustment of the instrument's eye separation. *Eye separation*—the distance between a pair of eyes or the interpupillary distance—varies greatly from person to person. It may range from 1 7/8 inches to 3 inches. Generally it is measured in millimeters. Between the eyepieces, in the center of the front hinge, exists a small semicircular scale (Fig. 3-9), which demonstrates the eyepiece separation.

For proper eye separation adjustment, fold the binocular barrels inward until they are closest, then back them out until the full field of view can be seen with both eyes. Both circular fields should merge at this point. Note the scale setting so you can return to it if your glass is handed around or if it must be folded to fit the confines of its case.

The next adjustment will be to focus the right diopter found on all binoculars. Simply focus the left eye on a distant target by moving the center wheel in and out or adjusting the lever focus up and down. When proper focus is accomplished, close your left eye and look through your right while adjusting the diopter to clear focus. Recall the setting for future reference. Diopters are generally marked as follows:

$$2 \quad 1 \quad + \quad 0 \quad - \quad 1 \quad 2.$$

To focus, always look for a distant object exhibiting sharp detail and never focus through a window. Focus as if you were employing a camera. Use the center wheel on center-focus binoculars, keep both eyes open, never squint, and focus in and out until the image is crisp. Lesser-quality instruments will have little travel distance in focus before that crispness is lost. Quality optics will always maintain sharpness over a longer range of focus.

Individual focus on binoculars is a bit more difficult because two diopters are used. Simply adjust one eyepiece at a time while closing one eye and finding the best focus. Then do the same with the other eye. You may also focus with both eyes open, but I find that one eye open at a time works best for me.

Lever focus, or insta-focus, works with a lever instead of a wheel. Lever focus is faster, yet it is valuable only to bird watchers and naturalists. Astronomers don't require speed in focusing.

I should mention that holding your binocular steady is of the utmost importance when you are examining distant detail or attempting to split a double star. A lightweight and well-balanced instrument is easiest to hold. Grasping your binoculars at the point of best balance will minimize shaking and make them more stable to hold. When you are handling those heavier binoculars with 70mm or 80mm objective lenses, you might try holding them close to the objective end and bracing the eyecups against your eye sockets. I've found that this method cuts

Fig. 3-9. The eye separation scale or interpupillary distance scale (Photograph by Dan Stosuy).

Fig. 3-10. The author testing the innards of binoculars with Irv Miller and his wife behind the counter at I. Miller Optical (Photograph by Caroline Meline).

down a good deal on any unsteadiness. At times, resting your elbows on the arms of a deck chair or on a fence rail will also aid in steadiness.

TESTING BINOCULARS

Testing binoculars only takes a few minutes and if done properly can spare you headaches, eyestrain, and money thrown away on a poor optical instrument. Preliminary testing, at the purchase sight (Fig. 3-10) will give you a better candidate to take home for more rigorous testing. Keep in mind that binoculars, like any complex optical device, should only be purchased with a money-back trial period. No reputable dealer will offer anything less.

After you have made your selection of a pair of astro-binoculars, check its outward appearance. Are its objectives and eyepieces free of blemishes and scratches? Do nicks or dents appear on the barrels? If they do, this could

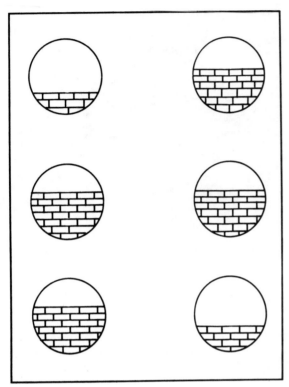

Fig. 3-11. Examples of proper alignment and misalignment (Drawing by Anne Sheppard).

be a hint of bad handling. Are the words "fully coated" engraved on the prism plates? Now check the coating. Point the eyepieces at a light source and notice if the reflections are uniform in color. White reflections are certain signs of uncoated surfaces.

To continue your preliminary testing, face the objective lenses toward the light and note the exit pupil disks. Are they the full bright circles of premium glasses or do the circles turn into shadowy rectangles because of cheaper glass prisms? Do you see internal dust, chipped prisms, dirt, lens cement separations, and chipped and bubbly lenses? Do the binoculars rattle?

Are the binocular barrels misaligned (Fig. 3-11)? Do you see a near perfect circle when you look through both eyepieces? Does the instrument feel balanced and comfortable in your hands? Is it too heavy to hold for more than several minutes?

Is the focuser wheel, diopters, or lever focus too stiff or too loose? Are the binoculars "American style" with superior unibody construction (Fig. 3-12)? Is the eyepiece adjustment scale movable?

If you wear eyeglasses, you must consider if the

binoculars afford you enough eye relief with the rubber eye cups folded down. If you are not an eyeglass wearer, are you getting a full field of view?

With astronomical binoculars the question of near focus does not arise, yet you may wish to take those 7×50s bird watching (Fig. 3-13). If you do consider near focus in your selection, then accept only glasses that focus down to 25 feet or less.

The circular edge of the visual field must be sharp. Fair amounts of farsightedness and nearsightedness can be tolerated without eyeglasses, but with astigmatism, glasses must be worn.

Check eyepiece holders. Do they bind during focusing? Watch for equal movement and smooth play from both oculars. Remember that very cold weather can make lubricants tacky and focusing sticky. You're better off testing the binoculars' moving parts at room temperature.

Is the eyepiece supporting bridge on center-focus binoculars machined well enough to give slight, smooth motions rather than jerky or rocky motions? Binocular hinges should be sturdy and move in a smooth motion when the eye separation adjustment is made. Is your nose pinched when the oculars are too close together?

Magnification is difficult to test, but the vast majority of manufacturers will give you a fair shake on the magnification stated on the barrels. If you really want to get crazy about it, take a millimeter tape measure and measure the binoculars' exit pupil and the clear aperture of the objective lens. Divide the aperture by the exit pupil

Fig. 3-12. American-style binoculars: the Bushnell Explorer (Courtesy Bushnell, Division of Bausch & Lomb).

Fig. 3-13. An armored 7 × 50 Bausch & Lomb Discoverer (Courtesy Bushnell, Division of Bausch & Lomb).

ment (collimated) with each other.

☆ the binoculars are held or supported in a steady fashion.

When you finally get those binoculars home, you will want to test them for sharpness, especially central sharpness. If a binocular test chart is unavailable then clear printing, artwork with fine detail, or even fine building detail will serve well. Making certain the test object is highly illuminated and some 30 feet away, focus carefully. Is the center of the field sharp? If it isn't, the binoculars are almost worthless. Pan the object being viewed. Does the object maintain its sharpness as it approaches the edge of the field? If it does, it's a plus. Most binoculars will suffer some fall off in sharpness at the very edge. This isn't such a bad situation because we tend to focus on objects in the center of view. The edges serve to locate an object when we are scanning. Remember, in wide-field and extra wide field binoculars, you can almost count on a drop in quality at the edge. Still, wide fields may be every bit as good or better in the center as the standard field.

In cheap wide-field glasses, be alert for *pincushion distortion*, the outward curving of the ends of straight lines. You might find pincushion distortion at the edge of the field.

Chromatic aberration or color fringing error can be witnessed when you look at a bright object such as a bulb, bright star, or planet. Chromatic aberration will show up as a blue or purple halo or haze around an object in view. At the edge of the field this aberration becomes more pronounced. Some degree of chromatic aberration should be expected in all binoculars.

Likely the most critical test for binoculars is the "Star test." A frosted 10-watt bulb placed behind a cardboard square with a pinhole in it will serve well as an artificial Star test. Make certain the artificial star is at least 30 to 50 feet away. Make the room dark for the pinhole star and then bring the artificial star in and out of focus in the center of the field. This same test can be conducted outside with a real star (preferably with a bright star near the zenith).

In a good pair of binoculars, the star should be able to be focused down to a fine bright point. If not, forget them!

Other possible aberrations encountered in binocular optics follow (Fig. 3-14):

☆ Spherical aberration, in which light from the outer edge of the lens comes to a different focus than the light from the lens's center, making a spread-out halo.

and you will find the magnification. If you have a 50mm clear aperture and a 7.1mm exit pupil, you will get a 7 × magnification. Again, though, most name brand optical manufacturers are on the up and up.

Field of view can be tested when you get your new instrument home. Like the test for magnification, the test for field of view is largely unimportant because there is a field statement on the binoculars' barrel plate. Major optical manufacturers are not going to create problems for themselves by misrepresentation. Simply look through the binoculars and see if you are visually satisfied with the field of view. Is it wide enough? Do you prefer the picture-window effect of fine wide-angle binoculars? Check if distortion at the edge of the field is too much. Comparison with a proven fine pair of astro-binoculars would help in this test, especially if it was the same field, power, and objective size.

How is the image quality? Do you see a sharp, clear scene from edge to edge in the binoculars' field of view? Does the central object stand out in crisp detail?

In order to test the optical components of binoculars it is important that:

☆ you do not look through air turbulence. It will be impossible to bring a star down to a fine point if air eddies are distorting the light paths.

☆ the binocular objectives are in correct parallel align-

Fig. 3-14. Some typical lens aberrations encountered in faulty binoculars.

☆ Curvature of image, in which a flat surface like a railing appears convex or concave.
☆ Divided image, in which an image appears divided. Divided image is a result of poorly made roof-prisms.
☆ Astigmatism, in which a star looks like a plus sign with radiating spikes. Astigmatism is caused by poorly aligned lenses and prisms.
☆ Curvature of the field, in which the sharpest focal plane of the eyepiece and objective share the center, but then curve away from each other like back-to-back saucers.

You might meet up with several of these aberrations at the same time and get some really weird visual effects. Every once in a while a pair of binoculars slips through production without being checked. I've seen a few that gave images you might not believe.

One item to remember is that in doing tests you might expect too much from your glasses. Even the best are not perfect. Because of their optical design, most possess errors, especially on the edge of the field. You might be a bit more certain of your instrument if you were to compare it to several others. Perhaps a few members of your astronomy club would lend you theirs for a comparative test.

ALIGNMENT

Alignment, or collimation of both optical barrels, is as important to binocular performance as sound working optics themselves. Poor alignment is responsible for more returned binoculars than any other reason and is generally caused by jarring during shipping or slipshod collimating at the factory.

Proper alignment means that both binocular objectives are parallel and aimed in unison at the same target. A well-collimated glass will have fields that merge perfectly into a single field. If this merging does not happen, the observer can suffer from eyestrain and from double vision. Eyes will often adjust to poorly aligned glasses. Headaches might be the eventual outcome of straining eye muscles attempting to compensate.

Three misalignment problems exist: vertical error, horizontal error, and rotational error (Fig. 3-15). Of the three problems, vertical error delivers the most eyestrain even if the objectives differ in only a few minutes of arc. Horizontal misalignment produces images separated side by side and will force the observer to look cockeyed if the images are widely apart. However, horizontal error proves less a problem if the images are close together because the eyes might tolerate some converging or turning inward. With rotational error, the eyes cannot compensate.

Checking alignment is no easy matter because of our eyes' tendency to fuse images. One sure-fire way of detecting poor collimation is to point the binoculars at a distant object, then swing them away, cupping one hand over an objective and keeping both eyes open. Immediately return to the object being viewed. Remove the hand over the objective. If the glass is poorly collimated, you will briefly note it before your eyes compensate for the error. The test becomes even more rigorous if your eyes are kept slightly back from their normal viewing position.

Please remember that headaches and eyestrain are almost sure signs of misalignment. Correctly collimated barrels will never cause those problems.

One final test for misalignment is to focus stabilized binoculars on an object or objects containing vertical and horizontal lines. A tower, chimney, or even an antenna will do. Standing slightly back, look through one eyepiece at a time. Is the object centered in one eyepiece and slightly off in the other? Do you see if the error is horizontal, vertical, or rotational? Glasses might even have all three errors in combination.

If you ever drop or extremely jar your binoculars, recheck the alignment.

Fig. 3-15. Examples of misalignment: rotational error (top), correct alignment (middle), horizontal error (bottom) (Drawing by Anne Sheppard).

CARE, CLEANING, AND REPAIR

Well-made and carefully handled binoculars should last a lifetime with a minimum of cleaning and maintenance. If you keep your instrument stored with its caps on, in its hard leather case, and away from excessive heat, then 96 percent of the battle is won. A pair of binoculars offers little room for malfunction because of its sealed optical systems and few moving parts.

Too much heat might cause the lens cement to soften and discolor and the lenses themselves to separate. Dropping or jarring binoculars might loosen the prisms or throw the alignment out of whack. If alignment problems do occur, there is little the astronomer can do to fix the problem unless he can lay his hands on an autocollimator (Fig. 3-16). Realignment or collimation is a task for the binocular repairman. If you live in a major urban area, there is a good chance you will find them listed under *Binoculars* or *Binocular Repair* in your yellow pages. If your area lacks one, I would suggest writing to the manufacturer. Most have service centers where you may ship your binoculars.

Unless you have a first-class working knowledge of optical instruments, you should not try to repair your own glass. The optical situation could be worsened and your warranty might get voided if you go inside the binocular itself. Care in handling, care in storing, and care in cleaning will literally save you a lot of headaches.

Under most circumstances your glass will never require lubrication. Most glasses manufactured today are permanently lubricated. Now and again you will be forced to wipe dust off the metal parts so grit does not make its way into the binoculars' movement.

Three brief notes about binocular care:

☆ Never leave your glass in the back window or back seat of your car on a hot day.
☆ Keep your fingers off the lenses.
☆ When your binocular is ice cold try not to bring it into a warm room right away because internal condensation can form if the air is moist.

As for cleaning the optics themselves, clean only the external lenses of the eyepieces and objectives. Blow loose dust off with a syringe. Canned gases are not recommended because grit might be ejected from the nozzle and might scratch the lens surface. Blowing directly on the lenses is not highly regarded, either. Tiny spittle droplets can smear.

If dust fails to be blown off, then you might wish to employ a camel's hair brush. Make certain the bristles are not sharply cut. Brush lightly! Even a soft camel's

Fig. 3-16. An autocollimator at I. Miller Optical (Photograph by Caroline Meline).

hair brush can sleek the magnesium fluoride coating. When you are brushing use quick, light strokes, making sure to flick the brush after each stroke to dislodge any dust it might have gathered.

A good second choice for dusting is a clean white facial tissue. Other choices are photographic lens tissue (make certain it is not silicone treated), a cotton ball, or a cotton swab. Always avoid needless harsh rubbing because it quickly will take off the optical coatings. Even find dust has abrasive qualities.

For dirt that is hard to dislodge and finger marks, alcohol or Kodak lens cleaning fluid will do the job. Fingerprints should be removed as soon as possible from a lens because body oils contain an acid that will etch coatings. Apply the alcohol or lens cleaning fluid directly to the cotton swab or cotton ball, then gently rub the smudge in a circular motion until it disappears. Alcohol or lens cleaning fluid should not be allowed to bead up on the lens. If not promptly removed after 20 seconds, both alcohol and lens cleaning fluid will leave a residue. This residue can be removed with acetone.

BUILDING BINOCULARS

Building binoculars from scratch represents a tremendous

challenge for anyone lacking a strong knowledge of both machining and optics, yet assembling a binocular from surplus parts can be plenty of fun. Some companies dealing in binocular optics are Edmund Scientific and A. Jaegers. You will want Edmund's industrial catalog and Jaeger's catalog. Their addresses are given in Appendix E and F, respectively.

Very little has been written about binocular construction. Henson's *Binoculars, Telescopes, and Telescopic Sights* from Chilton Books contains some good information about binocular construction, yet this book is out of print and difficult to find. Check your library or used book stores. More information about binocular construction can be found in the various armed services manuals on binocular and spotting scope repair. Surplus agencies carry these manuals and occasionally they pop up in used book stores. Dover Books publishes *Basic Optics and Optical Instruments* by the Bureau of Naval Personnel. It contains many fine pictures and diagrams.

Also check out "Gleanings from the ATM" in back issues of *Sky and Telescope* for stories on astro-binocular construction. You might find this fine magazine in your library. Also see *Telescope Making* magazine. Check Chapter 14 for mammoth binocular construction.

Chapter 4

Finding Your Way Around the Night Sky

Since you will use binoculars and they possess no setting circles to help you locate sky objects, you will be forced to learn about *star-hopping* if you want to find your way around the heavens. Star-hopping, even though it proves more difficult than using setting circles, offers the great advantage of teaching the night sky to the observer. With star-hopping you will rapidly learn the whereabouts of the bright stars and constellations. During the process of star-hopping you will also discover many curious objects that you did not set out to view.

Before I go any further with star-hopping, I will bring up the topic of star atlases. Almost as important as choosing good astronomical binoculars is choosing a star atlas for locating positions in the heavens. Without a star atlas, finding your way through the night sky would be akin to traveling down a highway with no signs. A good atlas must have several key features. Aside from the fact that stars at least to the sixth magnitude must be plotted, the atlas must also have nonstellar objects like galaxies and nebulae shown so the binocularist can find them. The atlas must be accurate within its epoch (1950, 2000 etc.).

A good atlas must have several features:

☆ It must be able to be easily held in hand and read at night under a dim red light.

☆ Its paper and binding must hold up under dewing conditions.

☆ It must contain a reference catalog with positions, magnitudes, and other key data listed, or provide this information in a companion volume.

☆ There must be a grid superimposed over the atlas charts so that measurements can be made.

After looking through nearly 20 atlases, I came to the conclusion that several of them would suit the night binocularist just fine. My choices for those owning binoculars within the 50mm to 80mm range are:

☆ *The Edmund Scientific Mag 6 Star Atlas* by Dickinson, Costanzo, and Chaple. This is a wonderful, easy-to-use, spiral-bound atlas with fine information for the beginner. The Mag 6 is easy to use because of its construction and good-sized charts to the sixth magnitude.

☆ *A Field Guide to the Stars and Planets* by Menzel and Pasachoff. This second edition contains first-rate atlas maps by Tirion to a magnitude of 7.5. Part of the Peterson field guide series, this book is chock-full of information and will fit in a windbreaker pocket.

☆ *Norton's Star Atlas and Reference Handbook* edited by Inglis, Moore, and Satterthwaite. Here's an old standard with lots of information and nice charts. For many years it was the premier atlas for amateurs.

For those binocularists employing instruments with apertures of 100mm or more and having a bit more money to spend, my choices are:

☆ *Sky Atlas 2000.0* by Tirion. This is a super, easy-to-manage atlas with stars to the eighth magnitude. Having a deluxe color edition, this atlas is fast becoming the most popular large atlas among amateur astronomers. A companion catalog comes in two volumes and provides lists of double stars, galaxies, clusters, nebulae, and the like.
☆ *A.A.V.S.O. Variable Star Atlas* edited by Scovil. This is a very fine atlas with an accent on variable stars.
☆ *Skalnate Pleso Atlas of the Heavens* by Becvar is an old standard with a reference catalog available.

There is also an atlas for those binocularists who wish to know more about our solar system: *Atlas of the Solar System* by Moore and Hunt. This book offers excellent reading and really good planetary and lunar maps.

Many of the previously mentioned atlases can be found in either university bookstores or the larger urban bookstores. If you fail to find them there, you can order them through three excellent mail-order houses: Willmann-Bell, Inc., Sky Publishing Corporation, and Herbert A. Luft. Addresses are located in Appendix E.

Besides atlases, these mail-order houses offer a wide assortment of astronomy books. If you can't locate an astronomy book in their catalogs, the book is very likely not in print.

A final note on atlases: The ones with star charts to the sixth magnitude will prove less confusing to the novice because their charts will be less crowded with stars.

Another useful item for the binocularist attempting to find his way around the heavens is a device called the *planisphere* (Fig. 4-1), or as it is often called the star finder, star wheel, or star-locater wheel. Like a portable planetarium on a circular cardboard or plastic card with a center pivot, the planisphere has a dial that can be set for any date or time, and only stars above the horizon are shown. A real help to the neophyte attempting to locate constellations and bright stars, the planisphere will give you a good perspective before you hunt up superior detail in a star atlas. The better planispheres are two-sided, with both Northern and Southern hemispheres displayed.

Most planispheres are computed for an average latitude of 40 degrees in the North and 30 degrees in the South. For this reason the sky you're viewing will be slightly different than that shown on the planisphere.

To use the planisphere, rotate the disk until the month, day, and hour are correct. Hold the card overhead, maintaining a North-South alignment to the compass directions. The planisphere's stars should almost match what you see in the sky.

Before you head outside, check your planisphere for what constellations will be available that night. Now find those constellations on your atlas charts and familiarize yourself with some of their detail. Have a good idea where the brightest constellations are, such as Ursa Major (the Big Dipper) and Orion (Fig. 4-2), because you might wish to use them as your celestial stepping stones to the night sky. These larger and brighter constellations possess straight lines of stars, which you can visualize as pointers in order to help you locate other constellations, bright stars, and nonstellar objects.

Star-hopping is basically hopping from bright star to bright star until you locate your intended target. At first it would be best to view the heavens with your naked eyes until you have a grasp of what is happening up there. When you advance to binoculars, you will find it convenient to know the degrees in your instrument's field of view. You can then compare your binocular's field to the atlas sky chart field in an attempt to further your orientation.

Some quick tips for the new binocularist:

☆ Keep your eyes centered in the eyepieces, yet never touch them.
☆ A star is in focus when it appears as a pinpoint of light.
☆ When you are viewing very dim objects such as galaxies, nebulae (Fig. 4-3), and some clusters, use a technique known as *averted vision*. With averted vision you can increase visual acuity by as much as one or two magnitudes. Get the sky object in the center of your binocular field, then direct your gaze a little to the side. The center of your eye offers you the sharpest resolution while the eye's outside portion is best for gathering light. Some old-timers have told me that rapid deep breathing also promotes additional light sensitivity. Remember too, that if you've just left your home, give your eyes at least 15 to 20 minutes to adapt to the dark. Your expanded pupil will gather more light, making it easier for you to observe dim objects.
☆ Try not to look over roofs during the winter because heat waves rise off them and will create turbulence, distorting what you view. Generally, atmospheric conditions will not affect the sky objects you view through binoculars except for twinkling stars because binocular objective lenses are small and the instrument's

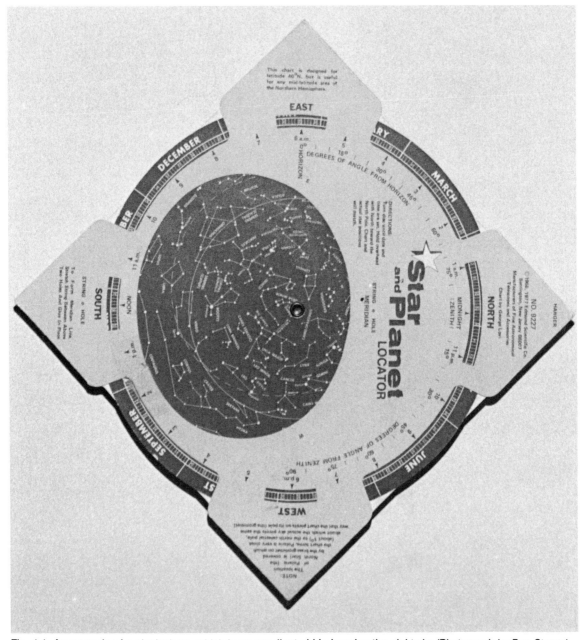

Fig. 4-1. An example of a planisphere, which is an excellent aid in learning the night sky (Photograph by Dan Stosuy).

power is low. However, poor conditions might make it difficult to split marginal double stars.

☆ Keep away from external lights because they might cause your eyes to lose their dark adaptation. Also you just might see your eyes reflected back in the eyepieces.

☆ The magnitude limit for the average eye under truly dark conditions is about 6.2 magnitude. Under the darkest skies you might just see 4000 stars.

☆ Join an astronomy club or start one. Astronomy clubs are excellent places to learn more about your hobby and to share your interest with others. Star parties

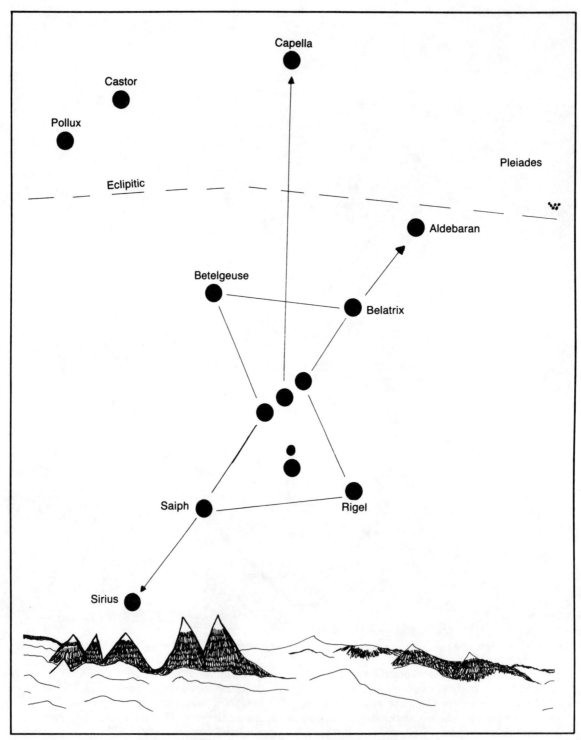

Fig. 4-2. The constellation Orion as a pointer to the heavens (Drawing by Anne Sheppard).

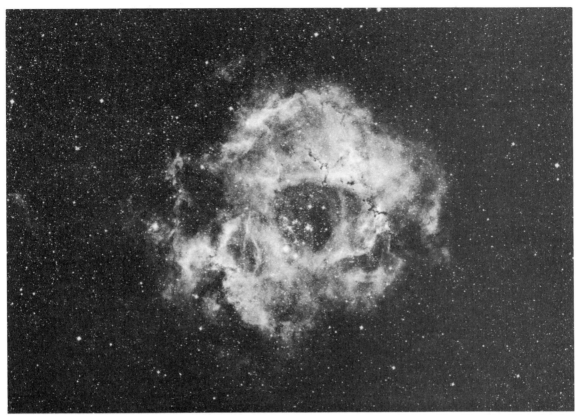

Fig. 4-3. NGC 2237, The Rosette Nebula, in Monoceros, a formless aura of gray light in 11 × 80s. This 61-centimeter Schmidt camera photograph was taken at Cerro Tololo, Chile (Courtesy National Optical Astronomy Observatories).

and club meetings can be great fun. Later in this book I will discuss how to start and run a club. Affiliation is at least a third of the pleasure of amateur astronomy.

☆ On very cold nights, warm clothing is required if you wish to stay out for any extended period. Try not to stand on concrete because it will rapidly absorb heat from your feet. Well-insulated boots are a must. Wear several layers of clothing that are loose fitted to the body so air pockets are created. Your entire body should be covered, especially your face and hands. Lightweight clothing is preferred because heavier clothing, like coats, can prove tiring after several hours. Wear a pair of thin cotton socks with a pair of woolen ones over them. If your feet become too warm, they will perspire and that will cause rapid heat loss. Wool caps are best for your head. Mittens are the choice over leather gloves because mittens can be easily removed when you are adjusting your binocular or marking your star charts. Mittens also retain heat better. An insulated, nylon-covered jacket, with

oversized pockets for warming your hands, would be a good first choice. Two sweaters, a scarf, a change of socks (in case a pair becomes damp) and all-cotton long-johns that don't fit too snugly are recommended. You might also consider bringing along a thermos of warm soup or hot chocolate.

☆ Learn where Polaris (the Pole star) is in the North. The two brightest stars in the Big Dipper's ladle form a straight line that points to Polaris (Fig. 4-4). The topmost stars of Orion point toward the Big Dipper. Polaris will help orient you to the heavens if you live in the Northern Hemisphere. All the stars in the Northern skies appear to revolve around Polaris.

☆ If you visit the Southern Hemisphere, you will find the location of the South Celestial Pole a less simple matter. No stars exactly mark the South Celestial Pole; however, the Southern Cross (Crux) points toward the general area of the South Pole.

☆ Remember the Earth turns eastward, making the stars appear to drift westward across the night sky. You

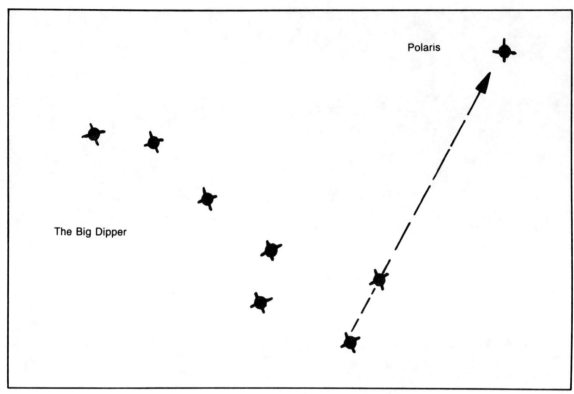

Fig. 4-4. The Big Dipper's ladle serves as a useful pointer to Polaris, the North Star.

might wish to learn the constellations that can be viewed in your area each season. Also find the ecliptic on your atlas charts and then learn the constellations of the zodiac. In its year-long journey around the Sun, the Earth traces a path among the stars, called the *ecliptic*. The 8-degree band on either side of this path is known as the *zodiac*. Along the ecliptic and among the constellations of the zodiac, you will find the Sun, the Moon, and the planets. Venus strays somewhat from the ecliptic from time to time. The zodiac constellations are Scorpius, Sagittarius, Capricornus, Aquarius, Pisces, Aries, Taurus, Gemini, Cancer, Leo, Virgo, and Libra.

☆ Learn about the *celestial sphere*. Outer space can be viewed as a large sphere. Like our own globe, the celestial sphere possesses a North and South pole and an equator. The North celestial pole is centered above the North horizon the same number of degrees as the latitude of your immediate area.

☆ The *Summer Triangle* (Fig. 4-5) is an excellent celestial landmark and it is formed by the bright stars Deneb, Vega, and Altair. The Summer Triangle is al-

most immediately recognized.

☆ To find out whether the object you are viewing is a star or planet, ask yourself these two questions: Does it twinkle? If it does then it is likely a star. Is the object far away from the Ecliptic and near the zenith? If it is, it can't be a planet.

☆ If you have to resort to using a light, use a red-filtered flashlight to help keep your eyes adapted to the dark.

☆ When I am speaking of magnitude, I am referring to *apparent magnitude*, or magnitude as the measure of a star's brightness as we observe it. The brighter planets and stars are brighter than first magnitude and will be expressed in negative values. For example, the Sun is –26 magnitude.

☆ If you wear glasses and are only farsighted or nearsighted, you do not need to wear them when you are using binoculars. If you have astigmatism, however, you must keep your glasses on.

☆ Check out "Celestial Calendar" and "Rambling through the Skies" each month in *Sky and Telescope*. In *Astronomy*, look for the monthly appearance of "The Backyard Astronomer" and "Eye on the Sky."

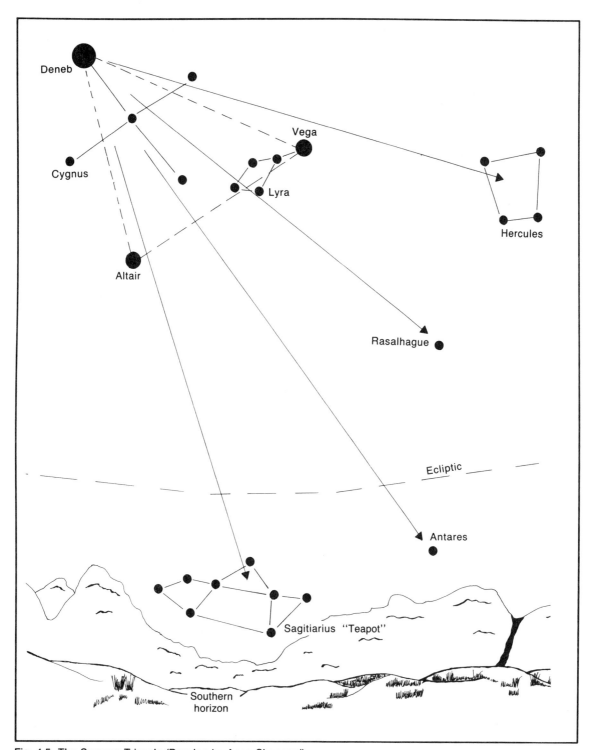

Fig. 4-5. The Summer Triangle (Drawing by Anne Sheppard).

Fig. 4-6. Bushnell Sportview binoculars (Courtesy Bushnell, Division of Bausch & Lomb).

These features, in both fine magazines, are chock-full of information about the monthly observing situation.

☆ Don't worry about having to do useful or worthwhile research. You don't have to be a serious amateur astronomer in order to enjoy the hobby. The casual observer also can have fun.

☆ Watch out for aperture fever (a bug that haunts telescope enthusiasts as well). You don't have to keep buying larger and more elaborate binoculars in the search for the ultimate instrument. Learn to enjoy what you have. Remember, it isn't the instrument that gains the clues to the enigmas and mysteries of the night sky, but the observer. A pair of 7×50s (Fig. 4-6) can keep you absorbed for a lifetime.

☆ Remember, there will be nights when the seeing is bad, the weather is too hot or too cold, the skies are clouded over, the skies are light polluted, the mosquitos are large and extra pesky, and the Moon is too bright. On those nights get out a good astronomy book and enjoy it.

Chapter 5

The Sun

The Sun's diameter is 109 times larger than Earth's.
The Sun's volume is 1,300,000 times larger than Earth's.
The Sun's mass is 332,000 times larger than Earth's.
Central temperature: 14,000,000° to 20,000,000° K.
Surface temperature: 6000° K.
Rotation period: 27 days.
Surface gravity: 27.99.
Sunspot temperature: 4000° to 7000° K.
Sunspot maximum: 11 years.
Reverse of sunspot magnetic polarities: every 11 years.
Complete sunspot cycles: 22 years.
Sun loses approximately 10^{-13} of its mass yearly.
Age of Solar System: 4.6 billion years, estimated.
Speed of Solar Wind: 250 to 500 miles per second.
Sun rotates at different speeds varying with latitude.
Sun's rotation fastest at equator.
Sun's rotation: 26.87 days at 0° Solar latitude (Earth view).
Sun's rotation: 29.65 days at 40° Solar latitude (Earth view).
Sun's diameter: 864,000 miles.
Sun's mass: 2.2×10^{27} tons.
Sun's density: 1.41 that of water.
Sun's gravity: 900 ft./sec.^{2}.
Apparent magnitude: -27.

Sun contains 99.9% of the Solar System's weight.
Sun's home galaxy: The Milky Way.
Sun is located 30,000 light years from the Milky Way's center.
Sun's star type: Population I (comparatively young star).
Sun's rotation period around galaxy: 225 million years.
Sun's distance from Earth: 93 million miles.
Nearest star from sun: Proxima Centauri.
Spectral Type: G2 V yellow dwarf on the Main Sequence.
Photosphere temperature: 4,300° at top, 9,000° at bottom.
Photosphere contains: 90% Hydrogen, 8% Helium, 2% heavy elements.
Sunspot sizes: 900 miles across to 90,000 miles across.
Sunspot Umbra temp.: 4240° K.
Sunspot Penumbra temp.: 5680° K.
Sun's composition: 75% Hydrogen, 24% Helium.
Sun's angular diameter: 32 minutes of arc.
Sun's luminosity: 3.90×10^{26} watts.

THE SUN

Composed of hydrogen and helium, the Sun (Fig. 5-1) generates its energy by a *thermonuclear process:* the proton-proton chain reaction taking place deep in the core

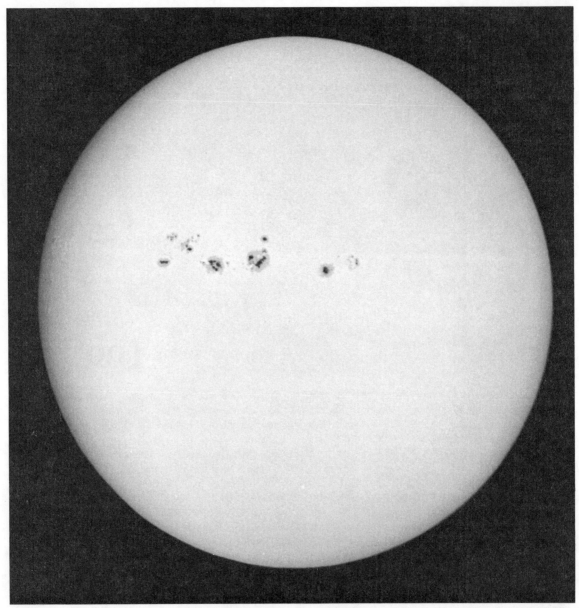

Fig. 5-1. The Sun, active with sunspots; photographed in white light by Paul Maxson (Courtesy Richard E. Hill and ALPOSS).

of this yellow-dwarf main-sequence star. Outside the core exists an envelope of unevolved matter, through which the core's energy is radiated to convective cells on the surface. The *photosphere*, or solar surface, is the boundary between the opaque convective surface and the transparent atmosphere. The photosphere is several hundred kilometers thick and from it the Sun's energy is radiated into space. The granulation's mottled appearance (Fig.

5-2) is a permanent feature of the photosphere.

Sunspots, or dark regions on the solar disk, and *faculae*, or brighter patches, are striking features when seen in white-light observations of the photosphere. Sunspots and faculae can be seen transiting the Sun's disk; in doing so, they disclose the differential rotation of the solar globe. Why a differential rotation exists remains a puzzle to the astronomical community. There has been some suggestion that the solar core's rapid rotation might affect the photosphere's differing movement. The photosphere shows a drop in temperature from 6000° K to 4000° K from the base to the top.

Above the photosphere is the *chromosphere* (Fig. 5-3), an envelope several thousand kilometers thick in which the temperatures rise as high as 50,000 K. A transitional region lies between the chromosphere and the rarified gas *corona*. Temperatures in this transitional region are said to be 500,000° K, while the corona might sustain temperatures of 200,000° K at the height of 75,000 kilometers. The corona might extend many millions of kilometers into the interplanetary medium where streams of hydrogen particles, called the *solar wind*, are sprayed out

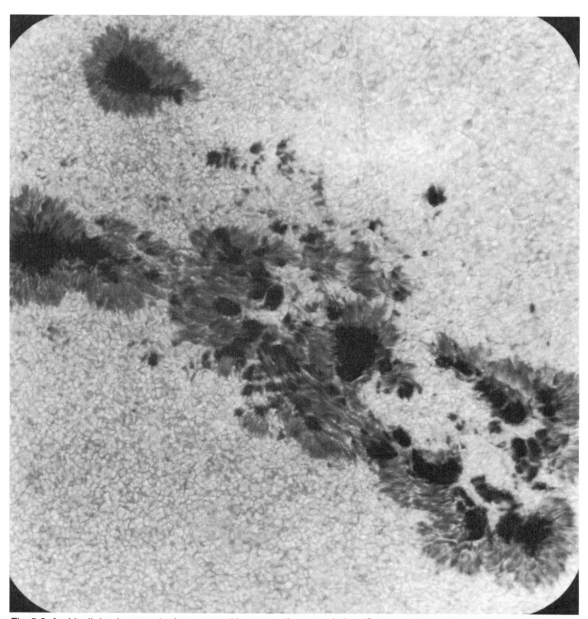

Fig. 5-2. A white light photograph of sunspots with surrounding granulation (Courtesy National Solar Observatory, Association of Universities for Research in Astronomy, Inc.).

45

DATE JUL 1 3 1982

TIME 1630 U

B OU

NOAA

SESC
BOULDER

N

Fig. 5-3. The solar chromosphere photographed in H-Alpha (Courtesy Space Environment Services Center, Space Environment Laboratory).

beyond the solar system.

Briefly I will mention three curiosities of the chromosphere. They are *flares*, or sudden short-period brightenings of small areas of the upper chromosphere (Fig. 5-4), *plages*, or bright patches occurring in the solar chromosphere; and *filaments*, or gas clouds witnessed in the upper chromosphere.

SUNSPOTS

Sunspots, those dark markings on the solar disk as seen in white light, range in size from pores—which are the size of solar granules—to highly evolved structures covering several thousand million square kilometers. Most sunspots, save the smallest, form two distinct regions: the *umbra*, which is the dark core, and the *penumbra*, which

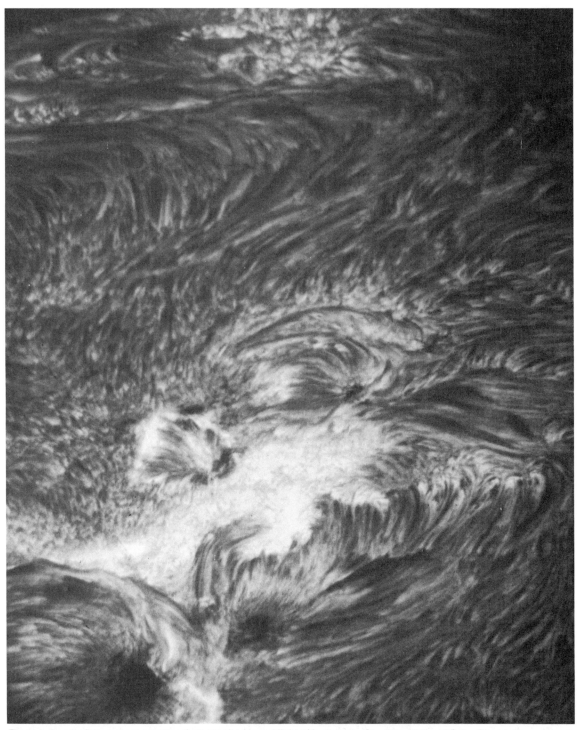

Fig. 5-4. A solar flare near sunspots, photographed in red light of hydrogen (Courtesy National Solar Observatory, Association of Universities for Research in Astronomy, Inc.).

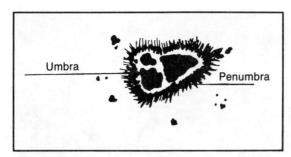

Fig. 5-5. A sunspot's basic structure.

is the umbra's light surrounding area often resolved into radial filaments (Fig. 5-5).

The majority of sunspots tend to form in groups rather than singularly. The formation and final decay of sunspot groups might last from weeks to even months, although most last only a few weeks.

Intense magnetic activity is centered in the sunspot. These magnetic fields are believed to suppress streams of hot gases rising from the convective zone prior to its arrival in the photosphere. The strongest magnetic fields lie in the umbra, and it is here where convection currents are almost completely inhibited.

In the penumbra, with its more horizontal field, the *Evershed effect*, or radial flow of material, takes place. The umbra is cooler than its surrounding penumbra, and in turn the penumbra is cooler than its surrounding granulation. This surrounding granulation possesses temperatures in the vicinity of 6000° K, while the umbra may be in the 4000° K range and its surrounding penumbra 5600 K.

The magnetic field in sunspots enhances the flow of heat and converts about 75 percent of the outflow into *magneto-hydrodynamic waves*, or Alven waves. These Alvén waves propagate rapidly along the magnetic field lines without dispersing.

Sunspot groups display much diversity in size and structure. Their classifications are set by their respective magnetic field's configuration. Sunspots can be unipolar, bipolar, or complex. Most likely to occur are *bipolar* groups, which consist of two main spots of opposing magnetic polarity. The *line of inversion* divides spot regions into opposite polarities where the vertical constituent of the magnetic field becomes zero. There you will find both a stable filament and the well-known violent flares. Both phenomena happen in the upper chromosphere (Fig. 5-6) and in the inner corona above the sunspot group.

Sunspots fluctuate in number over a period of 11 years, which is the sunspot cycle. The easiest seen of all the solar activity, the sunspots, along with faculae, plages,

flares, and filaments, make up the Sun's active regions, extending from the photosphere, through the chromosphere, and up to the corona.

OBSERVING THE SUN WITH BINOCULARS

Warning: Never look at the sun with unfiltered binoculars!

Binocular astronomy need not end with the coming of daylight. Our Sun, the nearest star and the only star Earthbound astronomers are capable of resolving into a disk, offers the binocularist an interesting target.

Before we begin our journey to the center of our Solar System, let me warn you that one brief look at the Sun through binoculars will likely destroy your ability to see. The Sun can only be safely viewed through binoculars with specially coated glass, and mylar filters (Fig. 5-7) and through battleship glasses having removable eyepiece and prism systems, with Herschel wedges. The specially coated glass and mylar filters are employed in front of the objectives. Preobjective filtration keeps unwanted heat out of the binoculars.

Stay away from any filters that are fitted over the eyepiece, unless they are used with Herschel wedges. The intense heat of a short-focus instrument might crack these filters, and in most cases they do not block enough ultraviolet waves.

Avoid projecting the solar image with your binoculars. Using projection with your instrument could spell disaster for most binocular eyepieces, which are generally Kellners or Erfles. The cement used in eyepiece lenses will be fried or yellowed by the Sun's focused heat, and the lenses themselves just might separate. Binocular objectives might bear up to the Sun better than eyepieces, yet after a time glass does absorb heat, thus harming its cement. I've only seen a few air-spaced objectives employed in binoculars and those were 150mm babies. Most binoculars possess cemented doublets.

In my opinion, the best solar filtration system is the Herschel wedge, but these can't be used with 99 percent of production binoculars. A close second are those specially ground and polished glass filters coated with iconel or other such substances. These filters give excellent resolution, yet they are expensive and their coatings might break down over a period of years. Mylar filters (which look like aluminum foil) give good enough images for the casual observer. They are least expensive. All filters, used in front of the objective, should be in a snug-fitting cell.

Sunspots

Binoculars generally do not produce enough magnification or resolution to warrant their use in sunspot re-

Fig. 5-6. The upper chromosphere showing a field of spicules; photographed in red light of hydrogen (Courtesy National Solar Observatory, Association of Universities for Research in Astronomy, Inc.).

search. However, a pair of binoculars will show you some of the larger sunspots, sunspot groups, and some detail if you're using higher-powered optics and have a keen eye.

Look daily at the Sun and you will note the day-to-day parade of sunspots toward the Western limb, or edge.

If you are persistent and the group you have been watching is large, you might see it reappear on the Eastern limb some two weeks later. Often groups grow rapidly. At times sunspots grow so large they can be viewed by the eye with only an optical glass filter. To be viewed with-

Fig. 5-7. A mylar sun filter mounted in its cell: Solar-Skreen (Courtesy Roger W. Tuthill, Inc.).

out an optical instrument, the sunspot must be at least 15,000 miles in diameter (including penumbra). In recorded history the largest sunspot group ever seen was on April 7, 1947. This sunspot group was bipolar, had a diameter in the neighborhood of 200,000 miles, and had an area of 6000 million square miles—some 20 times the Earth's area.

Through properly filtered binoculars you will be able to learn about Sporer's law. At the onset of each new sunspot cycle, the majority of spots show up at high latitudes (in the neighborhood of 30°) and begin dropping toward the equator as the cycle progresses. At maximum you will find them grouped in both 10-degree latitudes. By minimum you will witness two distinct sunspot zones: low-latitude groups from the past cycle and high-latitude groups signaling the approach of a new cycle. Sunspots rarely show up at the equator and never at the poles.

Eclipses

Solar eclipses occur when the New Moon passes in

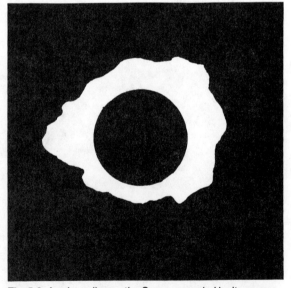

Fig. 5-8. A solar eclipse—the Sun surrounded by its corona.

front of the Sun (Fig. 5-8). If the New Moon passes exactly through the plane of our planet's orbit, the New Moon will partially or totally block out the solar disk. The Sun and our Moon will appear almost the same size because the Sun, 400 times larger than the Moon, is almost 400 times farther away. A perfectly aligned eclipse will spell totality. In certain instances—when the Sun is crossed by the Moon at a point in its not quite circular orbit around the Earth—the Sun fails to be completely covered. On occasion the Moon is so far from the Earth that the lunar disk appears to have shrunk in size.

For any eclipse the region of totality on the Earth's surface is quite small, the shadow a bit under 100 miles wide. This fact hurts the chances of any location witnessing an eclipse more than once in a 360-year time span. If you want to see this most famous of solar phenomena, be prepared to travel. However, arriving at the right location is no guarantee you will see the eclipse because there must be cloudless skies for you to be able to witness the event. I've heard many a tale of folks traveling to distant and exotic places only to be rebuffed by clouds. I don't feel too badly for them because traveling in itself can be fun.

Even as you observe an eclipse, you must keep in mind that the Sun's rays still provide a good measure of danger for your vision to the point of eclipse totality. Proper filtration of your instrument is a must! Only at that brief moment of totality, during a total eclipse, it is permissible to remove the filters. At full eclipse the Sun's radiant intensity is not much more than a full Moon's. Still, those filters must remain on until the last instant. Danger exists in glimpsing even the narrow solar crescent.

At the height of a total eclipse, the *corona* (the bluish-white outermost part of the solar atmosphere) and the *prominences* (bright reddish cloudlike projections on the Sun's limb) can be viewed through binoculars (Fig. 5-9). Also look for *Baily's Beads,* those beadlike fragments of light caused by the Sun shining through the mountains and valleys on the Moon's eastern limb. (See Table 5-1.)

Partial eclipses are not to be neglected. At First Contact, when the Moon's eastern limb begins to blot out the Sun, you will be inspired to awe as you watch. The duration of a partial eclipse depends on the Moon's phase. Some partial eclipses might last no more than 40 minutes while others might extend up to 2 hours. The longest duration of totality is only 7.5 minutes; most are quickies. Watch for flowers closing and opening, and listen to the birds singing during an eclipse. Bright stars and planets will appear.

Our Sun offers other phenomena of a highly pleasing visual nature. Anyone observing El Sol at sunset will often be treated to some refractive goodies. The Sun's limbs might appear to flatten as they dip into the atmospheric soup at the horizon. Often the Sun's edges look serrated and at times the solar disk might appear to divide into sections. The latter occurs when the atmosphere is divided by heat zones whose light refractions are different.

Fig. 5-9. A massive prominence erupting on the Sun's limb.

Table 5-1. Table of Solar Eclipses (1985-1995) and Where Viewed.

Date of Appearance	Type	Where Viewed
October 3, 1986	Total	North Atlantic
March 29, 1987	Total	Argentina, Atlantic, Central Africa, Indian Ocean
September 23, 1987	Annular	China, USSR, Pacific
March 18, 1988	Total	Indian Ocean, East Indies, Pacific
March 7, 1989	Partial	Arctic
August 31, 1989	Partial	Antarctic
January 26, 1990	Annular	Antarctic
July 22, 1990	Total	Finland, Pacific, USSR
January 15 to 16, 1991	Annular	Australia, New Zealand, Pacific
July 11, 1991	Total	Mexico, Pacific, Brazil
January 4 to 5, 1992	Annular	Central Pacific
June 30, 1992	Total	South Atlantic
December 24, 1992	Partial	Arctic
May 21, 1993	Partial	Arctic
November 13, 1993	Partial	Antarctic
May 10, 1994	Annular	United States, Mexico, Canada, Pacific
November 3, 1994	Total	Peru, Brazil, South Atlantic
April 29, 1995	Annular	South Pacific, Peru, South Atlantic
October 24, 1995	Total	Iran, India, East Indies, Pacific

Green Limbs and Green Flashes

If you live on the plains, by the shore, or anywhere with an unobstructed view of the horizon, you will eventually be in for two treats at sunset: *green limb* and *green flash*. Green limb occurs when the final fraction of the solar disk lingers on the horizon and alters in coloration from gold to blue-green. A clear sky is all important in witnessing this phenomena. The Sun can not be glimpsed until the final moment. The coloration in green limb is a result of the atmosphere's absorption and refraction of the Sun's rays.

Rarer is green flash, which exhibits itself as a sharp ray of light shooting from the top-most solar limb toward the *zenith* (the point directly overhead) at the moment of sunset or sunrise. Extreme turbulence in our atmosphere is associated with this event.

Sun Dogs

Another curious happening is the *sun dog*. Airborne ice crystals refract the sunlight and form circular arcs, sometimes showing color. These sun dog halos have 22° radii.

Auroras

A more well-known solar-related phenomenon is the *aurora* or, as it is sometimes called, the *Northern Lights* or the *Southern Lights* (Fig. 5-10). An aurora is an atmospheric event caused by the bombardment of the upper atmosphere by solar atomic particles trapped by the Earth's magnetic field. Most commonly observed near our planet's magnetic poles, the aurora is named aurora borealis in the Northern Hemisphere and aurora australis in the Southern Hemisphere.

These phenomena appear as diffuse light areas in the sky, often in shades of green, yellow, and red. Assuming the shape of archways, loops, and drapery folds, auroras shimmer and pulse. Truly these are outstanding visual effects.

Occurring at heights above 60 miles, the aurora is most frequently observed during the maximum period of the 11-year solar cycle, when particles are blasted out into space by the Sun's flare activity.

Auroric coloration is believed to be produced by oxygen and nitrogen molecules under bombardment by solar electrons. Recently it has been learned that aurorae in both Northern and Southern hemispheres are linked by atomic particles oscillating back and forth between the hemispheres along our planet's magnetic lines of force.

Zodiacal Light

Another solar-induced phenomena is *zodiacal light*, a diffuse cone of very faint light along the ecliptic, appearing in the sky at the last of twilight in the evening and at the first of dawn in the morning. Zodiacal light is caused by sunlight reflecting off a disk-shaped cloud

Fig. 5-10. An aurora near the Big Dipper (Photograph by Dr. Steve Simmerman).

of fine dust particles in our solar system. This cloud has an estimated mass of 30 million million tons.

In order to view zodiacal light, you will need dark and transparent skies. Observers in the Northern Latitudes will find zodiacal light observation best before sunrise in the fall and after sunset in the spring.

Gegenschein

One final solar-induced phenomena is *gegenschein*, a diffuse and very faint patch of hazy light near the ecliptic. This phenomena appears opposite the Sun in our sky.

Gegenschein means *counterglow* in German. In 1854 Danish astronomer Theodor Brorsen noted that this phenomenon at maximum is a glowing patch about 20° across and is composed of dust particles reflecting sunlight. Quite similar to zodiacal light, gegenschein appears a bit fainter than our Milky Way and is best viewed against an almost starless background.

The solar-induced phenomena like green limb, green flash, Sun dog, aurorae, zodiacal light, and gegenschein are best observed with the naked eyes or a low-power binocular. You will have to be away from urban light polution.

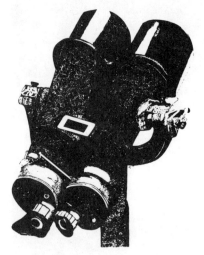

Chapter 6

The Moon

The Moon's diameter: 2160 miles.

The Moon's mass: 8.1×10^{19} tons.

The Moon's volume: 5.2×10^9 cu mi.

The Moon's density: 3.33 that of water.

The Moon's nearest distance to Earth: 221,463 miles.

The Moon's farthest distance from Earth: 252,710 miles.

The Moon's average distance from Earth: 238,857 miles.

The Moon's gravity: 5.31 ft/sec^2.

The Moon's inclination to the ecliptic: 6.6°.

The Moon's inclination of orbit to the ecliptic: 5.1°.

The Moon's synodic month: 29d 12h 44m.

The Moon's sidereal month: 27d 7h 43m.

The Moon's noon surface temperature: 212° F.

The Moon's midnight surface temperature: –238° F.

The Moon's atmosphere: none.

The Moon formed: 4.6 billion years ago.

The Moon's orbit: elliptical.

The Moon's albedo: 0.07.

THE MOON

Our Earth's only satellite, the Moon (Fig. 6-1) is a barren, lifeless world with no atmosphere to guard it from the baking midday Sun and the night's great cold. The cratered lunar surface testifies to over 3 billion years of meteor bombardment.

While the Moon orbits the Earth, we observe varying amounts of the sunlit side in the form of phases. A complete set of phases (Fig. 6-2) takes 29.5 days. The Moon's closeness to our planet makes for a reaction in the Earth's atmosphere, crust, and seas, as witnessed in the tides.

The other planets, save for perhaps Pluto, have satellites of no more than a few thousandths of their mass. Our Moon's mass ratio is 1:81 that of our planet's, causing our Earth-lunar system to be referred to as a *double planet.*

Rugged highlands and dark, smooth lowlands make up most of the lunar surface. Craters, pocking most of the Moon's surface, are 16 times more plentiful on the highlands than on the lowland plains. The majority of lunar craters result from the impact of large meteorites. Similar impact craters were discovered on our planet, but they are heavily eroded.

Cratering has been found elsewhere in the solar system. Mars and Mercury exhibit craters. Some small lunar craters—those in chains—may result from volcanic activity. The majority of Moon craters are near perfect circles—a pretty fair sign of nonvolcanic origin.

An ejecta blanket, which is made of crushed rock blown out by a meteor impact, surrounds some craters

Fig. 6-1. The Moon, photographed with a Meade 10-inch Schmidt-Cassegrain (Courtesy Meade Instruments Corporation).

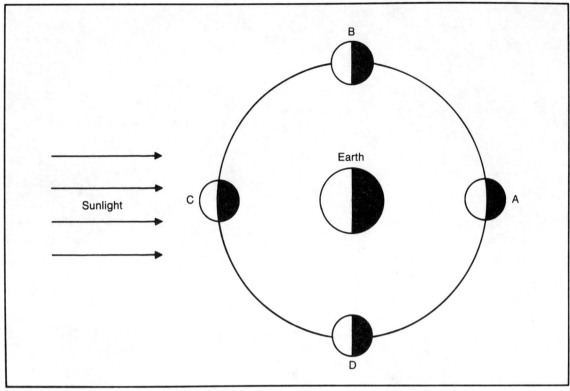

Fig. 6-2. The lunar phases (Drawing by Anne Sheppard).

and occasionally forms long rays. The ejecta is bright around recent craters, but darkens with age.

Lunar craters (Fig. 6-3) demonstrate differing ages. Some are sharply defined, while others are eroded and almost entirely filled. This weathering process is attributed to further meteorite impacting.

The Moon's largest features are its dark, often circular , plains called *maria* (sing. *mare*), or seas (Fig. 6-4). Mare Ibrium, a giant lava-filled crater 420 miles in diameter, is rimmed by rugged mountain ranges. Conjecture has it that Mare Ibrium was the product of an asteroid impact. Evidence of this impact is seen in the valleys and secondary craters visible for more than 1000 miles in all directions. The crater was later filled with a lava flow from the lunar interior. The maria appear formed from lava flows over a considerable period. The lunar far side evidences a few large basin areas yet filled with lava.

The dark lunar plains possess beveled ridges several hundred feet high, formed from the contraction of maria centers. Valleys, known as *rills* and fairly similar to our own rift valleys, have steep, parallel walls and flat floors. Rills can be hundreds of miles long and are found close

to the edges of maria. Sinuous rills are believed to be lava tubes that have collapsed beneath the mare surface. *Faults*, some up to 100 miles long and as high as 1200 feet, dot the lunar surface.

As a result of detailed first-hand investigation, high-resolution photography, and laboratory analysis, we now believe the lunar surface to be quite ancient. Almost 3 billion years of meteorite impacting has left an impressive pile of rubble and debris. Huge boulders and rocks of various sizes intermingle with vast amounts of extra-fine dust, much of which is glass and spheroid in shape. The heat of meteorite impacts is believed to be the cause of the glass dust.

The *regolith*, the layer of dust and broken rock, is some 60 feet deep and made of nearly 2 % meteoric material. Beneath the regolith resides a region of shattered, yet denser, rock that likely goes to a depth of 10 miles. The meteor bombardment continues to contribute to the regolith. Micrometeoric impacting also adds to the erosion.

Almost no lunar atmosphere exists. What little occurs is in the form of gases released by heating, radioac-

Fig. 6-3. The heavily cratered Tycho and Clavius region as photographed by the Lick 36-inch refractor (Lick Observatory Photograph).

Fig. 6-4. Mare Crisium, an elliptical plain covering 66,000 square miles; photographed with a 10-inch Cassegrain reflector by John E. Westfall (Courtesy ALPO).

tive decay, volcanic venting, and meteoric impact melting. The solar wind helps disperse these gases. The lack of atmosphere leads to extreme temperatures, ranging from 212° F at midday to –238° F during the lunar night.

Lunar rocks differ greatly from the rocks found on Earth. They are four times poorer in magnesium, sodium and iron, yet 6.5 times richer in aluminum, calcium, and titanium. Mare rocks differ greatly from their lighter counterparts in the highlands.

Seismically, the lunar surface appears quiet. Moonquakes, only a thousandth as strong as earthquakes, produce intense short-lived signals that are dampened by the cratered and rilled surface. A network of seizmometers left by the Apollo landings told of about 40 major quake sources at depths of 370 to 750 miles. The quake sources differ greatly from Earth's because earthquakes generally occur in the upper layers.

The Moon's interior consists of several regions: a 40-mile-thick outer crust that has a density triple that of water, a 740-mile-deep lunar mantle, and a 600-mile across central core with a temperature estimated to be 1500° C. The Moon does not possess a large nickel-iron core.

The dating of lunar rocks and soil samples has permitted geologists to construct the Moon's history. The Moon is believed to have formed along with the solar system almost 4.6 billion years ago. A heavy meteorite bombardment melted the Moon's surface. At 3.95 billion years ago, the lunar highlands formed and during this period the meteorite impacting began to taper off in intensity, leaving a blanket of dust and rubble across the lunar surface. From 3.9 to 3.3 billion years ago, liquid magma flowed up through the nearside surface and formed the marias.

The Moon originally formed with a molten core that grew solid with a powerful magnetic field encased within it. Molten crustal rock solidified in this magnetic field, then became magnetized. Later this same core melted as a result of radioactive heating, losing its magnetic force in the process.

Presently receding from Earth, our companion in space was once as close as 40,000 miles. Lunar origin theories focus on whether the Moon was formed at a distance from our planet or was captured. Some theories suggest the Moon at one time was a part of our planet and was formed from material gouged out of the Earth's equator. Another theory maintains that both the Moon and our planet were formed as a double planet from the same dust cloud. Dissimilar mineral compositions appear to kick dust in the face of these theories. Capture seems the most likely explanation.

OBSERVING THE MOON WITH BINOCULARS

A 7- or 8-power pair of binoculars will show you a fair amount of lunar detail. The 10- and 11-power binoculars will show you a bit more if you can hold them steady or mount them on tripods. A 20-, 25-, or 30-power model will offer you some outstanding lunar views and a grasp of all the major Moon details.

The secret of lunar observation with binoculars, besides patience and a steady hand, is to watch the *terminator*, that shadow line between day and night, as it moves nightly across the Moon's surface. Another important factor in learning about our nearest neighbor in space is to get your hands on a good lunar map or book containing maps. Celestron and Phillips both put out adequate folding maps. Excellent books containing good Moon maps are *Atlas of the Solar System* by Moore and Hunt, *A Field Guide to the Stars and Planets* by Menzel and Pasachoff, and *Pictorial Guide to the Moon* by Alter.

To learn the Moon's phases, rising, and settings check your local newspapers or purchase one of the many fine astronomical calendars now on the market.

The Moon's phases are as follows:

☆ *New Moon*—the Moon is closest to the Sun in the sky.The Moon is invisible and gradually moving toward the crescent stage. Its night side is facing Earth.
☆ *First Quarter*—the Moon has made 1/4 of its orbit around the Earth (each phase lasts about a week). The quarter is a half-illumined Moon.
☆ *Full Moon* (Fig. 6-5)—the entire lunar face is illuminated and ultra bright.
☆ *Last Quarter*—the Moon rises toward morning. After its 29 1/2-day cycle it is on the road to becoming *New* again. The terminator is moving East as the quarter shrinks.

OBSERVING THE LUNAR SURFACE

When you view the Moon's near side through binoculars, you will note how the lunar craters and mountains sharply highlight themselves against the terminator's shadow. With the Sun hanging low in the lunar sky, the Moon's features cast their shadow and stand out in bold relief. At lunar midday our pockmarked sister in space appears washed out, almost featureless (what we see when we look at a full moon). Only during the lunar morning or late afternoon is it worthwhile to study the Moon.

Observations of the lunar surface immediately point out the two major surface contrasts: the dark maria and the brighter land masses. Maria are vast dark areas with a relatively smooth appearance. Made of solidified lava, the maria are covered with a narrow layer of dust.

Craters pock the uplands. Hundreds can be viewed in low-power 7× binoculars; thousands with much higher powered, 20× to 30× binoculars. Craters are circular depressions, often with beveled walls and a huge mountain in the center. Your binoculars will show you quite a few cratered regions in the Southern Lunar Hemisphere. Craterlets can be glimpsed in the larger craters if you can mount those higher-powered glasses. Clavius, a 150-mile-wide giant lost to the South Lunar Pole, is a fine example.

Fig. 6-5. A full moon photographed with a 10-inch reflector (Photograph by Dr. Steve Simmerman).

As you observe the Moon change steadily from its initial thin crescent to the First Quarter, you will become more aware of the eastern limb. Here is the home of Mare Crisium (sea of crisis), a lunar maria some 300 miles across and marked with tiny craterlets that are invisible through low-powered binoculars. Mare Crisium, bordered by mountains and crisscrossed by curved ridges, is a good spot to behold *lunar libration*, the barely detectable swinging of the Earth-facing hemisphere from East to West, then gradually back again. Having an eliptical orbit, the

Moon will travel more rapidly as it nears the Earth. At apogee (when it is farthest from the Earth's center), the Moon slows and at perigee (when it is nearest the Earth's center), its speed increases. At all times, its axial rotation remains at the same rate. Ultimately libration permits us to view five-ninths of the lunar surface. Every so often the Moon's axial rotation and orbit get out of sync. Mare Crisium during one observation might border the limb, while two weeks later it might have swung entirely clear of the edge.

North of Mare Crisium is Cleomedes, a fair-sized crater. South of Mare Crisium lies four large craters: Langrenus, Vendelinus, Petavius, and Furnerius. All are 80 to 100 miles in diameter. Vendelinus is overrun with lava, while Petavius sports a deep valley slanting to the southeast wall and a tall central peak.

If you are curious as to why the near side came to have so many Latin names, you can blame an Italian priest named Giambattista Riccioli. In 1651 he published a map of the Moon based in part on the observations of Francesco Grimaldi. Riccioli introduced lunar nomenclature, naming the main craters after famous men. The system survives. Curiously Riccioli did not believe in Galileo's notions of the solar system, which is quite possibly why the man from Venice has only a small crater named after him, while two fairly important lunar formations carry the names Riccioli and Grimaldi.

As the terminator passes through Mare Tranquillitatis, you will note another chain of large craters toward the Southern boundary: Theophilus, Cyrillus, and Catharina, all fine examples of impacting by large meteorites perhaps several miles in diameter. Occurring over 4 thousand million years ago, these impacts clearly left evidence on the surrounding surface where blasted-out subsurface material remains.

Hyginus Valley, near the Moon's center, is a key volcanic feature. Craters vie for space as the terminator passes into the Southern Hemisphere. Atlas, Endymion, and Hercules are fine crater examples close to the North Lunar Pole.

During the Moon's First Quarter you will note the long string of craters along the central meridian. The most prominent are Arzachel, Ptolemaeus, and Alphonsus. Below them lie Walter, Regiomontanus, and Purbach—all wondrous sites under the gaze of even a low-power binocular. At near dead center of the Moon is Ptolemaeus, a 90-mile-wide crater which is a fantastic sight when it is close to the terminator. Nearby sits the craterlet Lyot with its low ringed mountain. Hipparchus, a neighboring crater, is small and has been eroded by early lunar upheavals. Mare Tranquillitatis rests in the Northern Hemisphere with its neighbor Mare Serenitatis. The Caucasus and Haemus Mountains border Tranquillitatis' western shore. The famed Alps are due North of the Caucasus (Fig. 6-6). They are home to the sharp-cutting Alpine Valley. Surface collapse likely took place there.

The Apennines, a fine mountain range, is visible just after the First Quarter. Look again toward the central meridian.

Mare Ibrium, a spectacular mare, is bordered to the west by the Apennines. Tiny craters dot this lunar sea and some of them—Autolycus, Aristillus, and Archimedes—will strike your curiosity. Another famous crater, Plato, resides on the northern shore. Clear-cut in outline, Plato's 60-mile floor appears almost featureless.

Perhaps one of the most outstanding craters is Copernicus. Almost perfectly formed, having 17,000-foot walls and being 55 miles in diameter, Copernicus has a giant central peak stabbing 22,000 feet in the air. Copernicus's ray system is the second largest on the lunar surface. The rays, those bright streaks radiating like wheel spokes from impact craters, are believed to be debris from intense impacting. Some rays are several hundred miles long. Tycho's ray system extends over 1,000 miles (Fig. 6-7). Rays are best seen during a full moon.

Sinus Iridium, the Bay of Rainbows, is a semicircular cliff configuration on the northern shore of Mare Ibrium and is over 100 miles across. The southern cliff of this aesthetically pleasing remains of a crater is washed away and its floor is covered with lava. In the shadows of the terminator, Sinus Iridium appears as a wreath.

Clavius, one of the more eye-catching craters and a bit south of Tycho, is 150 miles across. A line of craters dot Clavius's floor. Nearby sits Bailly with an even larger diameter of 180 miles. Because of its proximity to the limb, Bailly is not so easily observed.

Detail on the lunar surface becomes washed out and difficult to view as the full moon approaches. Larger objective binoculars, with big exit pupils, will make full-moon observation somewhat uncomfortable because the lunar surface shines almost intolerably bright. Recall, too, that lunar features will not cast shadows and thus heighten contrast during this phase. Only the brightest features can be seen under full-moon conditions. Grimaldi, a giant crater 120 miles in diameter, is one such feature. Because Grimaldi is so close to the limb, only a sloping view may be had of its dark gray floor. A glimpse of this feature will tell you it is close to being the darkest spot on the lunar surface. Grimaldi is also a fine location to judge libration.

Near Grimaldi rests the highly contrasting Aristarchus, a 23-mile-wide crater in Oceanus Procellarum (Fig. 6-8). A gray deposit, in all probability volcanic ash, coats the lunar highlands and makes Aristarchus bright during earthshine conditions.

During the full moon period you will have the occasional opportunity to see the lunar eclipse phenomenon. At rare times the full moon phase will happen almost exactly in a straight line between the Earth and the Sun. When this alignment occurs, the sunlight is cut off by Earth and we view the Earth's shadow on the full moon's face.

Fig. 6-6. The Alps of the Moon; photographed by the Lick 36-inch refractor (Lick Observatory Photograph).

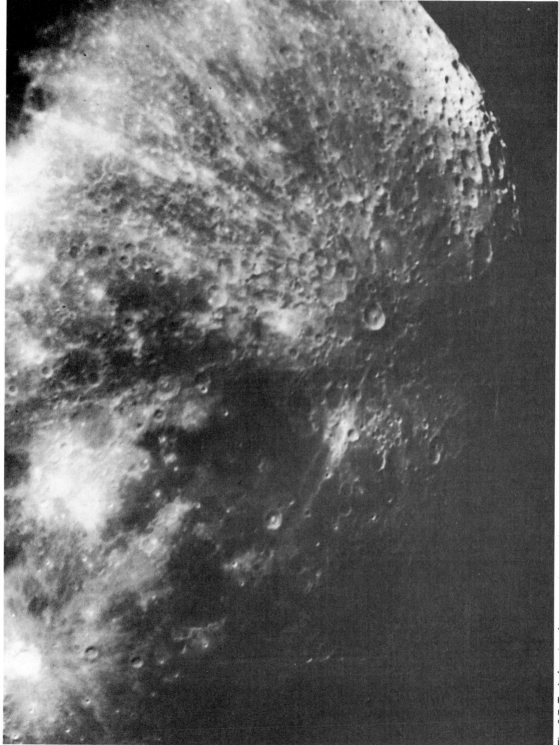

Fig. 6-7. Tycho's extensive ray system as photographed with a 10-inch reflector (Photograph by Dr. Steve Simmerman).

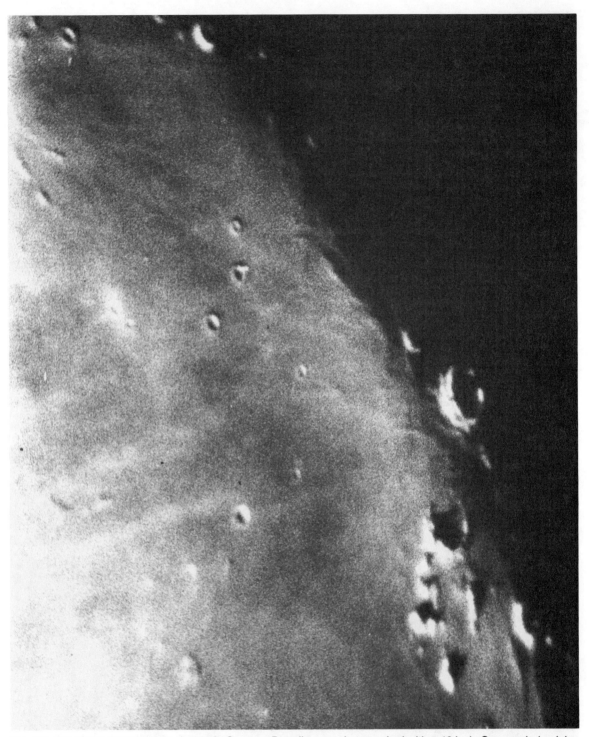

Fig. 6-8. The crater Aristarchus in the maria Oceanus Procellarum, photographed with a 10-inch Cassegrain by John E. Westfall (Courtesy of ALPO).

64

The Earth's shadow, 5700 miles wide when the Moon is at its mean distance, consists of two tapered cones pointing away from the Sun. The narrow umbra shadow converges and disappears at a distance of 1 million miles, quite beyond the Moon, while the other shadow—the much broader penumbra—diverges and continues endlessly (Fig. 6-9). The Moon does not vanish altogether when it moves into the umbra. The Earth's shadow on the Moon is lit up by sunlight refracted by our atmosphere. Because red light is most easily refracted, you will generally find the lunar surface colored salmon pink during an eclipse.

The Moon might remain totally eclipsed for up to 1 2/3 hours. If you total up the time the Moon spends wholly or partially in the umbra and penumbra, the total duration might be as long as 6 hours.

When you are observing an eclipse with your binoculars, you might notice that the eclipse is darker than average. If this is the case, the sunlight, passing through our atmosphere and being refracted into our shadow, likely passed through heavy cloud cover. If the earthshine is bright, then a clear Earth atmosphere is to be suspected. At times severe volcanic activity on our planet might affect our shadow. This effect was witnessed back in 1883 after the Krakatoa Event and even more recently in 1983 after some Mexican volcanic activity.

LUNAR ECLIPSE DATES

10/17/86
8/27/88
2/20/89
8/17/89

All of these dates are for total lunar eclipses. Your area newspapers will likely give you the starting times for them.

LUNAR OCCULTATIONS

Traveling in its westward path across the sky, the Moon often passes in front of stars and *occults*, or eclipses, them. The extremely accurate timing of an occultation, just as the star blinks out behind the lunar edge, offers important clues about the orbits of our planet and its satellite and any alterations in the speed or distance of that orbital motion. Lunar occultations also supply information about changes in sidereal time. On rare occasions double stars are discovered.

Because the Moon is a relatively large heavenly body, it offers the binocularist an opportunity to make precise occultation timings and to do valuable amateur research. I might add that your first occultation experience will teach you one grand fact about our neighbor in space. The Moon has no atmosphere and you, the binocularist, will grasp this notion when you observe a star instantly vanish behind the lunar limb. If an atmosphere existed, then you would have witnessed a flickering or fading seconds before the star flashed out. However, it bears mentioning that when a planet is occulted (Fig. 6-10), it will fade several seconds prior to its complete disappearance. Unlike stars, planets have a perceptible disk, and it takes the Moon a bit more time to make it completely invisible. Lunar dark-limb occultations can be wondrous sights when the star's abrupt flash-out occurs against the Moon's unseen face and the naturally dark sky.

Even though the lunar occultation timing is a fairly

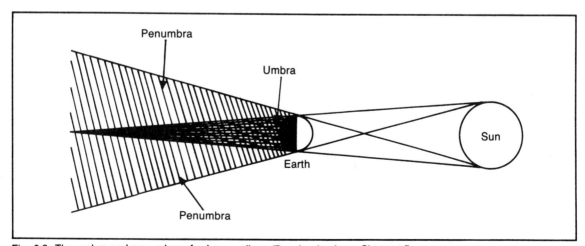

Fig. 6-9. The umbra and penumbra of a lunar eclipse (Drawing by Anne Sheppard).

Fig. 6-10. The Moon about to occult the planet Venus; photographed with a 10-inch reflector (Photograph by Dr. Steve Simmerman).

uncomplicated event, you must exercise caution during the observation. When the star flashes behind the lunar limb you must know the exact time to the nearest 0.1 second, using WWV time signals. You also must be certain what star has been occulted.

For accurate occultations, your binoculars—even 7× models—must be firmly mounted on a stable tripod. Wind, vibration, the slightest motion can destroy exactness in timing. The larger your binocular objectives, the more stars will be visible. It is best to avoid stars at your instrument's magnitude limits. Poor atmospheric conditions or atmospheric turbulence can cause the observed star to blink out and thus create havoc with your timing.

A good stopwatch, such as those used in a track event, is best used in timings because you will require 0.1 second accuracy at the instant of occultation. A shortwave radio, tuned to WWV time standard signals, is a must. The signal frequencies are 5, 10, 15, and 20 MHz. Not all frequencies can be heard at any one location. As with much shortwave reception, the difficulty of stations fading in and out will be encountered—and sometimes right before the occultation! If a fade-out occurs prior to occultation and you're employing a stopwatch, you can

measure, while the stopwatch runs, the next recognizable time mark after the occultation.

A tape recorder is almost mandatory for occultations. A small cassette recorder offers advantages. The only drawback can be cold weather, when drive speed variations occur. In this situation I'd recommend keeping your recorder warm and in your coat pocket. Battery power can also contribute to drive rate fluctuations. A possible remedy for tape recorder drive problems is to employ two tape recorders simultaneously. This solution is more expensive, yet reliable.

During your observation, make comments on any events that might affect the quality of your timings. If you run up against fading WWV signals when you're employing the recorder, the timing can still be made good by measuring from the previous minute's announcement.

Predictions on Occultations

If you plan serious lunar occultation research with your binoculars, I would encourage you to get a prediction schedule from The United States Naval Observatory, Occultation Timing Division, Washington, DC 20390. The

Naval Observatory's predictions are computer-generated and are based on your location; so you will attain timing accuracy. When you are making occultations you should be doing it from a fixed location where the latitude and longitude are known down to within 25 feet. Carefully timed meridian transits of stars with known positions are a must for deducing latitude and longitude. This work for your area has already been done. Get your hands on a United States Geological Survey topographical map from your local library or the United States Geological Survey Commission, Denver, CO 80225.

If you request predictions from the Naval Observatory, expect to receive a questionnaire regarding your observing experience, instrument, observing location, and your intentions.

If you have only a casual interest in lunar occultations, you can receive predictions of some of the better-known events for Canada and the United States from *Sky and Telescope*. Write their Occultation Prediction Department, 49 Bay State Road, Cambridge, MA 02138. The *Sky and Telescope* predictions are prepared by the Nautical Almanac Office of the Royal Greenwich Observatory in England.

The permitted margin of error in occultation timings is only 0.5 seconds, which would not seem exceptional with more experienced observers who can achieve results to about 0.03 seconds or better. A good sweep hand on your stopwatch is a must. The electronic stopwatches are considered the best choices for accurate timing because they can record down to 0.01 seconds. If you're about to choose an electronic stopwatch, a two-metal watch is best because contraction problems happen in very cold weather.

To test your stopwatch, run it for 60 minutes and find out its inaccuracy rate down to 1 minute. Test the stopwatch against the WWV time tick. Learn how your watch behaves under all kinds of weather conditions.

Methods for Timing

The three major methods for timing occultations are: the stopwatch method, the tape recorder method, and the eye-ear method. The *stopwatch method*, the most commonly employed method, gives the least accurate timings owing to its own character. Stopwatch timing goes as follows:

☆ Observe the star as the lunar limb approaches.
☆ At the instant of occultation quickly depress the stopwatch button.
☆ Let the watch run until the next voice signal announces the minute on WWV.
☆ At the exact instant you hear the tone signal, halt the stopwatch.
☆ Now subtract the elapsed time between the occultation and when you stopped the stopwatch to locate the true value of the occultation timing.

Example: 7:49:00.0 Next time tone after occultation.
        −   :32.8 Elapsed time.
            7.48:27.2 Time of occultation.

This method has its problems. You must start and stop your stopwatch instantly. If you anticipate or lag in your button pushing, you will screw up the timing accuracy, which will destroy your one chance at the event.

As previously mentioned, your stopwatch must work accurately; if it doesn't you should know its error. Mechanical problems often found in stopwatches are: delayed starts, effects of moisture and temperature, failure of the sweep hand to reset at zero, gravitational influences on a watch when it's held in different positions, and overwinding. The last major difficulty in the stopwatch method is your own reaction speed.

In essence, the tape recorder method is the simultaneous recording of the WWV radio signal and the observer's voice signaling the occultation. Tune to any 5, 10, 15, or 20 MHz frequency that gives you clear reception for 5 minutes prior to the occultation. At the same instant turn your tape recorder on so the time signals can be recorded. Remember: the tape recorder's accuracy must be known. If the WWV signal fades out right before the occultation, you'll still have a record of your voice signals. At the instant of the event, note the occultation quickly. Many people say Z the moment of the event because Z is easy to say and hear.

Later you can listen to the tape recording and determine the occultation's actual time. The tape can be played repeatedly until you are certain the timing obtained is accurate. A stopwatch giving timings to 0.1 seconds will be required. The stopwatch will be started at the precise instant of the minute tone prior to the occultation and halted after the voice signal. You can repeat this procedure enough times to ensure accuracy. You might wish to repeat the tape, remake the timings, and then determine an average.

In these event timings you must take account of your *personal delay*, or reaction time, between the occultation's actual time and the time noted on your tape recorder or stopwatch. When you report an occultation, you should mention if you've reported your personal delay. If you fail to make a statement about your personal delay, the folks examining your data will automatically add on a

0.3-second reduction to your timing. If you're just a neophyte in this business, it would be best that you use 0.3 seconds as your personal delay. Later as you become more efficient, your personal delay might drop to as low as 0.1 second.

Time delays can be caused in initially starting the watch and in stopping it. In using the tape recorder method, the delay might exhibit itself in the time it takes for your nervous system to make your voice respond that the occultation has occurred. The delay problems brought on by using a stopwatch to time the tape recording is almost entirely eliminated when you replay the tape several times and take an average.

Prior to the arrival of the ship's chronometer and the stopwatch, occultation timings were made with only the one-second tick of a clock. The old method in many instances proved every bit as reliable as using today's instruments with 0.1 second ticks. Simplest and least efficient, the eye-ear method offers only one advantage over the tape recorder and stopwatch, and that is that the eye and mind respond more rapidly to stimuli than the hand. I don't look with much confidence on this method, even though it is still used. I would stick with either the stopwatch or the tape recorder.

Problems in Making Accurate Timings

Occultation timings can be affected by atmospheric conditions (seeing), transparency, and personal bias. *Seeing* makes stars twinkle and flash in varying brightness. Faint stars might blink out altogether, causing a false alarm for the occultation observer. Beware of the Moon's proximity to the horizon when you are following an occultation. Any time our neighbor in space resides down in the atmospheric soup near the horizon, you can count on turbulence and its blinking effect on stars.

Transparency has a great deal to do with accurate occultations. Many false occultations have been caused by stars blinking out prematurely behind clouds and haze. Watch the skies carefully.

The final major problem in making accurate occultations is bias. Since you know from predictions the time an occultation is to happen, you might be tempted to slant your timing toward what is expected. Try to forget the prediction. Time only the occultation.

For more information on lunar occultations write:

International Occultation Timing Association
P.O. Box 596
Tinley Park, IL 60477

International Lunar Occultation Center
Astronomical Division, Hydrographic Department
Tsukiji-5, Chuo-ku
Tokyo, 104 Japan

Chapter 7

The Planets

Our solar system offers more than the Sun and the Moon to observe. Within the light grasp of even 7 × 50 binoculars is the possibility of sighting every planet save for Pluto, which requires at the very least an 8-inch aperture. In hunting Pluto a 10-inch aperture, a keen eye, and an atlas with stars to the tenth magnitude might prove a greater assistance.

Generally the planets will appear starlike in binoculars, save for the higher-powered instruments with which some of the planets will be discerned as disks (Fig. 7-1). At 25 power and up, depending on how its rings are displayed, Saturn will show rings.

Mercury and Venus, owing to their positions within our planet's orbit, are never found far from the Sun in our sky and are thus called *inferior* planets. When an inferior planet is both East of and at its largest angular distance from the Sun in the evening sky, the planet is said to be at *Eastern elongation*.

When an inferior planet is at its largest angular distance from the Sun in the morning, or furthest West, the planet is said to be at *Western elongation*. At *inferior conjunction*, the planet is nearest the Earth, yet too near the Sun's glare to be observable. The planet's night side is facing us much like a new moon. At *superior conjunction* the planet is at its greatest distance. The *synodic periods*,

or the time inferior planets take to complete their paths through our morning and evening skies, take into account both the Earth's rotation around the Sun and the inferior planets' orbits around the Sun. The synodic period for Venus is 584 days and the synodic period for Mercury is 116 days.

The most favorable time for seeing inferior planets is during their greatest angular distance from the Sun, either at western or eastern elongation (Fig. 7-2). At eastern elongation Mercury might remain in the sky some two hours after the Sun. Venus might last as long as four hours after sunset. Elongations are not always favorable because they depend on the Earth's axis tilt, which is 23 1/2 degrees.

Shining in the reflected light of the Sun, one or several of the planets can be viewed on almost any clear morning or night. Their positions in the sky vary little for observers anywhere on our planet. Yet over a period of several days the planets' motion can be noted if you chart them among the stars.

Since the solar system is flat for the most part, the planets are confined to a narrow path through the constellations known as the ecliptic. The Sun traces this same path during its daytime excursion. The ecliptic is essentially the projection of the Earth's orbit on the sky, ow-

MARS

JUPITER

SATURN

Fig. 7-1. Three planets: Mars (top left), Jupiter (top right), and Saturn (bottom); photographed with Lick 36-inch refractor (Lick Observatory Photograph).

ing to the fact that the Sun lies in the plane of our orbit.

If you are just starting out in astronomy, there are several tests for a planet. These tests appeared in Chapter 4, but I believe they bear repeating.

The tests for a planet are:

☆ If that bright object seems almost stationary and can't

be found on either your star locater wheel or on the map charts of your star atlas, then very likely you're viewing a planet.

☆ If that bright object twinkles then most likely it isn't a planet. However, at times Mercury twinkles because of its poor positioning in the atmospheric soup of the horizon.

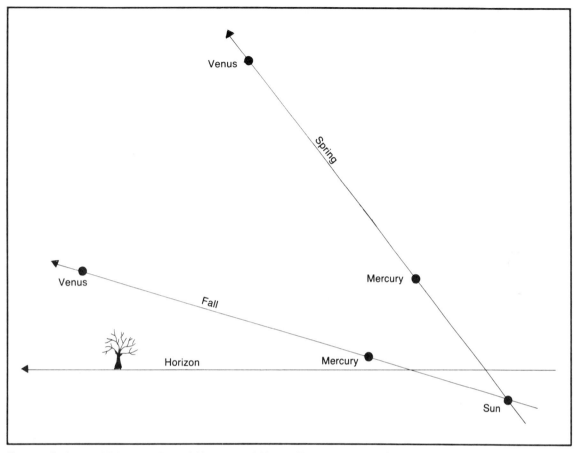

Fig. 7-2. Spring and fall elongations of Mercury and Venus (Drawing by Anne Sheppard).

☆ If that bright object travels far from the ecliptic, it will not be a planet. If you live in the Northern Hemisphere and you observe a bright object in the north or high in the south during the summer, then it will not be a planet. The planets' path along the ecliptic places them low in the south during the summer and high in the winter.

☆ If that bright object lingers near either the North Star or the South Pole, it can not be a planet. Planets never come within 50 degrees of the poles.

Before you embark on planetary observation it would be wise to keep several facts in mind. Without very powerful binoculars you will be unable to discern a planet's disk. In more powerful binoculars (25 × and up), the inferior planets will show crescents while some of the outer planets will appear full.

Each planet possesses a unique color, which will help in its identification. Mercury is the color of lead. Venus is almost silver. Mars has a reddish tint. Jupiter appears white (Fig. 7-3). Saturn gives a yellowish tint. Uranus and Neptune have a hint of green.

Positive identification can be made by finding out which constellation the planet resides in, then checking that against the information supplied by that month's issue of *Sky and Telescope* or *Astronomy*. A planetary ephermeris might also prove of value.

Brightness is also useful in determining identification. Compared to the stars Rigel and Vega, the planets have a relative brightness as follows: Mercury about the same. Venus is 40 times brighter. Mars is 4 times brighter. Jupiter is 6 times brighter. Saturn is nearly the same.

MERCURY

Mercury's distance from the Sun: 36 million miles (average).

Fig. 7-3. Jupiter (above) and M4, a globular cluster in Scorpius; photographed with a 12-inch f/5 Astromak (Photograph by Jim Riffle).

Mercury's eccentricity of orbit: 0.206.
Mercury's orbital inclination to ecliptic: 7 degrees.
Mercury's synodic period: 116 days.
Mercury's sidereal period: 88 days.
Mercury's rotational period: 58.65 days.
Mercury's angular diameter: Varies from 5″ to 13″.
Mercury's magnitude: At maximum − 1.9.
Mercury's surface: Densely cratered; some maria.
Mercury's atmosphere: Almost none.
Mercury's density: 5.4 g/km^3.
Mercury's diameter: 3,032 miles.
Mercury is the closest planet to the Sun.
Mercury's mass: 3.30×10^{20} tons.
Mercury's closest approach to Earth: 48 million miles.
Mercury's equatorial surface temperature (perihelion):
    415° C.
Mercury's equatorial surface temperature (aperhelion):
    285° C.
Mercury's dark side temperature: to − 175° C.
Mercury's core: iron-nickel.
Mercury's moons: none.
Mercury's albedo: 0.06.

Features of Mercury

An airless, arid world with a crater-strewn surface like the Moon's, Mercury is the closest planet to the Sun. Chilled by bitter temperatures at nightfall, this diminutive planet gets heated at noon to the melting point of lead.

To the Earth-based observer, Mercury—like its neighbor Venus—shows phases similar to the Moon's. At its greatest elongation from the Sun, Mercury shows a half phase to us.

Mercury on rare occasions can be viewed transiting the solar globe when this planet appears like a slow-moving speck. Look for these transit phenomena on November 12, 1986 and again on November 14, 1999. A transit is quite a curious sight in well-filtered binoculars.

A constant companion of the Sun, Mercury's greatest elongation is 28 degrees at *aphelion* (when it is farthest from the Sun) and 18 degrees at *perihelion* (when it is nearest the Sun). This elongation creates problems for Earthbound observers. Mercury, never much over the horizon, dwells in the atmospheric soup and is subject to bad seeing.

Rotating on its axis in a period of 58.65 days, the planet keeps the same face toward the Sun, maintaining one side as an oven and the dark side as a freezer. A rather unusual effect of perihelion is that Mercury's rotation becomes slower than its motion in orbit, causing the Sun, as viewed from Mercury, to halt its westward movement,

dropping back eastward for some hours before it resumes its regular motion.

Heat on the planet's equatorial surface reaches 415° C at perihelion when the Sun appears 50 percent larger in the sky. The dark side shows temperatures around − 175° C. The almost unrecordable atmosphere fails to retain any heat, resulting in the temperature extremes between night and day. The atmosphere is one one-million-millionths that of Earth's at sea level.

Mercury's surface composition, similar to the Moon's, possesses the same 7 percent albedo, the same radar reflectivity, and the identical polarization qualities. Bright areas and faint shadings on Mercury resemble lunar highlands and marias.

Mariner 10 photographs show a heavily cratered surface. The largest crater, Caloris Basin, is some 800 miles across and contains a lava-flooded floor covered with deep fractures.

Like the Moon, Mercury shows two distinct hemispheres: one with heavily cratered highlands, the other with sparsely cratered plains much like the lunar maria.

Mercury's craters are quite similar to the Moon's—both have ray systems and brilliant halos. Also both Mercury and the Moon's craters show the same erosion by meteor impacting. Shallower than lunar craters, the Mercurian versions have central peaks caused by movement in the underlying crust or by the terracing of crater walls. Secondary craters and *ejecta* (surrounding large craters) extend outward by only half the distance usually encountered by the Moon. This condition might be a result of Mercury's more powerful gravity.

Mercurian maria greatly resemble lunar maria. Both possess similar craters and craterlets. Irregular scarps up to 2 miles high might extend several miles and might cut through basins, craters, and maria. Near the Caloris Basin is terrain made of broken hills, large rugged valleys, landslides, and cratering. This terrain was likely the result of shock waves caused by heavy impacting in the basin.

Mercury's surface appears almost identical to the Moon's. The regolith, or surface soil, layer is perhaps 50 to 150 feet deep and made of rock debris imbeded in a glassy soil that was produced by the heat of meteor impacts. The soil covers a shattered rock mass. Mercury's density evidences a nickel-iron core. A weak magnetic field around the planet was detected by *Mariner 10*.

Mercury's history parallels the Moon's evolution. After the planet formed, the surface got melted by the intense heat of a meteor bombardment. Later the highland regions grew solid. Further impacts scattered rocky debris over the entire surface. Below the surface radioactive decay led to further melting, which filled the basin areas to form maria. Additionally evolved by small meteor cratering, the surface later formed scarps from the contraction of the cooling molten core. No Mercurian satellites have ever been detected.

Observing Mercury

Mercury, the seldom-noticed planet, is never more than two hand widths (28 degrees) from the Sun. Mercury is best observed within the week of greatest eastern or western elongation when the planet is seen as a 0 magnitude star (almost the same brightness as Vega). Through binoculars Mercury will appear as a leaden, starlike object. You would need at least 50 power to show this planet as a disk.

In the Northern Hemisphere the planet is better viewed on spring evenings than on fall evenings and better viewed on fall mornings than on spring mornings. Southern Hemisphere observers will find Mercury best seen on spring mornings than on fall mornings and best seen during fall evenings than on spring evenings. Southern Hemisphere observers will have the finest views of Mercury.

On November 13, 1986 Mercury will take a 5-hour transit across the Sun (Fig. 7-4). A repeat performance comes on November 6, 1993. You must use solar filters on your binoculars to observe this event.

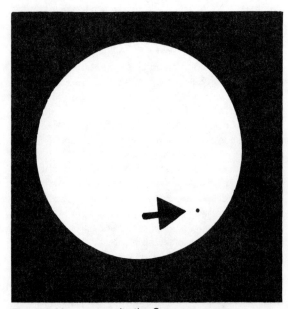

Fig. 7-4. Mercury transits the Sun.

Elongations of Mercury

Western

1/3/85	7/25/87	10/10/89	12/27/91	3/19/94
5/1/85	11/13/87	2/1/90	4/23/92	7/17/94
8/28/85	3/8/88	5/31/90	8/21/92	11/6/94
4/13/86	7/6/88	9/24/90	12/9/92	3/1/95
8/11/86	10/26/88	1/4/91	4/5/93	6/29/95
11/30/86	2/18/89	5/12/91	8/4/93	10/20/95
3/26/87	6/18/89	9/7/91	11/22/93	

Eastern

3/17/85	6/7/87	8/29/89	11/19/91	2/4/94
7/14/85	10/4/87	12/23/89	3/9/92	5/30/94
11/8/85	1/26/88	4/13/90	7/6/92	9/26/94
2/28/86	5/19/88	8/11/90	10/31/92	1/19/95
6/25/86	9/15/88	12/6/90	2/21/93	5/12/95
10/21/86	1/9/89	3/27/91	6/17/93	9/9/95
2/12/87	5/1/89	7/25/91	10/14/93	

VENUS

Venus' diameter: 7521 miles.
Venus' mass: 4.87×10^{21} tons.
Venus' axial rotation: 243 days in retrograde motion.
Venus' axis inclined: 3 degrees.
Venus' orbital speed: 22 miles per second.
Venus' average distance from the Sun: 67,238,000 miles.
Venus takes 224.7 days to orbit the Sun.
Venus' brightest magnitude: −4.3.
Venus' maximum elongation: 47°.
Venus' atmosphere: largely carbon dioxide with traces of nitrogen, carbon monoxide, and water vapor.
Venus' atmospheric pressure: 91 times that of Earth's.
Venus' angular diameter: from 10″ to 61″.
Venus' sidereal period: 225 days.
Venus' synodic period: 584 days.
Venus' albedo: 0.76.

Features of Venus

Venus, the second planet from the Sun, is rocky, hot, dry, and shrouded with a thick smoglike atmosphere (Fig. 7-5). Nearly the Earth's twin in size, Venus is both an evening and morning "star." The ancients called this

Fig. 7-5. A crescent Venus; photographed with a 10-inch reflector (Photograph by Dr. Steve Simmerman).

planet Hesperus and Phosphorus, and believed it to be two distinct bodies. After the Moon and the Sun, Venus is the brightest object in our skies, sometimes reaching a magnitude of -4.3. Visible in daylight, Venus can even cast shadows at night. This morning and evening star has the closest approach to Earth of any planet, yet its position inside the Earth's orbit makes the dark side face us from time to time.

Staying close to the Sun in our sky, Venus reaches a maximum *elongation*, or separation from the Sun, of 47 degrees. During maximum evening elongation, the planet shows itself as a half illuminated disk. In moving toward the Sun, Venus increases in size with its phase altering to a slender crescent. With rare frequency the planet transits the solar disk and appears as a slow-moving dark dot. Last transits occurred in 1874 and 1882. The next will take place June 7, 2004 and June 5, 2012. Again, use only properly filtered binoculars when you are viewing a transit.

For the Earthbound observer Venus offers little, save for its phases, owing to the nearly unbroken cloud cover. At inferior conjunction when Venus appears close to the Sun, the planet exhibits a fine crescent. Often Venus' outline is made visible through telescopes by light scattered by its atmosphere. Its clouds rotate in a retrograde direction (East to West) around the globe every 4 days. Venus demonstrates a slow retrograde motion, taking 243 days. The planet has no moons.

Venus possesses an extremely high surface temperature, reported to be $475°$ C. After the solar light and heat are absorbed by the planet, a greenhouse effect takes place. The heat is radiated into the atmosphere where it is trapped, causing high surface temperatures.

Because of the Soviet spacecraft *Venera 9* and *Venera 10*, the planet's surface is better understood. These space probes made soft landings and sent back panoramic pictures, showing a rock-strewn landscape with large and small boulders. The pictures disclosed a relatively young landscape, lacking the character of either the Moon or Mercury. Venus is believed to be much like our Earth internally, possessing the same liquid core surrounded by a mantle and granitelike crust.

The atmospheric pressure is said to be 91 times that of the Earth's. The cloud cover is more like thick smog than our planet's water vapor clouds. The Venusian atmosphere is composed of 90 percent carbon dioxide with some hydrogen, oxygen, helium, carbon dioxide, hydrogen chloride, hydrogen fluoride, sulfuric acid, and traces of argon. The main cloud cover ranges some 30 to 40 miles in altitude with a thinner haze above it. The clouds, made of sulfuric acid droplets, also contain hydrochloric acid, hydroflouric acid, and other minor constituents.

Venus' high temperatures never let water condense, but produce a permanent cloud cover, leading to a strong greenhouse effect that keeps carbon dioxide in the atmosphere and breaks up water molecules, which are lofted into the upper atmosphere.

High altitudes are marked by turbulent winds, while the atmosphere closer to the surface is quiet with occasional gentle breezes. Great cloud-cover belts girdle and equatorial and temperate latitudes. Heated by the Sun, the atmosphere forms jet streams and blows toward the poles.

Venus, unlike Earth, lacks a strong magnetic field. This lack is attributed to the planet's slow rotation. Venus is suspected of having an iron core.

Observing Venus

Other than the Sun and Moon, Venus can be the brightest sky object. It is certainly the brightest planet, and its dazzling silver light makes it unmistakable at twilight. This planet can also be glimpsed during daylight on many days of the year. Venus begins to show a crescent in 7- to 10-power binoculars that are firmly mounted.

At 19-month intervals Venus reaches its maximum height in the evening sky when the planet achieves its greatest eastward distance from the Sun. At this point Venus possesses a face like the Moon at First Quarter. Almost 30 days later the planet begins to vanish in the Sun's glare, where it becomes lost for nearly 21 days. Then Venus shows up again in the morning and rises higher each day until it fades into the morning glare. At its greatest westward distance from the Sun 60 days later, Venus is high at dawn in the sky. Once more it does its disappearing act at sunrise and remains out of sight for

60 days, again showing itself in the evening sky and repeating its cycle.

Venus, as a result of its great brilliance, produces glare, ghost images, and chromatic aberration in even the finest binoculars. Making out a firm Venusian outline will be next to impossible because of the glare, purple fringe, and I might add, the atmospheric seeing. Even though the image contrast will suffer during daylight observations, Venus will show its phases better then.

Elongations and Conjunctions of Venus

8/27/86	Eastern elongation
11/5/86	Inferior conjunction
1/15/87	Western elongation
8/23/87	Superior conjunction
4/3/88	Eastern elongation
6/13/88	Inferior conjunction
8/22/88	Western elongation
4/5/89	Superior conjunction
11/8/89	Eastern elongation
1/10/90	Inferior conjunction
3/30/90	Western elongation
11/1/90	Superior conjunction
6/13/91	Eastern elongation
8/22/91	Inferior conjunction
11/2/91	Western elongation
6/13/92	Superior conjunction
1/19/93	Eastern elongation
4/1/93	Inferior conjunction
6/10/93	Western elongation
1/17/94	Superior conjunction
8/25/94	Eastern elongation
11/2/94	Inferior conjunction
1/13/95	Western elongation
8/20/95	Superior conjunction

MARS

Mars is the fourth planet from the Sun.
Mars' average distance from the Sun: 141,636,000 miles.
Mars' orbital path: elliptical.
Mars' axial rotation: 24 hr. 37 min. 23 sec.
Mars' speed in orbit: 15 miles per second.
Mars' diameter: 4217 miles.
Mars' mass: 6.4×10^{20} tons.
Mars' mean density: 3.94 times that of water.
Mars' inclination of rotational axis: 25 degrees.
Mars' atmosphere: 95% carbon dioxide, 2% nitrogen, traces of argon, carbon monoxide, oxygen and water vapor.

Mars has the largest mountain in the solar system: Olympus Mons.
Mars' orbit time around the Sun: 1.88 years.
Mars' moons: Two: Deimos and Phobos.
Mars' synodic period: 780 days.
Mars' sidereal period: 687 days.
Mars' angular diameter: from 4" to 25".
Mars' magnitude: – 2.8 maximum.
Mar's albedo: 0.16.

Features of Mars

Fourth planet from the Sun, Mars is called the red planet because of its coloration. Having Earthlike qualities, Mars possesses atmospheric clouds, polar ice caps, and unchanging surface markings. Fly-by and landing pictures disclose volcanoes, rock-strewn deserts, canyons, craters, ancient river beds, and sand dunes. The red planet has a cold, dry climate visited by powerful dust storms. As yet no signs of life have been found.

The Martian surface offers a wealth of detail. Dark steel blue markings contrast bright orange desert areas and snow white polar caps. Minor cloud activity and thin polar caps demonstrate that water is lacking.

The 1976 Viking probes reported that the Martian atmosphere is 95 percent carbon dioxide with 2 percent nitrogen and traces of argon, carbon monoxide, and oxygen. During the winter a large percentage of the atmosphere becomes frozen in the polar ices. Because of the extreme cold, Mars possesses no liquid water. General consensus holds that Mars once had a more agreeable climate and a denser atmosphere. Clouds cover no more than 5 percent of the surface, even when they are most active. Blue clouds, much like our noctilucent clouds, have been spotted at 8 miles in altitude and are made of ice crystals around meteoric dust.

Weather varies greatly on the red planet. Large alterations in temperature exist between the equator and the poles and whip up westerly gales and intense low-pressure areas. Winds carry dust to extremely high altitudes. Powerful dust storms develop over the central highlands, lifting huge quantities of dust into a layer 12 to 18 miles in altitude. This layer might envelop the temperate and equatorial regions of Mars as it did in 1909, 1911, 1956, and 1971. In winter, dust is carried around the planet and in the spring as the polar cap retreats, the Martian surface reveals its blanket of dust that formed dark and light areas.

While the spring Martian temperatures climb, the gradient between the poles and the equator equals out. The westerly winds die down and gentle breezes replace the Westerlies around the equator. Easterly winds prevail during most of the spring day.

Mars' highlands, some 7 miles in height, are concentrated in the Southern Hemisphere. The Northern Hemisphere shows fields of recent volcanic activity. The southern highlands reveal heavy meteorite cratering, an indication of an aging process going on perhaps 3 1/2 billion years. Mars' two largest craters are Argyre and Hellas, both giant impact basins. Hellas—a dual-rimmed, 3-mile-deep bowl almost 1,000 miles across—is almost a mirror image of the Moon's Mare Ibrium. The uplands also have a fair number of weathered volcanic areas akin to the lunar surface. A 3,000-mile rift zone cuts across the southern uplands. A fault valley, with a 45-mile width and a 4-mile depth, dwarfs our Grand Canyon. Heavily eroded faults of various ages exist.

Mars' Northern Hemisphere contrasts the Southern and is home to plains and low, smooth basins. Young impact craters dot the region. The North 65-degree latitude is marked with youthful basalt flows. At the North Pole lies a long volcanic plateau 2 miles high and 250 miles across, with an extensive fault system and central calderas. Reaching 18 miles skyward, four giant volcanoes dot the equator. The largest, Olympus Mons (Fig. 7-6), reveals itself as a dusky spot to Earth-based telescopes. Having a 320-mile-wide base and a huge caldera on its mammoth cone top, Olympus Mons is the largest mountain in the solar system.

Dunes abound in the high Martian latitudes (Fig. 7-7), while giant stone blocks litter the northern equatorial plateau. Valleys with extensive tributaries are witnessed in the equatorial region. Small channels in the area hint of flowing water in the past.

Polar caps consist of frozen water and frozen carbon

Fig. 7-6. Mars' Olympus Mons, the largest mountain in the solar system (A Viking photograph courtesy JPL/NASA).

Fig. 7-7. Sand dunes on Mars' Chryse Planita Basin (A Viking photograph courtesy JPL/NASA).

dioxide. Mars is believed to be enveloped by a permafrost shell just below the planet's surface. The depressions and valleys are thought to be caused by the collapse of the permafrost shell. Each winter the polar caps reconstitute on sedimentary layers that in some instances may be as deep as 4 miles.

Mars, composed of a uniform mantle and crust, fails to show a liquid core. The red planet has two small moons, Deimos and Phobos, both orbiting in a circular motion around the Martian equator. Quite possibly Deimos and Phobos are captured asteroids.

Observing Mars

Mars proves an easy binocular object because of its bright redness and lack of blinking. You cannot see a planetary disk with binoculars when you are looking at the red planet. A telescope of at least 60mm to 80mm with powers above 140× would be required to see the most minimal surface detail, and that detail would only

be available during Martian *opposition*, when the red planet has its closest approach to Earth.

Mars' motion in the sky greatly differs from the inferior planets Mercury and Venus. At opposition the red planet rises at sunset and can be observed all night. Two months prior to opposition, it rises at midnight and can be viewed in the southeastern sky for several hours before dawn. At 60 days after opposition, Mars can be viewed in the evening sky before it sets at midnight.

Mars' motion among the stars appears erratic. During the majority of the year Mars moves eastward among the stars at almost 20 degrees per month, yet when opposition approaches, it slides back about 15 degrees in 60 days. This appearance of erratic motion is called *retrograde motion*, and it is caused by the Earth's orbital motion and our own Earthbound perspective.

Mars' two satellites, Deimos and Phobos, are simply too small and too dim to be perceived with binoculars.

Throughout an *apparition*, or time period for observing a planet, Mars' brightness changes considerably. Its elliptical orbit, its ever-changing distance from Earth, and its slight phase effect when it achieves its greatest angle between the Earth and the Sun, all contribute to the red planet's alterations in brightness. Arcturus (a Bootis), Aldebaran (a Tauri), and Antares (a Scorpii) offer fine comparison stars for Mars during the fainter stages of its observing period.

Mars' Oppositions

9/28/88	11/27/90
1/7/93	2/12/95

THE MINOR PLANETS

Asteroids, or minor planets, are small rocky bodies traveling in an elliptical orbit around the Sun. Ranging in size from 600 miles in diameter down to the size of small boulders, the minor planets are believed to exist in the thousands. Too small to have their own atmospheres, these sunbaked and meteorite-blasted asteroids lack environments that foster life. Collisions among these bodies can produce meteors.

There is an Asteroid Belt in the gap between Mars and Jupiter, and it is there where the large majority of the minor planets orbit. In 1772 Johann Bode predicted the existance of an undiscovered planet where the Asteroid Belt was later discovered. In 1801 Giuseppi Piazzi, an Italian astronomer, located the first asteroid, Ceres. In the next few years Pallas and Vesta were discovered by the German astronomer Heinrich Wilhelm Olbers. Another German astronomer, K.L. Harding, found Juno, the last of the four brightest asteroids. In the late 1800s the camera began the revolutionize minor planet hunting.

Some 2500 asteroids possess accurately known orbits, of which close to 1900 are officially numbered. An estimated 50,000 asteroids are believed to exist with magnitudes equal to or greater than 21. Estimated mass of the Asteroid Belt is said to be 2.5 million million million tons—somewhat twice the mass of the largest asteroid, Ceres.

Asteroids are classed into groups by their orbits: the main belt, the Apollo and Amor group, and the Trojan asteroids. Of the known asteroids, 95 percent make up the main belt and these travel in slightly elliptical paths between Mars and Jupiter. Those minor planets, moving along the sharp inner edge of the belt, stay in the plane of the solar system. Asteroids in the outer section of the main belt possess more highly scattered orbits.

Apollo and Amor group asteroids have elliptical and extremely inclined orbits. At the farthest approach to the Sun, they are in the main belt, yet at closest approach to the Sun, they dwell among the inner planets. Some asteroids come quite close to Earth.

The Trojan asteroids travel along Jupiter's orbit. It takes the asteroids from the main belt some 2 to 6 years to orbit the Sun, while Jupiter takes 11.86 years to do the same.

William Herschel, famed telescope maker and astronomer, coined the word *asteroid* almost 150 years ago. The asteroid has only a starlike appearance in even the largest telescopes, which made determining the minor planets' diameter measurements almost impossible until 1971 when two methods were developed. The accurate measurement of a minor planet's brightness at the infrared and visual wavelengths are included in the *radiometric method*. The measurements show whether an object of given brightness is reflective and small, or larger and not as bright, from which can be deduced both reflectivity, or *albedo*, and the asteroid's diameter.

Another method available is the *polarmetric method*, which involves the study of the polarization of sunlight reflected by a minor planet to find the asteroid's albedo. The albedo, when combined with the values for visual brightness, will give the diameter. Current studies reveal the minor planets as fairly dark bodies with odd shapes ranging from spherical and spindle-shaped to cylindrical. Their surfaces are similar to either stony or stony-iron meteorites or carbonaceous meteorites. The majority of stony asteroids have diameters in the 60- to 125-mile range, while carbonaceous minor planets are found more commonly in larger and smaller sizes that tend to predominate in the Asteroid belt's outer regions. Other Asteroids' spectra suggest iron-nickel and achondrite bodies.

Heinrich Wilhelm Olbers believed the asteroids were fragments of a disintegrated planet. The more current notion says that at the time of the solar system's origin, a cloud of some 2 to 4 A.U. formed an original family of nearly 30 large asteroids ranging in diameter from 60 to 600 miles. Collisions among the minor planets created the current system. Several asteroids in the Apollo and Amor group display highly tilted and eccentric orbits and thus may be the remains of short-period comets.

Observing Minor Planets

Appearing like yellow stars and residing in a belt between Mars and Jupiter, the minor planets offer the binocularist a true test of his eye and patience. Most of these objects are beyond the range of 50mm and 80mm objective lenses, yet a few will be treats when you find them. Well-mounted battleship binoculars having 100mm to 150mm objectives are best suited for this work.

The easier asteroids to locate with binoculars are those that become brighter than eighth magnitude at some point in their orbit. Likely the easiest asteroids (yet rather difficult) to locate are: Vesta, with the brightest visual magnitude of 5.1; Pallas, with a visual magnitude of 6.4; Ceres, with 6.7; Iris, with 6.7; and Eros, with 6.8 (Fig. 7-8).

Vesta, with its magnitude brighter than the naked-eye limit in the country, can be observed by the sharp-eyed without binoculars. When found, the minor planets appear starlike, but you will notice their movement from night to night through star fields. You will need an *ephemeris* (a table of positions, distances, magnitudes, and motions) to hunt asteroids and one can be obtained through subscription from:

Minor Planet Center
Smithsonian Observatory
60 Garden St.
Cambridge, MA 02138

If you would enjoy receiving a free monthly news-letter on asteroids by J.U. Gunter called *Tonight's Asteroids*, send a supply of long envelopes to:

Mr. J.U. Gunter
1411 N. Mangum St.
Durham, NC 27701

I should also mention that the more casual minor planet observer will find that both *Astronomy* and *Sky and Telescope* cover a small group of asteroids in each month's magazines.

Some of the brighter asteroids are:

4	Vesta	5.1 mag.
2	Pallas	6.4 mag.
1	Ceres	6.7 mag.
7	Iris	6.7 mag.
433	Eros	6.8 mag.
6	Hebe	7.5 mag.
3	Juno	7.5 mag.
18	Melpomene	7.5 mag.
15	Eunomia	7.9 mag.
8	Flora	7.9 mag.
324	Bamberga	8.0 mag.
1036	Ganymed	8.1 mag.
9	Metis	8.1 mag.
192	Nausikaa	8.2 mag.
20	Massalia	8.3 mag.
5	Astrae	8.7 mag.

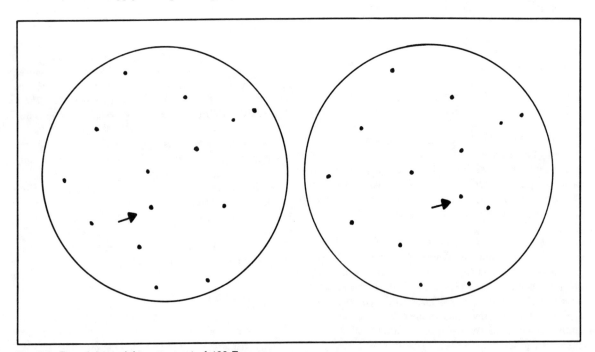

Fig. 7-8. The night-to-night movement of 433 Eros.

10	Hygeia	8.8 mag.
11	Parthenope	8.7 mag.
12	Victoria	8.1 mag.
14	Irene	8.7 mag.
16	Psyche	8.8 mag.
19	Fortuna	8.7 mag.
23	Thalia	8.9 mag.
25	Phocaea	9.0 mag.
27	Euterpe	8.5 mag.
29	Amphitrite	8.6 mag.
39	Laetitia	8.8 mag.
40	Harmonia	8.9 mag.
41	Daphne	8.7 mag.
42	Isis	8.8 mag.

Asteroid Research

The possibility exists of binocular research in the magnitude observation of several brighter asteroids. Most of these bodies possess irregular shapes and because each revolves on a rotational axis, their reflected light varies from asteroid to asteroid. For example, 15 Eunomia is suitable for 70mm and up binoculars; 433 Eros can be followed with 80mm and up glasses; 44 Nlysa can be observed with 100mm and up battleship glasses; and 43 Ariadne and 216 Kleopatra are suitable for study in 150mm battleship binoculars.

If you are interested in entering into amateur research programs concerning the minor planets, contact:

Association of Lunar and Planetary Observers
P.O. Box 3AZ
University Park, NM 88003

Minor Planet Bulletin
Rte. 7, P.O. Box 511
Tucson, AZ 85747

Minor Planets Division
British Astronomical Association
Burlington House, Piccadilly
London W1V ONL
England

The *visual photometry*, or visual estimation of magnitude or light intensity, is highly subjective. Deceptive alterations in magnitude can be brought about by haze, atmospheric refraction, and even your own eyesight and mental state. Because of the last-mentioned factors, it is sometimes best to attempt visual photometry with a partner so your findings can be confirmed.

Visual photometry with binoculars might help in learning the rotational rate of a minor planet through its light curve. The amplitude of a minor planet as it rotates can also be shown by its light curve. The value becomes the magnitude range at given a date. The relative shape and dimensions of an asteroid can also be gleaned from the previous information, as can axial angle. Light variation demonstrates the irregularities in the minor planet's shape or in its surface albedo. Shape, rotational rates, size, and odd surface features give the history and origin of the asteroid.

Your binoculars, if over 10×, should be well mounted. You will need a WWV time signal, a tape recorder, a note pad, a pen, and a flashlight. The recorder will help you retain a running record of magnitude change as it happens. I recommend the *A.A.V.S.O. Star Atlas* for this work because it contains stars close to the ninth magnitude.

Most asteroids travel quickly through their star-fields; so it is important to determine the minor planet's position during each hour of observing. Preplotting the asteroid's path on a star chart will speed up your search and give you the opportunity to find comparison stars along the predicted path before starting your observations.

Jot down asteroid positions for each day on your star charts. Plot the asteroid's daily path by connecting lines between the recorded dates on the charts. It is possible for even hourly rates to be recorded.

☆ The given position in the ephemerides for a minor planet on a specific date is given in right ascension and declination. You will note the minor planet's position change from one day to the next.
☆ Using the star atlas charts, you will plot positions for both dates and connect them with a faint pencil line.
☆ Using a ruler with a millimeter scale, measure the distance between the two points.
☆ The motion for one hour can be taken by dividing the motion for one day by 24. The total will be a rough estimate.
☆ Using the hourly progression in millimeters, mark the hourly movement on the line connecting the two days.
☆ Daily asteroid motions vary considerably from day to day during close apparitions. Compute every day separately. Even though your computations will be off, they will still help you locate that "little yellow star point."

Asteroid brightness is affected by two conditions: the minor planet's shape, which is often highly irregular; and the asteroid's irregular surface reflectivity and mineral content, which cause variations in albedo. A light curve may be used to monitor rotational variations and albedo variations.

A valid light curve may be found only if you observe the asteroid on as many dates as possible during the asteroid's apparition. Alterations in magnitude occur rather rapidly because of the irregular shapes of these objects. Estimate magnitude every 5 to 10 minutes. Record the estimate of magnitude along with the correct universal time. It's recommended that an observer make estimates of the asteroid's magnitude during a complete rotation.

The A.A.V.S.O. Star Atlas should be employed for asteroids brighter than 9.5 magnitude. Prior to observing, pick comparison stars close to the asteroid's path and label them with the correct magnitude from the companion catalog. Later you will compare these stars to the asteroid being plotted. Find a star that appears to match or closely match the minor planet in magnitude.

Magnitude estimates are useless if the asteroid is too faint. In such situations observe the relative change and forget about magnitude. After observing the relative change, find two stars close in magnitude to the minor planet, even though each star might be disimilar in magnitude from the other. The asteroid will then be estimated as dimming 0.3 or brightening 0.2. You will record this on the form as: +0.3, -0.2.

Such estimates prove difficult and often incorrect. Remember, the purpose of these observations is to find out the times of least intensity and brightest intensity, and if you know the times, you can construct a light curve and acquire worthwhile data.

When you are constructing a light curve graph, each hour of time should be separated by 3 centimeters and each magnitude by 1 centimeter. The time will be expressed in Universal Time and it will be written from left to right. Magnitude will be expressed vertically, with the dimmest on the bottom and the brightest on the top. Now you will be able to find out the amplitude and the period of rotation.

Amplitude studies give information on polar shifting and polar alignment, which helps us better understand light variations. Light variations are greater if the minor planet is oriented to us on the plane of its equator. Variations are smaller or almost absent if the asteroid's pole faces us.

Determination of amplitude is found by showing the light variation range from minimum intensity to maximum. This range is expressed in magnitude or tenths of magnitude.

Attempt to observe the asteroid on as many days as possible for alterations in amplitude. Mail the results to: ALPO and the Minor Planets Center.

Binocularists might be of great assistance in correcting and refining data on rotational periods for some of the asteroids. Some of these bodies might undergo abrupt unexpected alterations in brightness.

A minor planet's period of rotation is one complete 360° rotation on its axis. For an elongated or irregularly shaped asteroid, the light curve for a single rotation will take into account two minima and two maxima. You will use the light curve to figure the period of rotation. You can also measure from maximum 1 to maximum 3 or from minimum 1 to minimum 3 to learn the rotation period. Use the same chart for amplitude, except measure for duration instead of amplitude. To make certain no mistakes are made, measure a second time. Take the average of both determinations.

When you complete your observations you will supply the date, the beginning Universal Time, magnitude found at 5- and 10-minute intervals, unexpected changes in magnitude, amplitude, and estimated rotational period. Both ALPO and the Minor Planets Center will be interested in this data.

Your observations will be of great value. Too many asteroids exist for major observatories to monitor. Not enough is known about the minor planets' variability.

JUPITER

Jupiter's diameter: 88,730 miles.

Jupiter is the largest planet in the solar system.

Jupiter has 2 1/2 times the mass of all the other planets combined.

Jupiter's mass: 1.9×10^{24} tons.

Jupiter's density: 1.33 the density of water.

Jupiter's speed of orbit: 8 miles per second.

Jupiter's orbital path: elliptical.

Jupiter takes 11.9 years to orbit the Sun.

Jupiter's distance from the Sun: 483,631,000 miles.

Jupiter's axial rotation: 9 hrs. 50 min. 30 sec.

Jupiter's rotational speed: 22,000 mph.

Jupiter's atmosphere: mostly ammonia and hydrogen.

Jupiter consists of mostly hydrogen and a small amount of helium.

Jupiter's core: rocky.

Jupiter has 16 moons.

Jupiter's Galilean moons: 4—Io, Europa, Ganymede, and Callisto.

Jupiter's albedo: 0.34.

Jupiter's axial inclination: 3.12 degrees.

Jupiter's magnitude: −2.5 at maximum.
Jupiter's synodic period: 399 days.

Features of Jupiter

Jupiter, fifth planet from the Sun, is the largest planet in the solar system and has almost 2 1/2 times the mass of all the other planets combined (Fig. 7-9). Spinning faster than any other planet, this gas giant has a rotational period of 9 hours 50 minutes and 30 seconds, whirling around at the incredible rate of 22,000 miles an hour at the equator. The planet's low density, rapid rotation, and

flattened poles provide powerful evidence that Jupiter is a gas body.

Jupiter's surface shows dark belts and light zones running parallel to the equator that are generally reddish brown to yellow. Surface detail appears to change by the hour. Belt systems vary in prominence over the years. The South Equatorial Belt might show sudden and drastic alterations in shape and color, darkening and exhibiting bright and dark spots. Intervals of 6 to 10 years mark such changes.

Pioneer and Voyager photographs pointed out that

Fig. 7-9. Jupiter with its Great Red Spot displayed, photographed by Kitt Peak 84-inch reflector (Courtesy National Optical Astronomy Observatories).

regions around the Jovian equator appeared lacking in fine structure, yet consisting of huge swirls and cloud plumes. These markings are created by the planet's rapid rotational effects on the convection cells of hot gas rising beneath the cloud cover. Far above the equator the bands and belts show finer detail. At the poles little can be seen of any organized belt system. Visible convection cells exhibit dark and light patches, eddies, disorganized markings, and swirls.

The Red Spot, discovered in 1666, remains Jupiter's most curious and true permanent feature. Other smaller red spots have been observed from time to time at high latitudes. First observed in the 1920s, three small white ovals, in the vicinity of the South Temperate Belt, challenge the Red Spot for longevity by their intermittent appearances.

Jupiter emits almost twice as much heat as it receives from the Sun. The greenhouse effect keeps the temperature in the upper atmosphere, at both the equator and the poles, between 120° K and 133 ° K. The lower atmosphere is likely stagnant, while turbulence and storms reside in the upper 40 to 50 miles. The highest clouds are composed of methane. Ammonia condenses at intermediate levels and water condenses to form low-level clouds. Dark belts and spots are generally denser and hotter than light zones. Infrequently small dark features have been gauged at 310° K.

Jupiter's color might be attributed to different combinations of ammonia and hydrogen sulfide. Updrafts might carry coloring gases of red, orange, yellow, and brown to the upper atmosphere. Red phosphorus might account for the bright red in the red spot. Great changes in equatorial color over a 6- to 10-year period might be the result of heat being released slowly after a large build-up beneath a temperature inversion in the lower atmosphere.

Jupiter's features vary in rotational speed at different latitudes. The 20,000-mile-wide equatorial zone of the Jovian clouds rotates some 5 minutes faster than the planet's dense core, while material in the dark belt region can differ in rotational speed by up to 6 minutes.

Rich in the molecular building blocks of life, Jupiter shows the possibility of having living forms evolve such as highly adaptable bacteria. Below the cloud cover, Jupiter consists mostly of hydrogen and smaller quantities of helium. Hydrogen exists in combination with heavier elements. A rocky-metallic core, some 6000 miles in diameter, has a temperature believed to be 30,000° K. Pressure is said to be 100 million Earth atmospheres. The depths of the planet, around the core, is thought to be a helium and hydrogen mix. The core's gravitational contraction might possibly be responsible for the Jovian heat flow.

Having a powerful magnetic field and intense radiation belts, Jupiter's diapole magnetic field is ten times stronger than Earth's and has its North and South Poles reversed relative to our planet. The Jovian radiation belts—some 10,000 times more powerful than Earth's Van Allen belt and containing high-energy electrons and protons—emit bursts of radio waves somewhat influenced by the Jovian moon Io.

Jupiter has 16 moons, four of which are known as the Galilean moons (Fig. 7-10): Io, Europa, Ganymede, and Callisto. Discovered by Galileo, the four have been favorite observational objects for amateur astronomers. The 16 Jovian moons fall into three main groups. The innermost 5 have orbits of 12 hours to 17 days and move in almost circular orbits around the planet's equatorial plane. The next foursome have orbital periods from 239 to 260 days, traveling in elliptical orbits inclined 28 degrees to the Jovian equator. The last group of four small satellites move in retrograde ellipses at vast distances from the planet. Their orbital periods are from 631 to 758 days. The 16 moons are: Amalthea, Io, Europa, Ganymede, Callisto, Leda, Himalia, Lysithea, Elara, Ananke, Carme, Pasiphae, Sinope, 1973 J3, 1979 J1, and 1979 J2.

Observing Jupiter

Jupiter, second only to Venus in brightness, is a relatively simple planet to locate. White and almost nonstellar in binoculars, this giant planet is given away by its four orbiting moons, which at low power will appear as star points. At 7×, the Jovian moons are often difficult to see because of Jupiter's brightness and the glare they produce in binoculars. The four Galilean moons are best viewed when they are at their individual elongations. Io, closest to Jupiter, is most difficult. Callisto, the faintest moon, is also farthest out. Ganymede has been observed without visual aid by a few keen-eyed observers.

The four Galilean moons, first observed by Galileo in 1610, move exactly in the plane of the Jovian equator. Because Jupiter's pole is almost vertical you will view the orbits of the Galilean moons edge-on.

Jupiter's orbit is five times larger than Earth's and requires 12 years to complete. Moving at an average rate of one zodiacal constellation per year, this gas giant will be seen at opposition about 30 days later each year. Jupiter can be observed in the morning 5 months a year and in the evening 5 months a year. For two months it is lost in the Sun's glare. No surface features can be glimpsed with any binoculars except battleship glasses

Fig. 7-10. Jupiter with its Galilean moons: Io (left), Europa (below Jupiter), Ganymede (lower left), and Callisto (lower right) (A Voyager photograph courtesy JPL/NASA).

with interchangeable eyepieces.

Jupiter's Oppositions

9/10/86	10/18/87
11/23/88	12/27/89
1/28/91	2/28/92
3/30/93	4/30/94
6/1/95	

SATURN

Saturn's diameter: 75,100 miles at equator.
Saturn's mean distance from the Sun: 886 million miles.
Saturn's nearest approach to the Sun: 835 million miles.
Saturn's farthest distance from the Sun: 938 million miles.
Saturn's axial rotation: 10 hrs. 14 min. at equator.
Saturn's speed of orbit: 6 miles per second.

Saturn's axial inclination: 26.73 degrees.

Saturn's orbit: elliptical.

Saturn's sidereal period: 29.46 years.

Saturn's synodic period: 378 days.

Saturn's core: rocky; 12 miles in diameter.

Saturn's albedo: 0.33.

Saturn's mass: 5.684×10^{26} kg.

Saturn's color: copper-yellow.

Saturn's atmosphere: Mostly methane and hydrogen.

Saturn's magnitude: -2 at maximum.

Saturn's ring diameter from rim to rim: 170,000 miles approx.

Saturn's temperature at cloud tops: $-170°$ C.

Saturn's density: 0.7 that of water.

Saturn's moons: 23—Phoebe, Iapetus, Hyperion, Titan, Rhea, Dione, 1980 S6, 1980 S13, 1980 S25, Tethys, Enceladus, Mimas, 1980 S1, 1980 S3, 1980 S26, 1980 S27, and 1980 S28.

Features of Saturn

Sixth planet from the Sun, second largest, and well known for its attractive ring system, Saturn, like its neighbor Jupiter, is composed mostly of gas and is enveloped with a thick cloud cover (Fig. 7-11). Its shape flattened by its rapid rotation, Saturn's disk exhibits bands and belts similar to Jupiter's. The Saturnian belt system is fewer in number than its Jovian neighbor and these belts show little detail. Gold-yellow dominates the color. Colors are less pronounced than on Jupiter. Equatorial banding appears yellow-white with an orange-yellow equatorial belt. Orange belts exist among the yellow tropical and tem-

Fig. 7-11. Saturn with moons: Dione (front), Tethys, Mimas (right), Enceladus, Rhea (left), and Titan (distant top) (A Voyager photograph courtesy JPL/NASA).

perate zones. The darkest parts of the Saturnian surface are the polar areas, and they appear greenish.

The extremely cold cloud tops are recorded at around −170° C, almost 50° colder than neighboring Jupiter. This colder condition is a result of Saturn's greater distance from the Sun. The lower temperature keeps activity relatively minimal at cloud level. Saturn has few distinct markings. Back in 1933, a great equatorial white spot was recorded; it slowly spread until the whole equatorial zone brightened. Dark and white spots, appearing in the upper latitudes, show up every few months and prove difficult to observe.

Saturn's outer atmosphere is mostly made up of hydrogen, helium, and methane. The atmosphere is so bitterly cold that ammonia freezes into clouds at lower altitudes. Saturn's general composition resembles Jupiter's, yet it has somewhat lesser quantities of hydrogen.

The Saturnian core consists of rock with a diameter of 12,000 miles, nearly half the size of Jupiter's, and jacketed with 3000 miles of ice. This ice jacket is locked in a 5000-mile-thick layer of metallic hydrogen. Hydrogen in gas form accounts for the remainder of the planet, giving Saturn the average density of water. Pressure at Saturn's center is said to be 50 million atmospheres with a temperature of more than 15,000° C. The planet radiates a bit more heat than it receives from the Sun.

Forming a band encircling Saturn's equator and having a diameter of about 170,000 miles from rim to rim, the ring system makes this planet one of the most aesthetic observational sites in the whole solar system. Three main rings (A, B, and C) dominate two fainter ones. The C ring, or *Crepe*, is flanked on the outside by the bright, wide B ring. Outside B is ring A. The two share a common dark border called the *Cassini Division*. D ring, discovered in 1969, nearly touches the planet's surface. Scattered debris form a ring outside of A.

Galileo first noticed an odd shape to Saturn's disk, but owing to poor optics he was unable to truly discern the rings. In 1655 Christiaan Huygens discovered the true nature of the fantastic rings. There are two periods during the 29 1/2 year orbit around the Sun during which the Saturnian rings are tilted edge on to us and cannot be seen.

The rings are composed of independently orbiting particles. Voyager fly-by photographs of the bands have shown the presence of braiding. Density of the bands varies, which might be attributed to the gravitational effects of the nearest Saturnian moons. Mimas is most suspect in this event. The planet's sphere can be clearly observed through the Crepe ring. Ring particles have 70 percent reflectivity, making them brighter than the planet.

The composition of the ring particles remains a question. Likely the particles range from fine dust to the size of bricks and are coated with ices. Perhaps the rings are the remains of a moon or moons shattered by the planet's gravitational force. The rings lay within the Roche limit that predicts a satellite's destruction if it wanders too far inside a planet's gravitational field.

Some 23 moons inhabit the Saturnian system, eight of which travel in near circular orbits in the ring plane close to the planet. Phoebe, the most distant satellite, moves in a retrograde elliptical orbit, while Iapetus travels in an orbit inclined some 15 degrees.

Observing Saturn

To glimpse Saturn's ring system, you will need 25× to 30× binoculars and a firm mounting. In 7×50s under dark skies you will be able to see the planet's largest moon, Titan, as a star point. Coppery-yellow in color, Saturn appears in the same constellation for almost a year because of the planet's almost circular 30-year orbit.

No surface features are visible to the binocularist. Saturn's considerable alterations in brightness are not so much a result of changing distances at opposition than a product of the ring system's changing positions. At their widest appearance of 28 degrees, the rings reflect more light than the entire sphere.

Saturn's Oppositions

6/9/87	6/20/88
7/2/89	7/14/90
7/26/91	8/7/92
8/19/93	9/1/94
9/14/95	

URANUS

Uranus' mean distance from the Sun: 1,783,000,000 miles.

Uranus discovered: March 13, 1781 by W. Herschel.

Uranus' orbital inclination: 0 degrees 46 min.

Uranus' axial rotation: 10 hr. 45 min.

Uranus' albedo: 0.34 − 0.5.

Uranus' mass: 8.6978×10^{25} kg.

Uranus' equatorial diameter: 29,900 miles.

Uranus' magnitude: 5.7 maximum.

Uranus' angular diameter: 3.8″.

Uranus' inclination on axis: 98 degrees.

Uranus' sidereal period: 84.01 years.

Uranus' synodic period: 369.7 days.

Uranus' nearest approach to Earth: 1.61 billion miles.

Uranus' density: 1.25 that of water.

Uranus' moons: 15—Miranda, Ariel, Umbriel, Titania, 1985U1, 1986U1-9, Oberon.

Uranus' color: green.

Uranus' shape: slightly oblate.

Uranus' core: rocky and 10,000 miles in diameter.

Features of Uranus

The first planet discovered with a telescope, Uranus is a gas giant nearly four times the size of our Earth. The seventh planet from the Sun and possessing a rich atmosphere, Uranus is just visible to the naked eye during opposition. Early in astronomical history Uranus was regarded as nothing more than a star. Not until 1781 was it located by William Herschel during a systematic search of the heavens. Orbital motion irregularities in Uranus led to a calculation that paved the way to Neptune's discovery.

Uranus rotates on its axis in a retrograde motion while its orbital motion is direct. An odd feature of the planet is that its axis is close to the plane of Uranus' orbit, inclining the Uranian North Pole at 98 degrees to the vertical. Extremely long seasons result from the highly tilted axis. Each pole undergoes a 42-year summer and a 42-year winter.

Thin rings of rocky debris were discovered around Uranus in 1977. An estimated nine rings are now believed to encircle this greenish planet at distances from 42,000 km to 51,000 km from the planet.

Slightly oblate in shape, Uranus is colder and smaller than the other gas giants, Jupiter and Saturn. Uranus is composed of a smaller proportion of helium and hydrogen than Jupiter or Saturn, yet has a larger proportion of heavy elements than its giant brothers. Believed to be banded and belted, Uranus has an atmosphere with high quantities of methane, which may account for the planet's green coloring. Ammonia likely exists, but owing to the cold temperatures (near $-210°$ C) in the upper atmosphere, the ammonia has condensed into low-level clouds. The atmosphere's major constituent is hydrogen. Helium also is believed to be present. Methane and ammonia clouds cut off sunlight from the planet's surface.

Uranus is thought to possess a rocky core some 10,000 miles in diameter and coated with an ice layer 5,000 miles thick. The temperature at the core is considered in the neighborhood of 4000° C. The ice envelope and rocky core make up 4/5 of the planet's mass.

Uranus has 15 known satellites; Miranda, Ariel, Umbriel, Titania, 1985U1, 1986U1-9, and Oberon. Orbiting in the plane of the planet's extremely tilted equator, the moons travel in the same direction as Uranus' rotation.

Observing Uranus

If its position is known, Uranus is a relatively easy planet to locate. Appearing like a pale green star in binoculars, this gas giant reaches 5.7 magnitude at its brightest and is visible to the naked eye under dark country skies. Uranus takes 84 years to complete its orbit around the Sun. Uranus' magnitude changes can be studied using the same methods employed in the visual photometry of the minor planets.

Uranus' Oppositions

6/16/87	6/20/88
6/24/89	6/29/90
7/4/91	7/7/92
7/12/93	7/17/94
7/21/95	

NEPTUNE

Neptune is the farthest planet from the Sun from January 1979 to March 1999.

Neptune's diameter: 30,750 miles.

Neptune's mean distance from the sun: 2.8 billion miles.

Neptune's eccentricity of orbit: .008.

Neptune's magnitude: 7.6 maximum.

Neptune's angular diameter: 2.5″.

Neptune's albedo: 0.34 – 0.5.

Neptune's inclination of axis: 29 degrees.

Neptune's synodic period: 367.5 days.

Neptune's sidereal period: 164.8 years.

Neptune's mass: 1.028×10^{26} kg.

Neptune's equatorial rotation: 15.8 hr.

Neptune's density: 1.77 that of water.

Neptune's color: blue-green.

Neptune's satellites: 2—Triton and Nereid.

Neptune's core: rocky; 10,000 miles in diameter.

Neptune's nearest approach to Earth: 2.77 billion miles.

Features of Neptune

Because Pluto's eccentric orbit brings it inside Neptune's path around the Sun, Neptune is the outermost planet from January 1979 to March 1999. Prior to Neptune's discovery, the existence of this planet was calculated by nineteenth-century mathematicians who noted the perturbations in newly discovered Uranus orbit. In 1845 J.C. Adams, an English mathematician, forecast the

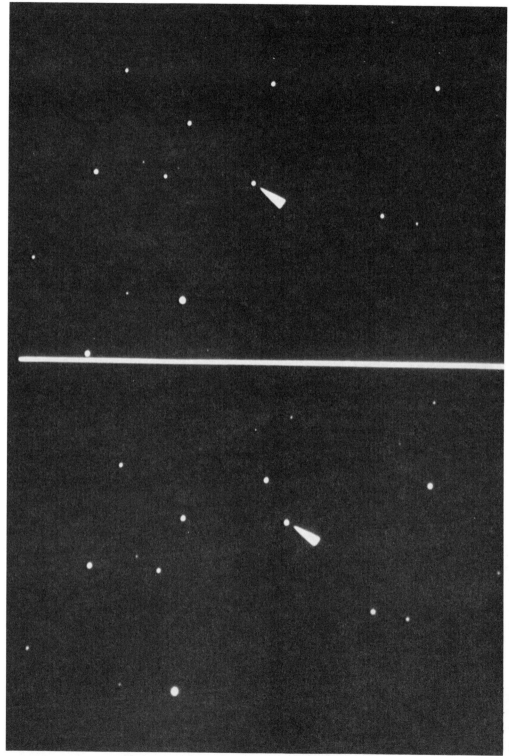

Fig. 7-12. Exposures of Pluto taken 48 hours apart. Note the planet's movement. This photograph taken with a Meade 10-inch Schmidt-Cassegrain (Courtesy Meade Instruments Corporation).

position of the unseen planet and sent results to Sir George Airy, the Astronomer Royal of England. Airy failed to begin the search. The next year a French mathematician, Urbain-Jean-Joseph Leverrier, reproduced J.C. Adams' results and passed them on to the Berlin Observatory where J.G. Galle made the discovery of Neptune. As with Uranus, Neptune was previously mistaken for a star.

Neptune is blue-green in color and appears starlike in all but the largest telescopes. Like the other gas giants, this planet is oblate in shape. Neptune exhibits almost the same size and structure as its neighbor in space, Uranus. Methane, responsible for the planet's coloring, is contained in large amounts in the Neptunian atmosphere. Hydrogen and helium dominate the atmosphere. As with Uranus, Neptune also has ammonia clouds below the atmosphere's visible layers.

Neptune likely possesses a warm stratosphere with a temperature somewhere in the vicinity of $140°$ K. The warm upper layers of the Neptunian atmosphere are attributable to methane's ability to absorb solar heat. Like Uranus, Neptune is suspected of having a rocky core almost 10,000 miles in diameter and covered with a layer of ice 5,000 miles thick. Almost 3/4 of Neptune's mass is thought to be contained in its core and ice.

Neptune has two known satellites: Triton and Nereid. Triton, one of the largest moons in the solar system, travels around Neptune in a circular retrograde orbit. Some conjecture exists that Pluto was once a Neptunian moon and had a close encounter with Triton. The encounter conceivably led to Pluto's ejection into a separate orbit around the Sun. This theory may explain why Triton now moves in a retrograde orbit.

Observing Neptune

Neptune is a fair test for the binocular astronomer. This planet appears like a slightly greenish star and at its brightest achieves a magnitude of 7.6. Taking 168 years for its orbital journey through the zodiac, this planet moves very little from year to year. The binocularist will need a star atlas to locate this gas giant and he will require several nights to chart its motion through the star fields. Like Uranus, visual photometry of this planet offers a chance for research.

PLUTO

Pluto was discovered in 1930 by Clyde Tombaugh.
Pluto's moons: 1—Charon.
Pluto's mass: 6.6×10^{23} kg.

Pluto's equatorial rotation: 6.3 days.
Pluto's albedo: 0.5.
Pluto's average distance from the Sun: 3.66 billion miles.
Pluto's nearest approach to the Sun: 2.8 billion miles.
Pluto's farthest distance from the Sun: 4.6 billion miles.
Pluto's eccentricity of orbit: .25.
Pluto's inclination of orbit to the ecliptic: 17 degrees.
Pluto's synodic period: 366.7 days.
Pluto's sidereal period: 247.7 years.
Pluto's maximum magnitude: 14.5

Features of Pluto

The farthest planet from the Sun, Pluto (Fig. 7-12) travels an odd and highly elliptical path that is inclined more than 17 degrees to the plane of the solar system. From 1979 until 1999 Pluto will be closer than Neptune to the Sun. Easily the smallest planet, with a diameter likely less than 2000 miles, Pluto is believed to possess a surface coated with frozen methane. Charon, a satellite, was discovered in 1978 and is thought to orbit the planet at a distance of 10,500 miles. Charon is believed to be 2/5 the size of Pluto.

With a density almost like water, Pluto is considered an icy ball of frozen gases. Because of its size and great distance from Earth, Pluto shows itself as no more than a star point in most earthbound telescopes. The planet has almost no effect on the orbits of Neptune and Uranus.

That Pluto is considered a true planet remains for debate. Over the years there have been arguments saying that Pluto is an escaped satellite of Neptune or that Pluto is the brightest of an asteroidlike swarm in the outer regions of the solar system.

The first planet discovered through the use of a camera and the second planet discovered through a deliberate search, Pluto was found by a 24-year-old astronomer, Clyde Tombaugh, using a 13-inch photographic telescope and a blink microscope on February 18, 1930.

Observing Pluto

Pluto cannot be viewed by the vast majority of binocular owners because most binoculars do not offer enough aperture to see this 14.5-magnitude planet. Dark skies and an aperture from 8 to 10 inches would be needed. I've never seen binoculars with objective lenses that size, yet I have heard of homemade, short-focus, Newtonian binoculars. At the Texas Star Party in 1984 one fellow showed up with 17 1/2-inch mirror binoculars. They must be a devil to transport, but I bet they give one heck of a view under dark sky conditions. Pluto would be a cinch to find with an instrument that large.

Chapter 8

The Comets

Spending most of its life in the frozen darkness far from the Sun, a *comet* (Fig. 8-1) is an icy body surrounded by a cloud of dust and gas that moves in an extremely elliptical orbit around the Sun. The comet, which periodically approaches close to the Sun, will heat enough to release dust and gas to form a gaseous head and a tail that always points away from the Sun (Fig. 8-2). The comet's tail has contributed much to its name; in Greek, *comet* means "long-haired one."

The comets were believed to be phenomena occurring in our own atmosphere until Tycho Brahe in 1577 showed that a comet had failed to alter position when tested by parallax, thus demonstrating its orbit lay beyond the Moon. Later, Isaac Newton set forth the notion that comets orbit the Sun in accord with his gravitational theories. He used Comet Kirch, discovered in 1680, to verify his theory. Edmund Halley and Heinrich Wilhelm Olbers added to the methods of determining cometary orbits.

Nowadays comets are named after their first three discoverers; for example, Comet IRAS-Araki-Alcock. Numerical designations for the year and order of perihelion passage are added, such as 1986I or 1986II. Comets are frequently discovered by professional astronomers studying photographic plates and by amateurs systematically scanning the heavens with binoculars and small, rich-field telescopes.

Clearly solar system objects, some comets have had their orbits disturbed so much by a planet's gravity that they have left our solar system. None are known to have come from deep space. So many comets have been observed over the last century that cometary orbits can be computed with reasonable accuracy.

Two kinds of comets exist: *periodic comets*, which travel in short-period elliptical orbits of 200 years or less, and *long-period comets*, which move in near-parabolic orbits, taking hundreds perhaps thousands of years to complete their slow circuits. Kohoutek 1973F will take 75,000 years to make one orbit around the Sun.

Perihelion distances vary for comets. A record of 75 million miles beyond Jupiter's orbit is held by Comet Van Den Bergh 1974g. Thome 1887I moves within 14,000 miles of the solar surface. Most comets cluster around 93,000,000 miles from the Sun. Short-period comets travel in ellipses close to the plane of the planets and have their aphelions close to the orbital paths of the giant planets. The gravitational attraction of planets likely causes the bunching process called *comet families*.

The vast majority of comets are faint, diffuse, and lacking much of a tail. The nucleus, the coma (head), and

Fig. 8-1. The Comet West (1975n) photographed on March 7, 1976 (Lick Observatory Photograph).

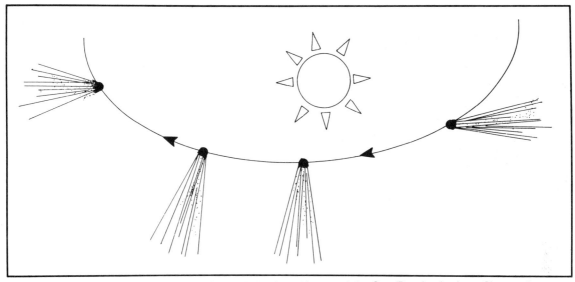

Fig. 8-2. The changing position of a comet's tail during its orbit around the Sun (Drawing by Anne Sheppard).

tail make up a comet (Fig. 8-3). The cometary nucleus is believed to be made of dust particles compacted in water ices bound up with carbon monoxide and methane. Weighing between 10 billion and 100 trillion tons, the nucleus has a low density. Diameters are estimated to be in the neighborhood of 1 to 30 miles. When the comet approaches the Sun, solar heat melts the nucleus and releases large volumes of gas, carrying away dust and ice particles.

The coma, or head (Fig. 8-4), is produced by gas made of carbon monoxide, hydrogen-oxygen molecules, water vapor with small quantities of carbon, hydrogen, and nitrogen molecules. The plasma (ionized gas) is produced by the nucleus gas' shattered molecules. If the comet is heated enough so that the nucleus melts, then the solar wind will drive the dust and gas outward to create the tail. Very long tails only occur when a highly active comet passes close to the Sun.

Cometary plasma consists, for the most part, of ionized molecules of carbon dioxide, carbon monoxide, methylidine, and nitrogen that are driven away from the coma at speeds approaching 400 miles per hour, forming a tail pointing away from the Sun.

Rich with dust about 1 micron across, the inner coma's tail is shaped like a fan. Tails are curved, yet often appear straight when our planet travels through the plane of the comet's orbit. An *antitail*, or spike, might be produced at such times when dust particles lead the comet. Comets might also release particles often as large as a centimeter or even a meter. Later these large parti-

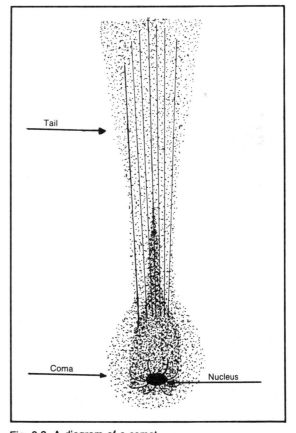

Fig. 8-3. A diagram of a comet.

Fig. 8-4. The head of Comet Brooks on October 21, 1911 (Lick Observatory Photograph).

cles might form a meteor shower. Brighter comets' tails can be extremely long. Some are 5 million to 25 million miles in length. The Great Comet of 1843I had a tail that was estimated to be almost 200 million miles long.

Comet gas can be excited to fluorescence by moving toward the Sun. Periodic comets tend to brighten more than dust-rich newer comets do. Because of changes in solar activity, comets will on occasion demonstrate brightness variation.

Short-period comets—those having 5-to-7-year periods—come to perihelion (the closest approach to the Sun) frequently and fade 2 or more magnitudes per century while decaying. At each perihelion passage, a comet will be expected to lose from 0.1 to 1 percent of its mass. Periodic comets seem to be gas-rich because they have lost the dusty outer layers of their nucleus. Their more compact core contained meteor-sized particles. See Table 8-1 for a list of short-period comets.

A periodic comet's nucleus has alterations in the force path of its escaping gas. This path change might increase with age, but in some comets the effect decreases. These alterations strongly hint that two types of nuclei exist. One possesses a central core of compacted stony material, eventually losing all its gas and leaving behind its rocky asteroidlike core. The other nucleus type is suspected of being a uniform conglomeration of ice that after a period of time will dissipate to nothing.

About 10 million comets are believed to have their perihelion points within Neptune's orbit. The majority of new comets travel great distances toward the Sun, and it is believed they had their origin in a huge cloud at a distance of 20,000 to 60,000 Astronomical Units. This cloud, known as the *Oort Cloud* (named after Dutch astronomer Jan Oort) is believed to hold in excess of 100 billion comets. The Oort Cloud is thought to have been evolved at the solar system's edge when the planets and the Sun came into being.

Moving in circular orbits within the Oort Cloud, the comets remain there until they are disturbed by passing stars and begin new orbits, taking them into the inner solar system.

OBSERVING COMETS

In binoculars, comets range in appearance from nebulous patches or smudges all the way to the generally held portrait of bright blurs with long and highly observable tails. Traveling slowly across a background of stars, it might be an hour or two before a comet shows movement.

Binoculars are an excellent instrument for observing a comet (Fig. 8-5). With binoculars from 7×50 on up, use-

**Table 8-1. Important
Short-Period Comets Making More Than One Return.**

Comet	Period in Years
Enke	3.3 years
Grigg-Skjellerup	5.1 years
Tempel II	5.3 years
Honda-Mrkos-Pajdusakova	5.3 years
Neujmin II	5.4 years
Tempel I	5.5 years
Tuttle-Giacobini-Kresak	5.6 years
Tempel-Swift	5.7 years
Wirtanen	5.9 years
D'Arrest	6.2 years
Kojima	6.2 years
Du Toit-Neujmin-Delporte	6.3 years
Di Vico-Swift	6.3 years
Pons-Winnecke	6.3 years
Forbes	6.4 years
Kopff	6.4 years
Perrine-Mrkos	6.5 years
Schwassmann-Wachmann II	6.5 years
Giacobini-Zinner	6.5 years
Wolf-Harrington	6.6 years
Tsuchinshan I	6.6 years
Brooks	6.7 years
Johnson	6.8 years
Tsuchinshan II	6.8 years
Gunn	6.8 years
Arend-Rigaux	6.8 years
Finlay	6.9 years
Daniel	7.1 years
Harrington-Abell	7.2 years
Faye	7.4 years
Whipple	7.4 years
Arend	7.8 years
Schaumasse	8.2 years
Wolf	8.4 years
Comas-Sola	8.6 years
Kearns-Kwee	9.0 years
Klemola	11.0 years
Van Biesbroeck	12.4 years
Van Houten	15.8 years
Crommalin	27.9 years
Tempel-Tuttle	32.9 years
Westphal	61.7 years
Olbers	69.6 years
Halley	76.0 years

jects change greatly in magnitude, brightening thousands of times in several days.

Comet-Hunting

Dark skies are of the utmost importance in observing these dim travelers of the solar system. Occasionally one of the brighter comets will be seen over urban areas, but not often. It's good to remember that your eyes should be dark-adapted before you go comet hunting. Give your eyes about 15 to 20 minutes in the dark to get ready. During this time of adaptation, you might wish to orient yourself to the constellations if you do not already know them. Depending on the sky light situation in your area, your pupils will dilate somewhere between 5mm and 7mm. If bothersome lighting is nearby, construct a pair of blinders or a light shield to keep extraneous light from interfering with your vision. Red filters are a must for your flashlight; your eyes can handle red light without losing their dark adaptation. Night vision might improve over several hours. Remember that every time you go back into your house or a lighted car, you will be forced to readapt your vision.

When you are hunting comets, use the technique of *averted vision*.

☆ Look directly at the star field.
☆ Now look away, yet keep your attention on the original star field.

Averted vision calls on your peripheral vision and will do wonders for your ability to see ultradim objects, such as nebulae, comets, and galaxies. Some observers report improvements of an entire magnitude in their vision.

In the majority of cases, comets are discovered by observers using rich-field reflectors, rich-field refractors, and battleship binoculars ranging from 4 to 6 inches in objective size (Fig. 8-6). Nevertheless, every so often a comet slips through the big boys' dragnet and winds up the catch of an 11×80s' man.

Always double-check star atlas maps whenever you sight and cannot identify a nebulous object. It is quite a thrill to discover a new comet and may be even as much a thrill to have your name tacked onto it. However, a lot of work goes into the search: standing around on cold mornings, missing sleep, giving your utmost concentration, and developing a sound knowledge of the heavens (knowing where galaxies, clusters, and nebulae are located).

Binoculars (Fig. 8-7) permit the observer a wide-field view, which is really important in hunting comets. With

ful research can be done on comets. Not only is it possible to discover one of these heavenly phenomena, you can also make magnitude estimates and observe changes in the coma. Magnitude estimates are especially valuable. Even though most comets show little variation in magnitude, which might not be predicted from alterations in their distance from the Earth and Sun, some of these ob-

Fig. 8-5. Large comet-hunting binoculars: the Fujinon 25 × 150 (Courtesy Roger Re and R.V.R. Optical).

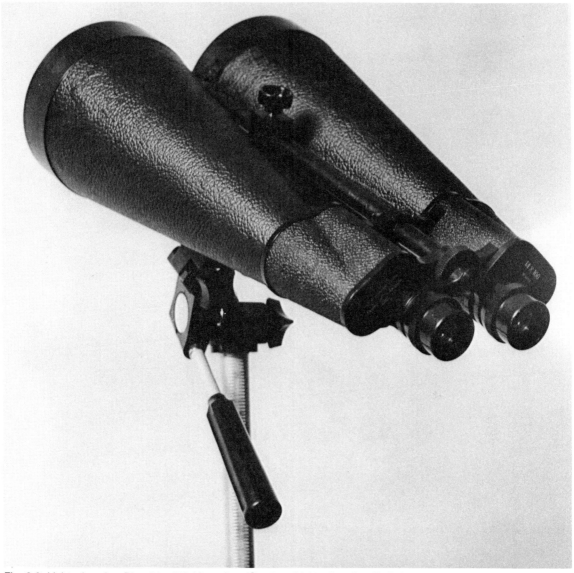

Fig. 8-6. Lichtenknecker Bino 14 × 100 binoculars (Courtesy Lichtenknecker Optics).

binoculars you will be able to sweep a wider area of the sky in a short time. Because binoculars are never equatorially mounted, you will be at an advantage. Comet-hunting requires sweeping to be done parallel to the horizon and not in arcs, which are the product of an equatorial mount.

Extra care is needed in examining a suspected comet because many deep-sky objects and even double stars possess the nebulous look of these visitors from the outer regions of the solar system. More than a few times I've mistaken faint unresolved galactic clusters for comets only to discover their true nature under a telescope's higher magnification. A telescope can be a valuable adjunct to binoculars in checking out cometlike objects.

When you are hunting for comets after sunset or before sunrise, make certain you have comfortable seating arrangements. Comet searches are long and fatiguing. Cold presents seat problems. Comfortable padding that won't conduct cold is valuable. Make sure your thermal-booted feet are not on concrete or asphalt.

Star charts are a must for a comet hunt; so is a pen-

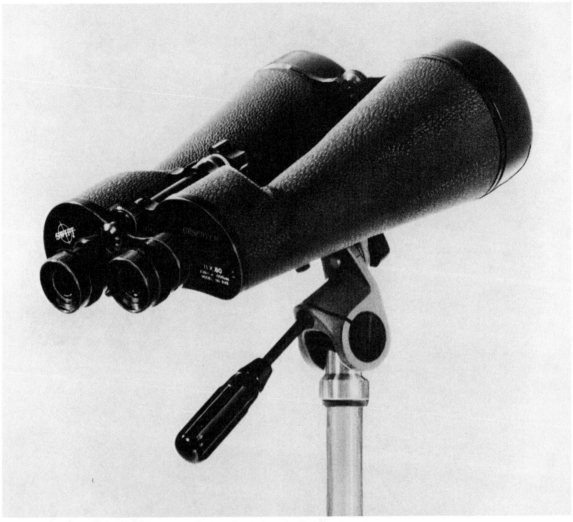

Fig. 8-7. Swift 11 × 80 Observer binoculars (Courtesy Swift Instruments).

cil or a felt tip pen because you will wish to mark the possible comet's position. The star charts will prove extra helpful if they list deep-sky objects to the twelfth magnitude. A good atlas helps you find the comet's rough position and its drift direction, which are of the utmost importance in reporting the comet and later finding it again.

The best time to go comet-hunting is three hours prior to sunrise in the Eastern heavens (Fig. 8-8) and about 40 to 50 minutes after sunset in the Western heavens (Fig. 8-9). The morning skies have historically been superb for visually locating comets. Comets are infrequent visitors to our skies and when these objects do come, they are

faint. Some comet hunters will spend an entire decade searching the heavens until they find their first "starry traveler."

Under a moonless evening sky, begin your search just after twilight. Start your hunt about 45 degrees north of where the Sun dips below the horizon, and then scan slowly over the horizon's lowest point. Sweep along a straight line, traveling from North to South until your binoculars take in a field some 45 degrees south of where the Sun left the sky. Take your time—perhaps a few minutes to travel one line.

Raise your binoculars up 3/4 of a field of view and sweep northward. Sweep back and forth until you reach

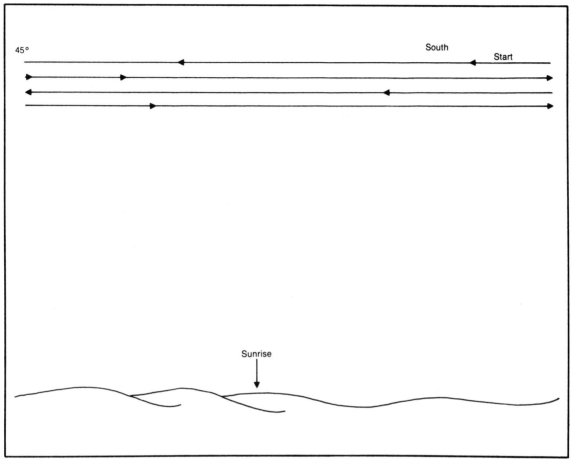

Fig. 8-8. A method for sweeping the eastern heavens for comets (Drawing by Anne Sheppard).

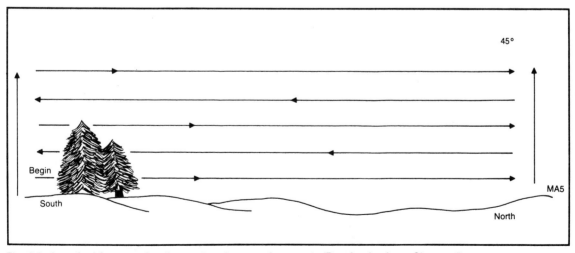

Fig. 8-9. A method for sweeping the western heavens for comets (Drawing by Anne Sheppard).

an altitude of 45 degrees above the western horizon. Searching might take up to 3 hours if done properly.

Hunting for comets in the morning is not much different. Start your search above the eastern horizon some 3 hours prior to sunrise. Reverse your evening search methods. Work your way down instead of up and scan from 45 degrees south of where the Sun appears to 45 degrees north of it. For morning comet-hunting, you must be up around 3 A.M. Again, the search will last close to three hours.

Comets are found every so often opposite the Sun. Keeping an eye on the ecliptic, sweep 30 degrees West and 30 degrees East of a point that will be directly overhead at 12 A.M. A star chart will be valuable here, giving you an area in which to confine your search. Do not neglect the areas around the celestial poles at midnight. On occasion a very faint comet is located near the poles.

Several methods help in proving or disproving that a suspected object is a comet:

☆ Because binoculars lack an equatorial mounting and setting circle for reference, you will need to locate that suspected object on a star chart and see if the starry visitor lies near known clusters, galaxies (Fig. 8-10, nebulae, or even double-star systems. If the suspect passes this test, then check it out with a higher-powered telescope if possible. Maybe the suspect is a deep-sky object that will better reveal itself at a higher power.

☆ If the suspected comet passes the initial tests, leave a mark on your star chart. Now make a rough reproduction of the star field on paper and note the suspect in relationship to the stars. Be careful!

☆ Using the faintest stars nearest the object's position, make a magnitude estimate and record it on your sketch. The star's approximate magnitudes can be found on an A.A.V.S.O. Star Atlas chart or in your charts catalog.

☆ Note the correct Universal Time and eyeball the suspect for a tail or nucleus.

☆ Does the suspect drift across the star field? You will note this occurrence in 20 or 30 minutes. If it drifts, then likely it is a comet. Watch the direction of the drift.

☆ Even if the object shows no apparent drift, this does not entirely preclude that the suspect is not a comet. Perhaps the suspect is distant and traveling slowly. To check further, mark the position again on your star chart. Locate the suspected comet on the next clear night and see if it has moved relative to the stars. If it has, you might well have a comet. Record the drift's

Fig. 8-10. M64, The Black-Eye Galaxy, in Coma Berenices, like many other deep-sky objects, is often mistaken for a comet. This spiral galaxy was photographed by Ron Potter with a 14-inch Schmidt-Cassegrain (Courtesy Dr. Jack Marling and Lumicon).

direction.

☆ Check IAU literature to make sure the comet is not a recent discovery or a known periodic comet. If you believe you've discovered a comet, then go to the telephone and send a telegram to:

Central Bureau for Astronomical Telegrams
Rapid Satellite CAMBMASS
60 Garden St.
Cambridge, MA 02138

The telegram should contain:

☆ Your last name.
☆ The fact that you located a comet.
☆ The epoch on which your star positions are based.
☆ The year, month, day, and Universal Time.
☆ The right ascension and declination.
☆ The comet's estimated magnitude.
☆ The degree of condensation in the comet's nucleus using a scale from 0 to 9, (with 0 meaning no condensation, 5 meaning a fair amount of condensation, and 9 meaning the nucleus appeared starlike).
☆ The comet's rate and direction of drift as shown by a new set of positions.
☆ The instrument or instruments employed in the discovery, including objective size, focal length, and type of instrument.

After you've given the information to the telegraph operator, have the operator read it back to you so you can check the numbers. A wrong numeral in either declination or right ascension could spell disaster for your discovery (if a nebula doesn't get it first).

After the Central Bureau receives your telegram, it will publish your claim in an attempt to verify the discovery. If your claim does hold up, the comet will bear your name as well as two other discoverers. If for example my comet was the third comet discovered in 1986, it will be called 1986c (third letter of the alphabet). Later this small letter will be replaced by a permanent Roman-numeral designation that gives the year and order of perihelion passage; for example, Mensing-Mewsing-Moosing 1986IV.

Before I continue on the topic of amateur research, I should mention a wonderful adjunct to comet study: the Arizona-Tonantzintla Catalogue, which is a highly accurate and commonly used bright star list. The Arizona-Tonantzintla Catalogue derives its accurate magnitudes from photoelectric photometers. The catalogue is available from Sky Publishing Corporation.

I also recommend the variable star charts sold by the American Association of Variable Star Observers. Also valuable are Wil Tirion's Sky Atlas 2000.0 and C.E. Scovil's A.A.V.S.O. Variable Star Atlas.

Determining Magnitude

A highly important area of amateur research on comets is the making of magnitude estimates. Two estimates—one of the coma (head) and one of the nucleus, if it can be observed—can be made. These estimates are a key to the comet's activity. Magnitude is the only available route for knowing about a comet's changing physical makeup.

The easiest and most reliable method of estimating a comet's magnitude is as follows:

☆ Center the comet in your field of view and observe the coma's brightness in focus.
☆ Next find stars on your star charts that are both close to the comet and are within the same magnitude range. Comparison stars should share the comet's field of view. Next center on the comparison star and out-focus on it until its size is the same as the comet's coma in focus. Is the star as bright, brighter, or dimmer?
☆ If you lack comparison stars of the same brightness as the comet, create a magnitude scale by selecting a dimmer star and a brighter star. Now estimate the

comet's brightness in relationship to the two stars. Mark Xs on the comparison stars. Indicate if you have used a magnitude scale.
☆ After observing, check out the comparison stars with a catalog like the Arizona-Tonantzintla Catalogue.
☆ Repeat the first three steps at least three times to ensure accuracy. Also, in your log book or observer's notebook record the star numbers from the catalog.

Binoculars (Fig. 8-11) are the instrument of choice in doing magnitude studies on the brighter comets. Binoculars give bright images and exceptionally wide fields, making the location of comparison stars an easy task. 7×50s and 11×80s are excellent for magnitude studies.

One warning: the brightest comets are often too bright to be compared with stars. If this proves a problem, you can compare the brightest comets with the planets or even the Moon if they are available in the same sky. When a comet gets this bright, you will be viewing quite a show.

Nuclear magnitudes pose problems because of the small nucleus' faintness and often hard-to-determine

Fig. 8-11. Steiner 15×80G binoculars (Courtesy Pioneer & Co.).

boundaries. The coma's light dispersion also creates hardships. If the comet has a bright center, you are in luck. Use comparison stars in making the magnitude estimate and keep them in focus along with the nucleus. As with the comet, the nucleus estimates can be made without the precise magnitude of a comparison star. You can use a relative scale between brighter and dimmer stars. Jot down the right ascension and declination of both stars from your star chart. The comet nucleus is generally fainter than the limiting magnitude of star catalogs, so the precise magnitude will be difficult to find. Some comets possess multiple nuclei as a result of splitting. Keep daily magnitude records of each nucleus. Also keep a record of their positions relative to each other. After the split the brightest nucleus is considered the *primary particle*, and it is this nucleus that will be estimated.

The secondary component of the split is measured as an angle in degrees from north toward east from the main component. Measured in seconds of arc, the changing distances of each secondary particle will be gauged from the primary. This information is invaluable to astrophysicists in determining the two nuclei's mass and velocity. From that information scientists can estimate the force of expulsion leading to the split between the two components.

Some comet nuclei exhibit a gradual condensation, rather than a clear one. The condensation resides in the central head. You might wish to record this condensation using the following graduated scale:

0—Diffuse coma showing no condensation; uniform brightness.
1—Diffuse coma; some brightening in central half.
2—Coma center showing brightening in comparison to outer region.
3—Coma differentiated and having two brightness levels.
4—Condensation, although still diffuse, in coma's center; condensation more than 25 percent of coma's diameter.
5—More condensation than 4; bright spot in center.
6—Condensation more evident than 5; coma has uniform brightness save for center; nucleus rounded.
7—Hazy starlike appearance to condensation.
8—Nucleus like a spherical blob of light, somewhat lacking in clarity.
9—Starlike.

Preplotting Motion

When you are studying comets, you will be called upon to preplot their motions across star fields. To preplot you will employ the same method used in preplotting as-

teroid paths. Preplotting gives you the opportunity to locate suitable comparison stars that will be in the comet's general area and will assist you in magnitude studies. Preplotting is also a valuable time-saver in that it lets you get right at the magnitude study without wasting valuable minutes hunting for comparison stars.

An accurate ephemerides is a must for preplotting comets. Some of the major monthly amateur astronomical journals contain ephemerides, yet these predictions might be too late for you to observe early apparitions. You would be wise to have a subscription to the International Astronomical Union circulars. These circulars publish ultrarecent comet discoveries. Positions, magnitudes, heliocentric oppositions, and the closest approaches to earth are predicted. Within a week's time any news of changes in a comet will be mailed to you.

Subscriptions are available by writing:

IAU Circular Service
Smithsonian Astrophysical Observatory
60 Garden St.
Cambridge, MA 02138

To make an accurate plot of a comet, you must find the center of the coma. If a nucleus is observed, you may use it as the center. Know the field of your binocular eyepiece and estimate, using the stars in your field of view.

When you plot a comet, use the date and Universal Time in your records. Also record the type of binoculars you used and the method you employed in arriving at the estimate.

Knowing how to plot will assist you in: finding errors in the predicted position of comets, making measurements of the comet's tail and other constituents, measuring the position angle of the tail and secondary constituents, and making approximate measurements of the comet's position from the field stars as noted in the catalogs.

Estimating Size

In order to estimate the size of the coma and the sizes of other comet constituents with binoculars, you will need to know your instrument's field of view. Generally the field of view will be listed on your binoculars (this might be approximate) or you can find it by observing a star cluster and marking the extent of the field on a chart. You will need to know the chart's scale in millimeters per degree of sky if you use the second method.

After your instrument's field of view has been determined, you will then be able to get an approximate estimation of the coma's size in relation to the binoculars' field of view. The coma's diameter will be an estimated fraction of the binoculars' field of view. Graduated reticles can be installed inside the binocular eyepiece barrels. The reticles work well with binocular eyepieces and will give more accurate portrayals of coma size. Graduated reticles can be purchased from surplus optic supply houses.

Likely the most used method of finding the coma's size is the drift method. In this method you will center the coma in the eyepieces of your binocular. Making certain your binocular is perfectly still (well mounted), you will let the comet drift toward the edge of the field. Observing this drift, wait for the exact instant, to the nearest second, when the coma makes contact with the edge of the viewing field and write down the time. While the comet continues to drift out of the field, you will await the last moment the comet is viewed and write down this time. Now determine (in seconds) the time between the first and last timings. A factor for the comet's declination will now be added. (See Table 8-2.) This factor, listed on the following table, will be multiplied by the interval in seconds between the first and last timings. The final value will be shown in minutes of arc. You will make two more timings and find the mean value for the coma's actual diameter.

Measuring Position Angle

Binoculars, because they are wide-field instruments, are excellent for measuring the position angle of a comet's tail. The comet's tail angle depends on the comet's position in relation to the Sun and Earth in space, and these positions alter as the comet and the Earth orbit the Sun. The comet's orbital speed, as well as the solar wind, might distort the tail and alter position angle.

Star charts are of the utmost importance in measuring position angle. The comet's center must be plotted. After the position has been located on the star charts, you can measure the length of the tail and the position angle. Measurements for position angle are always made from 0 degrees North toward 90 degrees East. The majority of star charts will show North at the top and West on the right.

The following method will assist you in finding the position angle:

☆ With the tail passing from the comet, locate a star in line with the tail. This star must be seen in both the binocular field and on the star chart.
☆ With the comet's coma already marked on the chart,

Table 8-2. Comet Declination Factors.

Factors	Approximate Declinations
0.10	65.3°-67.7°
0.11	62.8°-65.2°
0.12	60.2°-62.7°
0.13	57.5°-60.1°
0.14	54.8°-57.4°
0.15	51.9°-54.7°
0.16	48.9°-51.8°
0.17	45.8°-48.8°
0.18	42.5°-45.7°
0.19	39.0°-42.4°
0.20	35.2°-38.9°
0.21	31.0°-35.1°
0.22	26.3°-30.9°
0.23	20.5°-26.2°
0.24	12.3°-20.4°
0.25	0.0°-12.2°

pencil in a line from the coma mark to the star. This line will show the tail's direction. Stars on either side of the tail may be used if no stars lie in a direct line with the coma. The position will then be estimated.
☆ With the South at 180 degrees, the East at 90 degrees, the North at 0 degrees, and the West at 270 degrees, use a protractor and measure from the North to the line illustrating the comet's tail. Jot down the angle in degrees.
☆ Now hunt for any secondary tail and measure any that you locate.

Measuring Comet Tail Length

Comet tail length measurement is another area open to research with binoculars. For large comets, as a rule tails are measured in degrees and decimals. Measurements of short-tailed comets are generally expressed in minutes of arc. Use the following method to measure the comet's tail:

☆ First make a drawing of the tail as it appears in your binoculars.
☆ Employing field stars, place the tail relative to the comet's center on the star chart. This may be accomplished by marking off the distance from the comet's center to the stars on the chart.
☆ When the tail is correctly drawn to its length, measure the tail on the chart in millimeters.
☆ Now employ this equation:

$$\frac{1°}{\text{Chart scale in degrees (in mm)}} \times \frac{\text{Actual tail length in degrees}}{\text{Length of tail on chart (in mm)}}$$

Actual tail length in degrees = ?

In doing this equation, you will have to find your star atlas's chart scale (this must be exact).

☆ Remember to measure the comet's *antitails*, or secondary tails, which emanate from the comet's head.
☆ An illustration of a comet can be made inside a circle with a diameter of 3 1/2 inches. The circle will represent the field of your binoculars. Often drawings are superior to photographs in comet work because, when a comet splits into components, drawings of the sequences often reveal activity in the comet's center. Use quality drawing pencils because you will wish to render fine contrast and detail.

Abnormal Activity

At times comets behave unpredictably and exhibit sudden brightenings and dimmings, nuclei that split, explosions, and distortions of all kinds. If you observe these strange phenomena, send immediate notification to IAU circulars.

The Association of Lunar and Planetary Observers has a comet section that will be interested in your observations. Membership in this fine organization can be had by writing:

ALPO
P.O. Box 3AZ
Las Cruces, NM 88003

Preserving your observations is extremely important in comet study. It is wise to keep a record of your comet observations because your memory can distort what you have seen. For each comet, list:

☆ The seeing conditions, rated from 1 to 5 (1 is worst, 5 is best).
☆ The binoculars used.
☆ The sky transparency, rated from 1 to 6. These numbers are equivalent to the magnitude of the faintest stars visible to the naked eye. If you can see only fifth-magnitude stars, then the transparency is 5.
☆ The position angle of the tail and tail components.
☆ The degree of nucleus condensation.
☆ The length of tail in degrees or minutes.
☆ The magnitude of the nucleus, if applicable.
☆ The coma size in minutes of arc.
☆ The total magnitude of the comet.
☆ The comet's description—any strange activity.

☆ The drawing of the comet.

Another area of comet research is the comet occultation. Large bright comets may occult stars. Find yourself a radio that will receive time signals from WWV and a good tape recorder. Begin recording radio signals prior to the time predicted for the event. Signal with your voice the moment the star blinks out or dims behind the coma or nucleus of the comet. You will again signal when the star reappears or brightens. Afterwards you can time the recorded event to within 1/10 second.

HALLEY'S COMET

Halley's Comet (Fig. 8-12), easily our most famous comet, drew great public attention when it returned to our skies in 1985 and 1986. Being the only periodic comet bright enough to be viewed with the naked eye, this retrograde orbiter of our solar system might have been observed by the Chinese as far back as 467 B.C. Most historians assign 240 B.C. as the comet's first sighting.

Previously observed in 1910, Halley's Comet has an orbital period ranging between 74 and 78 years because of the comet's perturbation by the gas giants Jupiter and Saturn. In 1948 this magnificent traveler passed aphelion and went beyond Neptune's path. Since 240 B.C. the comet has been observed making 29 returns.

Halley's Comet, because of its altering position in comparison to Earth, fails to shine with equal brilliance on its various returns. Reported to be outstanding in 989, 1301, and 1456 (the year Pope Calixtus III called it the devil's agent and excommunicated it), the comet had a less than spectacular return in 1985 and 1986. When Halley's Comet pays a visit again in 2061 and 2062, it should be a real eye-catcher.

Since it was sighted in 240 B.C., Comet Halley has also been witnessed in the following years: 163 B.C., 11 B.C., 66 A.D., 141, 218, 295, 373, 451, 530, 607, 683, 760, 837, 912, 989, 1066, 1145, 1223, 1301, 1378, 1456, 1531, 1607, 1682, 1759, 1835, and 1910.

Over the centuries many historical events have been linked with Halley's Comet. Among them the comet was said to have foretold the death of the Roman ruler Agrippa in 11 B.C., the destruction of Jerusalem in 66 A.D., and the defeat of Attila the Hun in 451 A.D. In 87 B.C. Julius Caesar reputedly spotted the comet. Halley's comet appeared prior to the Norman Invasion in 1066 A.D. and was recorded on the famous Bayeux Tapestry said to be woven by William the Conqueror's wife. The comet proved to be a bad omen for King Harold, who perished at the Battle of Hastings. In 1301 A.D. the Florentine

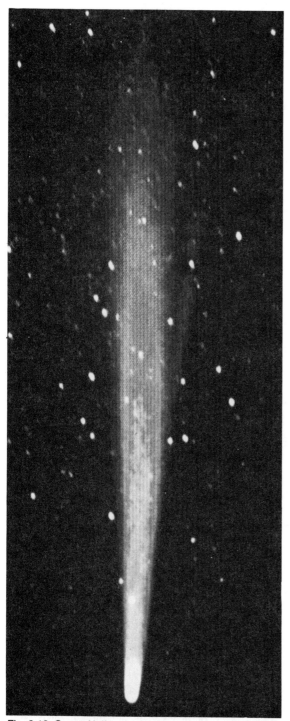

Fig. 8-12. Comet Halley: A KNPO computer reconstruction of a 1910 photograph taken at Lowell Observatory (Courtesy National Optical Astronomy Observatories).

painter Giotto di Bondone witnessed Halley's Comet and incorporated it into the Fresco of Padua, which pictured the Magi from the East.

The 1910 apparition of Halley's Comet was extremely bright, although not as bright as the apparition of 837 A.D. when the comet rivaled Venus in magnitude. In 1910 a brighter comet appeared several weeks earlier and was hailed the Daylight Comet. Many older folks, recalling Halley, actually observed the famed Daylight comet.

Edmund Halley (1656-1742) first demonstrated that comets travel around the Sun in accordance with Newton's theory of gravity. Halley, England's second Astronomer Royal after Flamsteed and a close friend of Newton, noted the similarity of the orbits of the very bright comets of 1531, 1607, and 1682 and conjectured from his data that the three were the same comet. After calculating this body's orbit, he predicted the comet's return in 1758. However, he never knew how close his predictions were because he died 16 years prior to the comet's return.

There are 16 comets known to be in the Halley class of comets that return to the Sun in less than 200 years. None stay far beyond Neptune's orbit. Halley ranks as the brightest of this class. Comet Halley's orbit is 18 degrees to our planet. The comet's solid portion is a dirty black snowball 3.1 miles across, a bit smaller than most asteroids. With a 50-million-mile tail, the comet reaches a maximum magnitude of 3.6. At its closest approach to the Sun, Comet Halley comes within 3280 million miles of the solar disk. The comet is associated with two important meteor showers: the annual Aquarids and the Orionids.

Over the years questions have been raised about Halley's Comet's loss of material through evaporation during each perihelion passage. Why does this comet fail to lose much brightness over the centuries? This riddle has yet to be fully answered, although bits of this puzzle may come forth from the data returned from the 1986 comet probes.

In 1910 when the comet was midway between the Earth and the Sun, an experiment was conducted with the hope of observing the comet's material. This material proved insubstantial. Later that year our planet traveled through the comet's tail with no visible results.

Amateur astronomers were not terribly disappointed with their views of the comet during the 1985-1986 apparition. The most stunning views of the comet and its tail came with binoculars, owing to their wide fields and low magnifications (Fig. 8-13); 7 × 50s, 10 × 50s, 8 × 56s, 9 × 63s, 10 × 70s, and 11 × 80s were all well suited for observing the comet.

Fig. 8-13. Tasco's Halley's Comet Series: 8 × 56 (top left), 8 × 56 armored (top right), 7 × 50 (bottom) (Courtesy Tasco).

Binocular astronomers had their best views from the tropics and the Southern Hemisphere. Those of us living in the Northern United States and the United Kingdom found the comet close to the horizon.

My first sighting of the comet came in early October with some difficulty. Using an 8-inch Schmidt-Cassegrain, not far from a city, I located Halley's Comet in a fairly dense starfield. At 60× the comet looked like a dim gray patch. In November observing began to improve, and by

December I had no problem finding the comet with 7 × 50 binoculars in the bright skies over Philadelphia. Toward the end of December, Comet Halley showed traces of a tail to observers under dark-sky conditions.

In 1986, after disappearing behind the Sun and then re-emerging from the glare, the comet grew more eye-catching as it continued on its path through the constellations (Fig. 8-14). During the last week of February, the comet appeared in the morning twilight in the East and

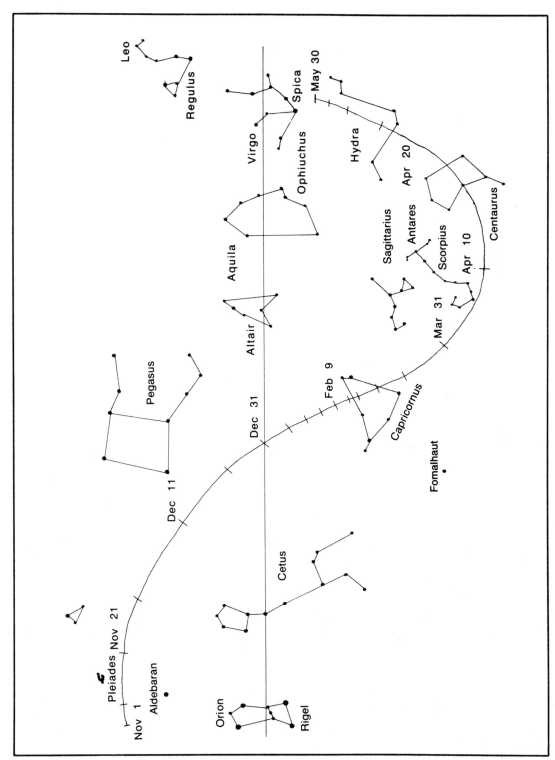

Fig. 8-14. Comet Halley's path through the constellations (Drawing by Anne Sheppard).

was observed with a bright, starlike nucleus and a fair-sized tail. By the end of March, Comet Halley showed a long, bright tail in the dawn Southeastern skies. I recall standing on a hill overlooking a pine forest in central New Jersey and marveling at our visitor from space as it hung a bit south of the Teapot in Sagittarius. The tail had grown brighter and more extensive since the previous month. The nucleus was extremely brilliant; the tail showed some detail. I had no problem finding the comet with the naked eye under dark skies.

In April, Comet Halley put on a poor display for folks in the Southern Hemisphere. Dimmer now, the comet hung low on the horizon for northern observers and lost some of its detail in the atmospheric murk. By May our visitor began to shrink in magnitude. If you missed our friend, you will have to wait until 2061 to see it again.

Chapter 9

The Meteors

Meteors, or *shooting stars*, are streaks of light caused by particles from outer space entering our atmosphere at high speeds and burning up (Fig. 9-1). Often as luminous as naked-eye stars, meteors occur at heights between 55 and 65 miles. Brighter examples called *bolides,* or *fireballs,* have a torchlike appearance as they arc across our heavens. Most meteors travel at 20 to 35 miles per second, depending on whether they overtake our planet or our planet overtakes them. The major indication that these bodies are members of our solar system is evidenced by the fact that no meteors possess velocities in excess of the escape velocity needed to leave our solar system.

Most meteors leave a glowing trail that often persists for several seconds or minutes. The trails are the visual effect of the recombination of ionized atoms and molecules. Extremely bright daytime fireballs, traveling at low altitudes, often leave dark trails behind them.

The majority of naked-eye shooting stars occur alone, and are thus called *sporadic meteors*. Visible sporadic meteors grow in number from 6 after sunset to a peak of 14 just before dawn. Large numbers of meteors are observed moving outward from the radiant point in a meteor shower. Orbiting the Sun in parallel paths at similar velocities, these meteors from a shower. Ten annual meteor showers exist, along with a fair number of minor showers that are almost indistinguishable from the activity of background sporadic meteors.

Formed by the remnants scattered by a periodic comet, a meteor shower occupies the same orbit as the comet. Starting as a dense swarm of meteoroids and then spreading out, the meteor shower gradually disintegrates. Young meteor showers might exhibit up to 1000 meteors per minute for several hours. Examples of these grand displays were seen in the Andromedid storms of 1872 and 1885; the Leonid meteor storms of 1799, 1833, 1866, and 1966; and the Giacobinid storms of 1933 and 1946.

Meteor showers are best viewed when their radiant is high in the sky. Showers get their names from either the constellation in which their radiant resides or from their parent comet. The predicted rate, with the radiant overhead, is called the *zenithal hourly rate*, but because the radiant is seldom directly overhead, the true observed rate is often lower.

The pioneer work in modern meteor astronomy began a little over a hundred years ago when naked-eye observers recorded the paths, velocity, and brightness of meteors. Today photographic methods have largely supplanted naked-eye observation. Radio and radar have also been added to the meteor observer's armaments, and with this modern instrumentation several daylight meteor

Fig. 9-1. A Perseid Meteor photographed with a 50mm f/2 lens (Photograph by Lee C. Coombs).

showers have been recorded.

The spectrum of shooting stars demonstrates that their composition is quite similar to either iron or stony meteorites. Scientists believe most meteors are composed of gas-rich carbonaceous chondrite, a kind of stony meteorite. Fireballs are likely scattered boulders from the nuclei of ancient periodic comets or the refuse from asteroid collisions, while meteor-shower meteors are undoubtedly derived from the outer layers of young, periodic-comet nuclei.

OBSERVING METEORS

Meteors and especially meteor showers offer the naked-eye and binocular observer some of the finest visual pleasures available. (See Table 9-1.) Anyone who has witnessed either a great shower or a bright, almost torchlike bolide arc across a dark country sky would likely agree with me. Meteors are one of the few celestial happenings where no optical equipment is required to undertake research (except for telescopic meteors where binoculars are the instrument of choice). No other form of astronomical observation is likely to be as relaxing as meteor watching, where the observer is often found sprawled in a deck chair with his eyes heavenward.

Although most amateur meteor observation is naked eye because of our eyes natural wide field, binoculars of 7×50, 10×70, and 11×80 ranges offer advantages in studying meteor trains, telescopic meteors, and fireballs. Fireballs can be spectacular (Fig. 9-2)! A few years ago, when I vacationed in southwestern Arizona, I had the great pleasure of being out on the desert late one evening in May when I suddenly noticed a bright shadow on the ground. My shadow. Turning, I looked up to observe a bright orange-blue torch hurtling through the sky—the largest and most brilliant fireball I ever saw. Instants later it boomed as it hurtled through the sound barrier and left a smoky trail in its wake. I doubt I would have been any more awed if I had seen the belt stars in Orion supernova.

Meteors, because they are mostly dim events, are best observed away from the bright skies of urban areas and when the Moon is not present. A fine time to view them is toward morning, due to our planet's path which is head on into the shower. In the evening only those meteors with velocities greater than our planet's velocity in orbit will overtake the Earth and make their descent into our atmosphere.

All the equipment you will require, aside from your eyes, and binoculars for telescopic meteors, is a comfortable reclining lawn chair or camper's mattress, a star atlas, a red-filtered flashlight, and if you're doing research, a shortwave capable of picking up WWV time signals.

RESEARCHING METEORS

A major field in amateur meteor research is discovering new meteor showers. Just about any dark night when there are no predicted showers, you will likely see from 10 to 16 meteors. You may wish to chart these "sporadic" meteors. If you find several coming from the same radiant or point of origin, you might have discovered a new shower.

Plotting a meteor's apparent path is a relatively simple undertaking. Using a star atlas chart, make a point where the meteor first appears, and then draw a line from it to where the meteor vanishes (Fig. 9-3). A ruler edge will do fine. If you are plotting meteors in a shower, it would be advantageous to study the star fields in and around the constellation where the radiant is listed. The lines must be drawn rapidly because you will need to return your attention to the sky so you will not miss what you came out to observe. Jot down the Universal Time, the length of time the meteor was visible, and its coloration above the line you drew.

Having a companion is a great help in meteor observation—one of you can record while the other is observing. Again note the Universal Time to the nearest second when you first sighted the meteor. Use either a watch set to Universal Time or a shortwave radio tuned to WWV (5, 10, or 15 MHz).

Meteor duration, or the interval between initial sighting and vanishing, is noted in the total number of seconds. The meteor's duration permits an estimate of the object's speed of entering and passing through the atmosphere. After you have determined the entry angle and altitude, which requires observations from several locations with accurately known positions, you can compute the speed. Most durations are shorter than 3 seconds. Fireballs can be seen for 2 or 3 seconds, yet because of some psychological factor attached to seeing a fireball's brilliant and spectacular show, these objects appear to endure much longer. The best method for timing duration is to count the number of ticks on the WWV broadcast.

Finding a meteor's brightness is an easy exercise because all you are required to do is to compare the meteor's brightness with nearby stars of naked-eye magnitude. On the other hand, fireballs present difficulties in that only bright planets can be used as comparisons. Quite often planets won't be available so your memory must be trusted. In such instances error might show itself.

Knowledge about the meteor train's length is useful

Table 9-1. Important Meteor Showers.

Date (approx.)	Name of Shower	Constellation Radiant
Jan. 1-6	Quadrantids	Bootes
Jan. 16	Delta Cancrids	Cancer
Jan. 18	Coma-Berenicids	Coma Berenices
Feb. 26	Delta Leonids	Leo
March 16	Corona-Australids	Corona Australis
March 22	Camelopardalids	Camelopardus
March 22	Geminids	Gemini
April 4	Kappa Serpentids	Serpens
April 7	Delta Draconids	Draco
April 10	Virginids	Virgo
April 15	April Fireballs	radiant erratic
April 22	Lyrids	Lyra-Hercules
April 25	Mu Virginids	Virgo
April 23	Grigg-Skjellerups	radiant erratic
April 28	Alpha Bootids	Bootes
May 1	Phi Bootids	Hercules
May 3	Alpha Scorpiids	Libra-Scorpius
May 4	Eta Aquarids	Aquarius
June 3	Tau Herculids	Hercules
June 4	Alpha Circinids	Circinus
June 5	Scorpiids	Scorpius
June 7	Arietids	Aries
June 7	Zeta Perseids	Perseus
June 8	Librids	Libra
June 11	Sagittariids	Sagittarius
June 13	Theta Ophiuchids	Ophiuchus-Sagittarius
June 16	June Lyrid Meteors	Lyra
June 20	Ophiuchids	Ophiuchus
June 26	Corvids	Corvus
June 29	Beta Taurids (daytime)	Taurus
June 30	June Draconids	Draco
July 16	Omicron Draconids	Draco
July 28	Delta Aquarids	Aquarius
July 30	Capricornids	Capricornus
Aug. 13	Perseids	Perseus
Aug. 20	Kappa Cygnids	Cygnus
Aug. 31	Andromedids	Andromeda
Sept. 1	Aurigids	Auriga
Sept. 6	Lyncids	Lynx
Sept. 7	Epsilon Perseids	Perseus
Sept. 21	Kappa Aquarids	Aquarius
Sept. 23	Alpha Aurigids	Auriga
Oct. 9	Draconids	Draco
Oct. 19	Epsilon Geminids	Gemini
Oct. 20	Orionids	Orion
Nov. 5	Taurids	Taurus
Nov. 9	Cepheids	Cepheus
Nov. 12	Pegasids	Pegasus
Nov. 14	Andromedids	Andromeda
Nov. 17	Leonids	Leo
Dec. 10	Monocerotids	Monoceros-Gemini
Dec. 10	Chi Orionids	Orion
Dec. 11	Sigma Hydrids	Hydra
Dec. 14	Geminids	Gemini
Dec. 16	Piscids	Pisces
Dec. 20	Delta Arietids	Aries
Dec. 22	Ursids	Ursa Minor

Fig. 9-2. A fireball blazes across the heavens.

information. The light trail, which follows brilliant meteors, can be measured in degrees when you know the approximate altitude of the meteor. Use this formula:

$$L = \frac{A° \times D}{49.6°}$$

where L = the actual train length

A° = the maximum angular length as figured by the observer

D = Meteor's altitude upon entering the atmosphere.

To find the angular length you must know the angular distance of a few known stars. Remember a full moon is 0.5 degrees.

A record of the meteor's color is invaluable in determining the meteor's temperature and chemical composition. Color estimates must be based on the head (the preceding portion) of the meteor. Describe what color you have seen. Record it on the trace line after the meteor.

Watch for unusual meteor behavior! Note when you have observed any sudden changes in these bodies, such as explosions, sudden flareups, loud reports, color alterations, and splitting.

Hourly Counts

Meteor shower hourly counts are much needed. The hourly count represents the number of meteors visible to an observer watching a specified area of the sky. The hourly count reveals the meteor shower's peak time, and in doing so, it also reveals the time in which our planet

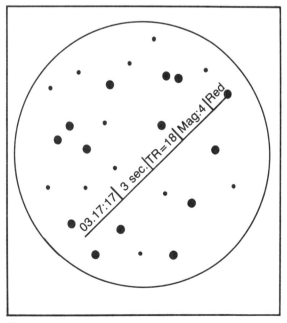

Fig. 9-3. A meteor's path recorded.

Instructions for AMS-R Sheet

    This form is to be used for all AMS visual (non-telescopic) observations and
supercedes all previous versions. Telescopic meteors and fireballs should be filed
on the appropriate forms. This form may be duplicated or copied as needed.

    The key to the numbered items are as follows:

(1) Under conditions include clouds,moonlight or artificial light. Do <u>not</u> give
    double date unless observations span the actual change of date (for example,
    if interval is 22:15 EST to 00:45 E.S.T. give double date). The use of
    Universal Time is encouraged.

(2) Time to the nearest minute or 0.1 minute is sufficient.

(3) Estimate the stellar magnitude to the nearest 1/2 magnitude (decimals may be
    used to facilitate recording,i.e. write 4 1/2 as 4.5).

(4) Give color on scale (R = red,O = orange,Y = yellow,G = green,B = blue,
    W = white,or combination YW = yellowish).

(5) Indicate if meteor is related to a shower or sporadic (i.e. Per. = Perseid,
    Spor. = sporadic,ect.).

(6) Give duration to the nearest $0.^{s}1$ if desired,otherwise to the nearest second.

(7) Give length in sky to nearest degree.

(8) Indicate if meteor left a train or wake and indicate color (if any) and its
    duration in seconds.

(9) Indicate accuracy of information.   (E = Excellent,F = Fair,P = Poor)

(10) Give a serial number here to indicate number for the year,i.e. 74 – 153
     indicates 153rd meteor for 1974.

(11) List here additional comments including any special data required by specific
     programs:

    (a) radiant and height solutions – give chart reference here.

    (b) magnitude and color solutions – give here an estimate of meteor end-
        point altitude (Alt =) or zenith distance (Z =). Quote to the nearest
        degree even though actual accuracy may not be better than $\pm 5°$ in some
        cases.

    (c) If magnitude is –2 or brighter a separate fireball form should be filed.

Fig. 9-4. The American Meteor Society's form for naked eye meteor observation, front and back (Courtesy Dr. David D.
Meisel and the American Meteor Society).

Observer Name _____   Double Date _____[AMS-R]

Mailing Address _____   Began _____ Type of Time _____

_____   End _____ Type of Time _____

Observing Site _____   (1) Conditions: Begin _____

                                                            End _____

(2) Time	(3) Mag	(4) Color	(5) Type	(6) Dur	(7) Length	(8) Train/Dur	(9) Accur	(10) No.	(11) Comments

115

Instructions For AMS T-1 Recording Form

Please mail these blanks when full or at end of year directly or forwarding to:

American Meteor Society

New or more blanks available upon request provided a postal address is supplied.
(1) Please mount this form on a piece of cardboard and take it with you to the telescope with your observing notebook.

Keyed Notes for completing this form (see reverse):
(2) List station if same for all observations; if different stations were used, list these instead on a separate sheet giving your other notes (13).
(3) List all instruments here and enter appropriate number in item (7) for each sighting.
(4) Number consecutively for year.
(5) Give month and day.
(6) Give time to nearest minute INDICATING EACH TIME-TYPE IN USE (E.D.T.,G.M.T., U.T.,etc.).
(7) Instrument Identification.
(8) Instrument position to nearest 1^m in R.A. and $0.1°$ Dec. if possible (or $0.\overset{°}{1}$ Alt. & Az., if possible), otherwise nearest $1°$ acceptable. Indicate which coordinate system is in use by circling either "RA" or "Alt". DO NOT MIX coordinate systems on each form. If it is necessary to use different coordinate systems, please use two reporting forms, one for each type of coordinate system. (This division of data is most convenient because of our specialized data-reduction system and saves a considerable amount of transcription time for us.)
(9) Give estimate of meteor magnitude here to the nearest $0\overset{m}{.}1$ if you can. Otherwise nearest $1/2^m$ or 1^m is acceptable.
(10) Record here observed meteor length in units of 0.1 of the total field diameter and classify the sighting on the following scale:
    A - beginning and end inside field
    B - beginning in field, end outside field
    C - beginning outside field and end in field
    D - both beginning and end outside field
(11) Give position angle of direction of motion so that the number indicates the direction in which the meteor was traveling or headed and duration to nearest $0\overset{s}{.}1$, if possible.
(12) Sky transparency should be recorded on scale, s = 0 overcast, s = 5 perfect with M added to indicate moonlight if present.
(13) Additional remarks such as color, train, etc. should be noted on a separate sheet and numbered. In this column put the corresponding number for each note.
(14) In order to check the statistical validity of this sample please estimate total hours logged and averaged sky condition represented by this report.

YOUR COOPERATION IS GREATLY APPRECIATED.

Fig. 9-5. The American Meteor Society's form for telescopic (binocular) meteor observation, front and back (Courtesy Dr. David D. Meisel and the American Meteor Society).

Telescopic Meteor Report Form   A.M.S.
                                                        T-1

Observer_____ Postal Address (1) _____
Station (2) _____ Longitude_____ Latitude _____
Instruments (3): (a) Telescope (b) Finder (c) Binocular (d) Other_____
Diameter/Focal Ratio   _____ _____ _____ _____
Magnification   _____ _____ _____ _____
Angular Field of
   View   _____ _____ _____ _____

(4)	(5)	(6)	(7)	(8)	(9)	(10)	(11)	(12)	(13)	
No.	Date 19__	Time and Type Used H M	Inst. I.D.	Field RA/Alt	Center DEC/AZ	Magn Est	Length and Class	Motion PA/Dur	Sky Trans	Notes

(14) Statistical Information: Main Program Being Undertaken_____
     Total Hours Observing represented by this log= _____ hours under
     Average Sky Conditions of s = _____ (s = 1 poor,s = 5 best)

117

travels through the densest region of the meteoric cloud. Only one observer determines an hourly count. A partner keeps time and records data. There is no role switching.

The simplest and best method for counting meteors, especially during active showers, is to record every meteor by making a mark on a note pad or by calling into a tape recorder. A new count will proceed every hour on the hour. If you face an extremely heavy shower, you better start a new count every 15 minutes so you will have a better handle on the shower's peak.

For slower showers you should be equipped with six sky charts, one for each hour of the observing night. A separate chart will be started each hour on the hour. If the shower becomes active, then a new chart will be employed every 15 minutes. The meteor is traced on the charts, along with the magnitude. This method is best for finding the shower's radiant and the magnitude of its meteors.

With either the note-pad/tape-recorder or the chart method, you must report the meteor totals witnessed during each hourly or 15-minute period. Graphs can be drawn demonstrating the shower's increased strength.

The American Meteor Society, a serious research organization whose members actively submit observations of fireballs, meteors, and meteor trains (Figs. 9-4 and 9-5), does not operate a large public observation program nor does it furnish free materials. The serious observer should contact:

American Meteor Society
Department of Physics and Astronomy
SUNY
Geneseo, NY 14454

Several observations you should make for the Society are:

☆ Determination of meteor altitude.
☆ The radiant point and its motion in space during a time interval.
☆ Determination of the shower's maximum activity to within 0.25 hour.

Determining the Radiant

Finding the meteor shower radiant is a simple enough task. It is the intersection of the meteoric material cloud and the Earth's atmosphere. To find the radiant or the point of the meteor shower's origin on your sky chart, simply trace back all the meteor paths to their starting points. Now jot down the point's right ascension and declination.

You will realize that a few of the meteors recorded on any observing night will not be a part of the shower. Keep a record of sporadic meteors because they might be part of a minor shower that is just peaking. This information is valuable and it might lead to the discovery of a new shower. When you are recording long-event meteor showers, record their positions over several nights. A shift in position can demonstrate the direction and amount of motion of the meteor cloud in relation to Earth.

Determining Altitude

A meteor's altitude can be determined by two observers some 30 miles apart. Your positions must be accurately determined with a geographic survey map. A base line must be determined between the two observation points and it must be measured by the map. An exact East-West or North-South orientation will help in rapidly reducing data; however, orientation is not all that important.

When finding the altitude, both of you will note the angle from true North at which the meteor is observed, as measured North to East. North will be at 0 degrees, due East will be at 90 degrees, South at 180 degrees, and West at 270 degrees. To determine the meteor's altitude, trigonometry will be employed. The meteor's direction must be determined on the ground by each observer. The measurement will be an angle measured from the North. Observer **A** notes the meteor's direction **AD**. Observer **B** notes the meteor's direction **BD**. Because of the base line's previous determination, a trigonomic calculation permits the meteor's height to be figured. To find the height, each observer views the meteor. This measurement will be an angle measured from the North. The angle for observer **A** is **NAD** and for observer **B**, **NBD**. After the angles are found, you will have:

Base line (**AB**) = Distance in miles.
Angle A = NAD′ – NAB = BAD′
Angle B = NBD′ – NBA = ABD′

Because both angles and an included side have been figured, you can find out the distance from each observer to point D. The complete answer has still not been determined, however.

Figuring that the angle ADD' is a right angle measuring 90 degrees, the angle DAD' was determined as the altitude above the closest horizon. Line AD was calculated earlier. Again employing both angles and including a side of the triangle, you can figure out the length of D'D (the meteor's height above the ground).

Chapter 10

Observing Artificial Satellites

Observing artificial satellites resides on the borderland of amateur astronomy (Fig. 10-1). Many amateurs question whether it is really an astronomical pursuit. Perhaps this arcane area of binocular observation belongs more under the heading of Earth Sciences since studies of artificial satellite orbits have offered valuable information about the Earth's shape and the odd behavior of our planet's upper atmosphere. By and large, the bulk of satellite orbits are recorded with large Baker-Nunn and Hewitt cameras (which are somewhat like Schmidt cameras), using radar and radio, and in more recent years using lasers aimed at reflector studded satellites. However, some need still exists for the binocularist to record orbits.

Satellite orbits are recorded in much the same way the amateur binocularist records the track of comets with a stopwatch. Studies of spin axis directions and spin rates of satellites are performed similarly to the way rotational light variations among asteroids are recorded. I will not go into detail here because these departments are nonastronomical and an excellent book on the subject has been written detailing the observation of artificial satellites: Desmond King-Hele's *Observing Earth Satellites*. I highly recommend it for anyone who wishes to undertake this curious hobby.

Another sound reason for watching Earth satellites is to find out where they go down when they re-enter our atmosphere. Observing satellites during their blazing plunge is another great heavenly spectacle. Like bolides and meteors, satellites shine by their own light during their decay. Considering that close to 5,000 satellites are in orbit at any given time, seeing a satellite's decay is highly rare, perhaps rarer than sighting a new comet.

The favorite instrument in artificial satellite observation is a pair of binoculars because of its wide field and hand-held maneuverability. The dual objectives of binoculars lend an almost stereoscopic effect to an artificial satellite zipping across a background of stars.

Satellites appear like stars moving through the heavens, and they often blink as a result of their end-over-end motion and reflectivity. Satellites travel a good deal slower than meteors. Because of their distance and size, satellites will only be starlike when they are visible, although I have had the infrequent pleasure of glimpsing some of their cylindrical shapes tumbling past the face of the Moon or Sun when I was observing with 4- to 8-inch telescopes at high power.

Dark skies—free of moonlight and with the Sun at least 10 degrees below the horizon—are best for viewing artificial satellites. These man-made objects are best

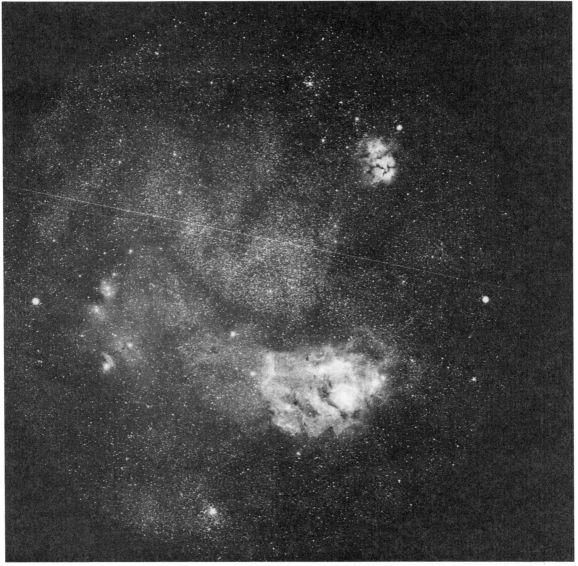

Fig. 10-1. A satellite trail in the M8/M20 region of Sagittarius; photographed with a 12-inch f/5 Astromak (Photograph by Jim Riffle).

viewed directly overhead. Close to the horizon's atmospheric soup, they lose some of their brightness. Winter proves the most difficult time to view satellites because the Earth's shadow extends more than a million kilometers, forming an indistinct and variable slender cone and eclipsing these objects. The summer ranks as the finest time for artificial satellite observation because it is the season when most of these man-made objects are beyond the Earth's shadow.

Some satellites at *apogee*—the orbital point farthest from Earth—are almost halfway to the Moon. At a height of 150 miles, a satellite will last almost 8 days before it makes its plunge back to Earth. At 750 miles up, the satellite might last several years in orbit.

A satellite's visibility depends on its size, surface reflectivity, distance from our planet, and angle of orbit compared to the Earth's equator. If the angle is small, observers in the Northern or Southern Hemispheres might

Fig. 10-2. The Celestron Classic Series: 7 × 50 (top left), 10 × 50 (top right), 7 × 35 (bottom) (Courtesy Celestron International).

not be able to observe the satellite at all. Satellite orbits are ellipses, with the center of the Earth as one of the object's foci.

The best method of locating satellites appears to be slowly sweeping the northen and southern skies well above the horizon. Low satellites can be found during the first hour or so after sunset and an hour or two after sunrise. Drifting longitudinally each night, often westwardly, satellites as a general rule possess limited visibility from 1 to 3 weeks. Those orbiting at higher altitudes near the poles have longer durations of visibility.

Some satellites might have partial illumination like the Moon or Venus because of their positions in the Earth's shadow. When completely illuminated, a satellite might be two times brighter than when partially illumined. Some of these objects might have negative

magnitudes. The space shuttle and Salyut are often observed at −1 magnitude.

Here are some addresses to write to if you care to find the orbits of some satellites:

Code 512
Goddard Space Flight Center
Greenbelt, MD 20771

The B.A.A. Artificial Satellite Section
Burlington House
Piccadilly, London
W1V ONL, England

British Satellite Prediction Centre
The Earth Satellite Research Unit
University of Aston, St. Peter's College
Saltby, Birmingham, U.K.

The Goddard Space Flight Center provides orbital elements of all satellites determined by the United States Air Force. Let them know you're interested in observing satellites.

The easier artificial satellites to observe follow:

☆ Cosmos rockets—Orbital inclinations 48 to 83 degrees; Mag. 4; some 200 have short-lived orbits.

☆ Cosmos satellites—65- to 83-degree inclinations; Mag. 2; recon satellites.

☆ Agena rockets—Mag. 2; launched in the sixties and seventies.

☆ Seasat—Mag. 3; motions are North to South or South to North.

☆ Ariel—Only one in orbit.

☆ Prospero—Mag. 7 and Mag. 9.

☆ Soyuz—Space craft; Mag. 1.

☆ Salyut—Space station; Mag. 0; orbit 51 degrees to the equator.

☆ Meteor—Mag. 5; 80 degrees to equator.

☆ Nimbus, NOAA, DMSP—Sun-synchronous orbits; 98 degrees.

☆ Big Bird—High latitude; large cylinder; Mag. 0 or −1; low-altitude surveillance platform.

☆ Comsats—Eastbound equatorial orbits; communications satellites; very dim.

☆ Space Shuttle—Orbital inclinations 28 and 57 degrees; between Mag. 0 and Mag. −1.

Chapter 11

Stars

Like our Sun, *stars* are self-luminous gas bodies energized by thermonuclear reactions. Because of their great distances from us, we see them as mere points of light. Under outstanding conditions we can view up to 4,000 or so stars in a single night without any optical help.

Stars show great variance in luminosity, size, and temperature (Fig. 11-1). The smallest stars yet known are neutron stars (the Crab nebula has a fine example) which might be only 10 miles in diameter. The largest stars might be red supergiants, which are a thousand times larger than our Sun. Stellar surface temperatures might run between 2000° K and 100,000° K. Temperature variation can be witnessed in color, from very hot stars that are blue, ranging through cooler red stars.

Spectroscopy, the study of the light spectrum, has taught astronomers much about the chemistry of stars. Atoms in a specific star's atmosphere absorb light at certain wavelengths and give off absorption lines in a spectrogram, thus showing a star's chemical makeup, density, and temperature. The majority of stars appear to be made up mostly of hydrogen, with lesser amounts of helium and traces of other elements.

Stars appear to have evolved out of collapsing dust and gas clouds (Fig. 11-2). The collapse is held to be started by cloud collision or alterations in cloud heating caused by nearby stars. Condensing and collapsing by its own gravity, a condensation, or *prestar*, continues to compress until its internal temperature rises to above 10 million degrees. Pressure in these gas clouds rapidly grows, halting the contraction. At this point the star is hatched. A dividing cloud might be the cause of multiple star births, such as witnessed in clusters like Trapezium. Double stars might be born out of the same rotating dark globule.

Nuclear reactions, in the extra-hot central regions of stars, provide a great energy output. Left with only their nuclei, atoms are jammed together, producing great quantities of energy. In very hot stars, with core temperatures above 15 million degrees, hydrogen is added to carbon nuclei to form nitrogen, which then splits into carbon and helium. At around 100 million degrees, helium changes into carbon and oxygen. At yet higher temperatures star material in the central core might become iron, magnesium, neon, and silicon. These alterations release further energy to heat the star. In our Sun and stars like it, a proton-proton chain is formed where hydrogen combines to form helium.

Our Sun and similar stars are suspected of initially evolving out of an interstellar gas cloud and having been 50 times larger than their present size, as well as almost 500 times brighter. As these stars contracted, they drew

Fig. 11-1. The red giant Antares blazes among the globulars in Scorpius; photographed with a 12-inch f/5 Astromak (Photograph by Jim Riffle).

on their gravitational energy to make up the debit of radiation lost to space. At this point no nuclear reactions took place because these star cores were too cool. When the star began to contract and the temperatures climbed in the center, the entire body grew less luminous. Then, 30 million years later, the core grew hot enough for nuclear reactions to get underway.

For the better part of a lifetime—about 10 billion years—the star remains the same, retaining the same size and luminosity as our Sun. This period is its *main sequence*, or hydrogen-utilizing period, and it lasts so long because hydrogen is in great reserve.

As the star uses up the hydrogen from its center, helium begins to form in the core. Gradually the fuel is used up in the core's shell, and at that point the star begins growing in size and brightness. After a period the

125

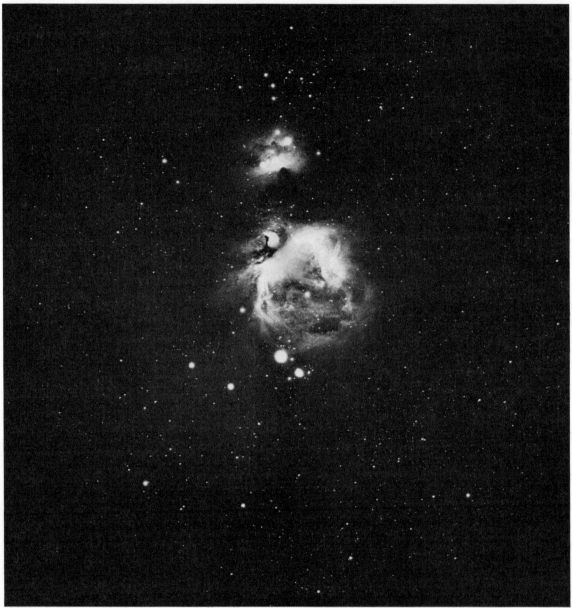

Fig. 11-2. M42, the Orion Nebula, and M43 are gas clouds where stars are being born; photographed with a 12-inch f/5 Astromak (Photograph by Jim Riffle).

star will become a red giant 1,000 times more luminous than our Sun.

During the star's evolution, the helium in the central region rises in temperature until it begins to burn. Now the star must suddenly adjust to its new fuel source. Within a few short days the star contracts, and in the process decreases its brightness. While the helium is employed, the star again grows in brightness and size, using up its helium to create a carbon core before it in turn burns the helium and hydrogen in the shells surrounding the new carbon center. At this point the star again grows in size, expanding up to 400 times the Sun's size. Brighter now, the star becomes so huge that its gravity can just about keep it together. In the future this star's surface layers will be blasted away. This material creates a shell that will expand away from the star and will form what we know as a planetary nebula (Fig. 11-3). The remaining star is a white dwarf, which will eventually cool into a black dwarf.

More massive stars than our Sun follow the same pattern of early evolution. These stars' central regions are so intensely hot that the carbon-nitrogen-oxygen cycle creates their energy. Failing to alter much when it uses up the hydrogen in its core, the star spends a good deal of its life on the main sequence. A star 10 times the solar mass possesses a luminosity about 10,000 times our Sun's. Since it uses fuel at a much greater rate, a star of this type evolves more quickly. In general, it remains on the main sequence for about 10 million years.

After the central hydrogen is depleted, the hydrogen burning travels out to the depleted helium core's shell. Contracting and heating up around 100 million degrees, the core begins to convert to carbon and oxygen. At this point the star expands into a giant or supergiant, remaining this way for its life as a star. While the central helium converts into carbon and oxygen, the stellar core compresses to the point when it alters carbon into magnesium. Later the magnesium burns into neon before the neon changes into iron. The central potion of a star's evolution is made up of one fuel burning up, then the core contracting and igniting the next fuel. All these reactions take place as lower temperature reactions occur in the outer shells away from the central region.

The star faces the end of its career after its iron core has formed. To change iron, the most stable element, into heavier elements takes energy instead of releasing it. At this point only gravitational contraction can supply the needed energy, and thus the central region collapses, making the outer shell fall inward. This collapse raises the temperature and hastens the nuclear burning in the areas where fuel remains.

A supernova results from sudden energy release that makes a star explode. During this explosion vast amounts of elements are manufactured and blasted into space. Often the star will be disintegrated, or in some instances the star's ultracondensed core might remain as a neutron star. Another possibility is that the remaining core is so huge that it draws inward on itself and vanishes from sight, becoming a black hole.

THE 30 BRIGHTEST STARS

1—A Canis Major (Sirius)—Mag. − 1.47

2—A Carina (Canopus)—Mag. − 0.73
3—A Lyra (Vega)—Mag. 0.04
4—A Bootes (Arcturus)—Mag. 0.06
5—A Centaurus (Rigil Kentaurus)—Mag. 0.06
6—B Orion (Rigil)—Mag. 0.08
7—A Auriga (Capella)—Mag. 0.09
8—A Canis Minor (Procyon)—Mag. 0.34
9—A Eridanus (Achernar)—Mag. 0.47
10—B Centaurus (Hadar)—Mag. 0.59
11—A Aquila (Altair)—Mag. 0.77
12—A Orion (Betelgeuse)—Mag. 0.80
13—A Taurus (Aldebaran)—Mag. 0.86
14—A Virgo (Spica)—Mag. 0.96
15—A Crux (Acrux)—Mag. 1.05
16—A Scorpius (Antares)—Mag. 1.
17—B Gemini (Pollux)—Mag. 1.15
18—A Piscis Austrinus (Fomalhaut)—Mag. 1.
19—B Crux (no name)—Mag. 1.24
20—A Cygnus (Deneb)—Mag. 1.26
21—A Leo (Regulus)—Mag. 1.35
22—Epsilon Canis Major (Adhara)—Mag. 1.50
23—A Gemini (Castor)—Mag. 1.58
24—Gamma Crux (no name)—Mag. 1.62
25—Lamda Scorpius (Shaula)—Mag. 1.62
26—Gamma Orion (Bellatrix)—Mag. 1.64
27—B Taurus (El Nath)—Mag. 1.65
28—B Carina (Miaplacidus)—Mag. 1.67
29—Epsilon Orion (Alnilam)—Mag. 1.70
30—Epsilon Carina (Avior)—Mag. 1.85

DOUBLE STARS AND MULTIPLE STARS

Double stars, or binary stars (Fig. 11-4), and multiple-star systems are linked by gravity (if they are not visual systems). In 1650 Italian astronomer Giovanni Riccioli discovered the first genuine double Mizar. Mizar represents a physical double, rather than an *optical double*, a situation where two stars appear close together in the sky, but are quite separated in space.

Of all stars, 46 percent are believed to be involved in double systems, where one star is gravitationally bound to another star and orbits it. Another 15 percent of the star population appear to be singular bodies like our Sun. The last 39 percent are involved in multiple systems of three or more members.

The separation between double stars ranges from stars separated widely enough to be observed through telescopes to contact binaries like W Ursae Majoris, where stars contact each other and share the same atmosphere.

The closest double stars, with orbital periods less than

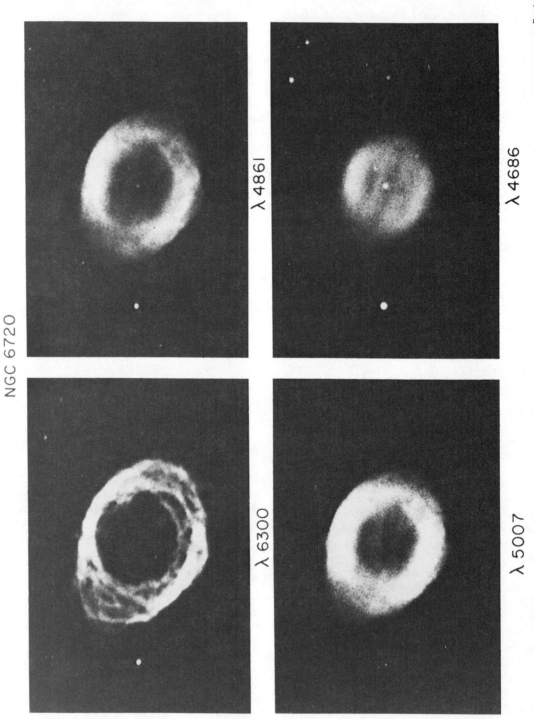

NGC 6720

λ 4861

λ 4686

λ 6300

λ 5007

Fig. 11-3. M57, the Ring Nebula, in Lyra. This planetary nebula has been photographed in four different lights by the Kitt Peak 2.1-meter reflector (Courtesy National Optical Astronomy Observatories).

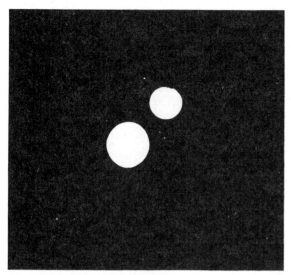

Fig. 11-4. A double star system.

orbital period (17 1/2 minutes), is a fine example. Certain X-ray novae, in which both stars were white dwarfs, have had periods of 120 seconds.

The *primary star* is the brightest in a binary; the *secondary* is the faintest. During its evolution, the primary expands while its atmosphere is attracted by the secondary. Gas is stripped away from the primary, the primary fills its Roche lobe, and the binary becomes semidetached. So much gas may be lost by the primary that the secondary now evolves into a new primary. The new primary expands, it fills its Roche lobe, and the binary star semidetaches, with its gas going to the new secondary. Algol fits this picture. The secondary becomes either a neutron star, a white dwarf, or perhaps even a black hole. X-rays are created when gas falls into such a small star. If enough material falls into a white dwarf, that its mass exceeds the Chandrasekhar Limit, or the maximum for such a star, the star will explode into a nova.

Observing Double Stars

Although double-star research is not open to the binocularist, you might have some genuine fun attempting to test your vision and your binocular optics on a pair of fairly widely separated doubles. For best results your instrument should be well mounted (Fig. 11-6). I have found that when binoculars are hand-held, their resolving limit appears half as much as when firmly mounted. With larger and more powerful instruments, holding them by hand becomes a chore.

It is important to remember that 1 minute is 1/60 degree. A full moon is roughly 30 minutes of arc. The average pair of 7-power, rigidly mounted binoculars is able to obtain a split down to 45 seconds of arc. By dividing 300 seconds of arc by your binoculars' power, you will be able to find the seconds of separation your pair of binoculars is capable of.

Keep in mind that a double star's components should be close in magnitude to be seen, otherwise the brighter companion's glare might overcome the secondary. A list of fine binocular binary systems will appear in the constellation-by-constellation deep-sky catalog at the end of this book.

100 years, were probably formed when a gas cloud that was becoming a star split into two or more sections. Double stars with long orbital periods appear to have formed separately. Some close binaries reveal themselves as being double when a spectroscope examines their light. Close binaries often reveal themselves when the Moon occults them, making their light fade in two steps. *Speckle interferometry* is a relatively new technique whereby a high-speed photograph of a star is unblurred by laser illumination and shows the images of two stars close together.

Features of Double Stars

Binary-star orbits lie at random angles (Fig. 11-5). They often fail to line up with the galaxy's plane. If the orbit is witnessed edge-on, the two stars will pass in front of each other, creating an eclipsing binary.

Closer doubles in general possess shorter orbital periods, and this is according to Kepler's third law. Eta Cassiopeiae has an orbital period of 480 years, the longest on record. Binoculars will reveal this double. However, doubles exist with periods so long they have yet to complete an orbit since observation began. Proxima Centauri's orbit around Alpha Centauri is estimated at about 1 million years.

Double stars' dualness can be inferred by the facts that they share the same motion and they have the same distance. The shortest-period doubles are those having a small star, such as a white dwarf, for their component. AM Canum Venaticorum, which has the shortest known

VARIABLE STARS

Variable stars are stars whose light varies in brightness. A variable star's light production fluctuates or its light might be briefly blocked by another star or dust cloud. Variability can be measured down to .01 magnitude by a photoelectric photometer which transforms the light of a star to a measurable electric current. Only one star can

Fig. 11-5. NGC 457, an open star cluster in Cassiopeia. Look for the many binaries that appear in this cluster. This photograph was taken with a Kitt Peak 2.1-meter reflector (Courtesy of National Optical Astronomy Observatories).

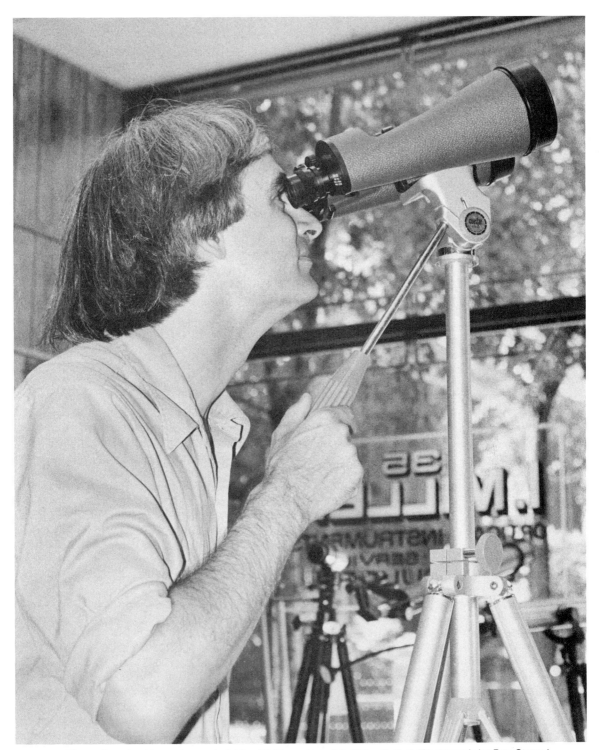
Fig. 11-6. The author checking out mounted 11 × 80 binoculars at I. Miller Optical (Photograph by Dan Stosuy).

be measured at a time. The general method used on variables is to take star-field photographs at different times and examine those pictures with a blink microscope. A keen-eyed blink microscopist will spot stars that change from plate to plate by as little as 0.2 magnitude.

Close to 26,000 variable stars are known. Except for stars already named prior to the discovery of their variability, these stars are named with a letter or a pair of letters and their constellation of origin, such as *RR Lyrae*. When this system is exhausted in a constellation then the variable stars are numbered with a prefix V.

Classifications of Variable Stars

The three major classifications of variable stars are: pulsating, eruptive, and eclipsing stars.

Pulsating variables pulsate like a beating heart. Cepheid variables are regular in their pulsations, while red giants are generally irregular. Changes in size and surface temperature affect a pulsating stars' brightness. A star is brightest when it is hottest. Maximum size does not always coincide with brightness. The stellar surface rises and falls while it pulsates, yet the pulsation does not penetrate the central core, which contains 95 percent of the mass. The ionization of helium and hydrogen causes the pulsating effect.

Pulsating variables include RR Lyrae stars, cepheids, and short-period Delta Scuti stars, which have periods of less than 5 hours. These pulsating variables occupy only a small region of the Hertzsprung-Russell Diagram known as the *instability strip*. Just about all stars are pulsators during at least one period of their lives. Other pulsating variables are Beta Cephei stars (often known as Beta Canis Majoris stars), which are fine examples of periodic variable blue stars. Variability is also witnessed in red giants known as Mira-type variables, semiregular variables, and irregular variables. These stars have low densities and their periods range about 100 days.

Eruptive variables have surfaces on which flares or explosions occur or the star itself explodes nova-style. Although unpredictable, eruptives are some of the most spectacular variables. Some increase in brightness up to 100 million times (the supernovae). Eruptive variable examples are T Tauri stars and UV Ceti stars, both flare stars, whose flares complete themselves in several minutes. Also included are Z Camelopardis and U Geminorum variables, whose slow flares last only a day or two. These last examples are close double stars that contain a white dwarf surrounded by a gas disk. Gas pours from the companion star to the white dwarf, contacting the disk to create a hot area which disappears and returns

as the stellar disk rotates. These variables demonstrate wide fluctuations.

R Coronae Borealis stars are the opposite of flare stars in light output. Every so often these stars lower their brightness, remaining faint for several weeks or months before they resume their normal brightness. Having excess carbon in their atmosphere, they periodically release some of their atmosphere into space. The released carbon cloud temporarily obscures the star.

Eclipsing variables are double stars in which one star passes in front of the other and in the process blocks out light. Even when no eclipse takes place, the total light might vary during each orbit because the gravitational pull of one star distorts the other into a nonspherical shape. When observed from the side, an ellipsoid shape has a greater surface area than when seen from its end; therefore the light from ellipsoidal stars will vary during rotation. In a double-star system the closer the two stars are, the more their distortion and variation. Beta Lyrae, a typical close, eclipsing variable, has a period of 12.9 days and a range of brightness of 0.7.

Alpha[2] Canum Venaticorum variables are examples of magnetic stars that vary during rotation because large spots are carried across their surface.

Observing Variable Stars

Because of their wide field and low power, binoculars are outstanding instruments for observing variable stars. Whether you use a small, hand-holdable 7×50, 10×50, 10×70, 11×80, or one of those battleship glasses, you will locate many surprises in the heavens. When observing variable stars, the amateur astronomer will have the opportunity to follow change as it takes place in the universe. These alterations, as witnessed in variable stars and novae, have made variable-star addicts out of a large and growing number of amateur astronomers. I'd wager that of those amateurs engaged in research, likely a third or better are out with their binoculars and telescopes every clear night, hunting those changing stars.

The term *binocular variable* generally applies to a certain classification of star of the red semiregular or irregular type whose variations in luminosity are between fifth and ninth magnitudes. This is 50mm-binocular turf! The smaller hand-held binoculars like the 7×50, 8×56, and 10×70 are also valuable in observing the brighter and very predictable phases of long-period variables. Hand-held binoculars can also be employed in observing the phases of several R Coronae Borealis type stars, even though the complete variations are not observable because these star's magnitude changes reside beyond the smaller binoculars' grasp.

Novae, part of the variable star family, offer surprises to the keen-eyed enthusiast. Light from distant novae or supernovae might be zipping through space at 186,000 miles per second toward Earth at this very instant. The novae offer the possibilities of discovery to the binocularist, and discovering a nova ranks right up there with the experience of finding a new comet.

Among the many curious variable stars available is the bright eclipsing star Algol (Beta Persei). Algol's 3-day period of variability is highlighted by the fact that it is 1/3 as bright during its several-hour eclipse. Another interesting example is the pulsating variable Mira in the constellation Cetus. Within a year's period it will go from third magnitude to ninth magnitude. Several other variables, such as CH Cygni (Mag. 6 to 7.8 with a 97-day period) and TX Draconis (Mag. 6 to 8.2 with a 78-day period) are other good targets for the casual binocularist.

If you wish to pursue research on variables, I would recommend that you contact either the American Association of Variable Star Observers or the British Astronomical Association, Variable Star Section:

American Association of Variable Star Observers
25 Birch St.
Cambridge, MA 02138

British Astronomical Association
Variable Star Section
12 Taylor Rd.
Aylesbury, Bucks HP 21
8 DR, England

The data variable star observers collect gets computed by the A.A.V.S.O. and the B.A.A. and is figured into light curves. These light curves are made available to the professional astronomical community where these records become important factors in the growth of human knowledge about stars, our galaxy, and the entire cosmos.

Variable-star research is almost entirely the domain of amateurs since most large professional telescopes are tied up in other areas of study. Thousands of amateur observers, with unlimited time, the ability to make rapid estimates, and suitable instruments such as binoculars and small telescopes, can follow many more stars than can all the major observatories in the world.

You must have a sound knowledge of the constellations when you are undertaking the study of alterations in stars. No setting circles are employed with binoculars, so you must know how to star-hop, and star-hopping

is not the swiftest way to travel around the constellations. However, familiarity breeds speed. I have known experienced amateurs who are able to estimate one variable per 1 1/2 minutes.

Choice of Binoculars

Hand-held 7×50s, if the optics are good, will be more than adequate for observing variables to 8.5 magnitude, perhaps a bit more if your eyes are up to it. Finder charts are a must for locating the majority of stars. The A.A.V.S.O. supplies "A" and "AB" charts, which are designed specifically for 7×50s. These charts show comparison stars known for their constant magnitudes. Without these charts, magnitude estimates are likely to be off base.

Because aberrations show up on the edge of most binocular fields (likely encountered with Erfle eyepieces) you must center the variable and then the comparison star in the middle of the field.

With 10×70 and 11×80 instruments you will be able to see many more fainter stars than with 7×50 and 10×50 binoculars. Those battleship jobs with their 4-, 5-, and 6-inch objectives will take you out to the range of many dimmer variables, and you will be able to observe some of the brighter novae through much of their cycles. See Table 11-1.

Key Words

Some key words you should understand when you are undertaking variable-star observation are: Purkinje effect, amplitude, and comparison stars.

The majority of observers' eyes are more sensitive to red than to other colors, so we tend to overestimate the brightness of red stars. This overestimation is called the *Purkinje effect*. In some instances blue stars are often underestimated, especially if red comparison stars are employed.

Table 11-1. Magnitude Range of Binoculars.

Aperture	Magnitude Limit	Recommended Limit for Variables
Naked-eye	6.2	1.0-4.5
50mm	10.3	4.0-8.5
80mm	11.2	6-10.5
100mm	11.8	7.0-12.5
125mm	12.3	7.5-12.5
150mm	12.7	8.0-12.5

The magnitude range of a star's variation in light is known as *amplitude*. Bright-star estimates, with minimal variation, permit vast discrepancies among variable-star observers. These variations result from the Purkinje effect, atmospheric effects, and the astronomer's physical and mental condition.

Comparison Stars

Comparison stars are simply those fixed-magnitude stars that the observer compares with his variables. Bright stars have fewer comparison stars, which adds to their difficulty. It is best never to compare stars outside the field of view. Memory can't be trusted to give sound estimates.

The A.A.V.S.O. variable star comparison charts (Fig. 11-7) are in a class by themselves and are available to all members of this fine organization. These charts vary in scale. The scales are meant to be used with specific fields of view and the star's brightness at a specific time in its cycle. Each chart provides quick identification of the variable-star field and the magnitudes of comparison stars in the field. These comparison stars possess an accuracy of 0.1 magnitude. Every so often errors crop up, so be careful when you are making comparisons.

After you have located the variable star in the field, you will begin the process of the brightness estimate. Locate several stars in the field that are comparable in magnitude. On occasion you might find a perfect match; most times, however, you will need to estimate the magnitude between two stars—a brighter and a dimmer star than the variable in question. The majority of charts have close sequences having 0.1 magnitude increments, offering fairly accurate comparisons.

Comparison Example. The variable is a tiny bit brighter than star **A** whose magnitude is 7.5, but not as bright as star **B** whose magnitude is 7.3. In this instance the variable appears to be 7.4 magnitude.

Often the binocularist will not have the luxury of having two comparison stars so close together in brightness as the preceding example. When this situation occurs a relative estimate is okay, using only those available comparison stars in the field. You may employ more than two comparison stars if possible. When the variable is only halfway between two comparison stars, say **A** 7.0 and **B** 7.6, then the magnitude would be 7.3. Remember, the variable star charts contain no decimal marks to show tenths. You will see 80, 82, 83 etc. The decimal point is omitted so that it will not be confused for a star on the charts.

Be cautious when you are selecting comparison stars, especially when the variable closes in on maximum. Many

of the stars you will observe with smaller binoculars will be red stars, and red stars will seem brighter to some observers because of the Purkinje effect. Overestimation is so easy with red stars and novae. Make your estimates of red variables with as much speed as possible because the longer you look, the brighter they will appear. Use the "quick glance" method.

Often during its cycle, the variable you are observing will be too faint for your binoculars. Even if you can no longer see the star, you should continue your observation. Record the faintest star visible in the field and jot down the variable's brightness as "fainter than—."

Beware of bias in making estimates. Previous experience with the same variables can poison your estimates. Be careful! Novae and long-period variables can cause bias because of their predictable light curves.

A final hint: You might consider defocusing your binoculars so that your star points become disks. It seems easier to estimate brightness spread over a larger area. Defocusing also minimizes the problem created by twinkling stars. However, defocusing will not work on extremely faint variables.

Defocusing slowly, with the variable in the field's center and your comparison stars nearby, can help you gauge which comparison stars are nearest in magnitude to the variable. Watch for the ones blinking out about the same time your variable disappears.

When you are outdoors you may record your magnitude estimates any way you wish. The A.A.V.S.O. supplies its members with standardized forms, which contain slots for recording the variable's designation, the magnitude, and the Julian day and the decimals for those days. The A.A.V.S.O. also supplies its members with a yearly Julian-day calendar. The Julian-day calendar makes it easier to compute your records because the 24-hour period is expressed in decimals on this calendar. The Julian-day calendar simplifies the compiling of light curves and eliminates the difficulties of having to alter dates when an observation is underway. It also permits rapid mathematical use of the variable-star recordings.

NOVAE

Abruptly flaring into brightness, the *nova* is a faint star becoming visible where no other star was previously noticed. Derived from the Latin word meaning *new*, novae increase in brightness by thousands or even tens of thousands of times. Often observed with just the naked eye, these erupting stars climb rapidly to their highest magnitude, sometimes within a day or two. Their fading might be a matter of days, weeks, months, or even years. Two

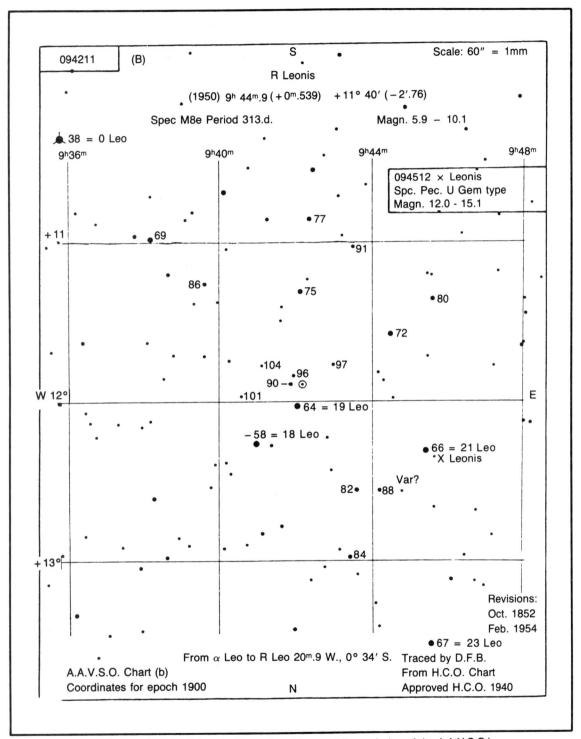

Fig. 11-7. A B variable star chart for R Leonis (Reproduced by special permission of the A.A.V.S.O.).

or three of these exciting stars are discovered yearly by amateurs.

A nova gets its name from its constellation and the year of its maximum brightness. Brightening by a factor of 10,000 in a single day and discovered by a Scots amateur, T.D. Anderson, Nova Persei 1901 became one of the brightest stars in the heavens. Spectral evidence showed that its gas shell got ejected at 1250 miles per second. The surface's rapid expansion was responsible for Nova Persei's sudden brilliance.

Features of Novae

A nova is not greatly disrupted by its outburst. Only .00001 of the star's original mass is thrown off. However, a star is almost completely destroyed during a supernova event. A nova's intrinsic brightness at its height reaches −7 or −8 magnitudes, almost 10 magnitudes less than a supernova.

The majority of novae are believed to be binary stars. A nova eruption is thought to be the product of gas flowing from a companion star to a white dwarf, where it fuels a nuclear explosion. Novae are known to erupt more than once. Nova Pyxis had four recorded outbursts, in 1890, 1902, 1920, and 1944. X-ray novae are now known to exist. Likely they too are binary stars having as one component either a black hole or a neutron star.

Features of Supernovae

Supernovae eject most of their matter at extremely high velocities. Their central cores often collapse into extremely dense neutron stars or perhaps even black holes.

During a supernova event a star might become as luminous as a small galaxy for days. Since 1937 systematic hunts have turned up nearly 500 supernovae. These events are listed in two major categories: Type I and Type II.

Brightening to an absolute magnitude of −19.4, Type I supernovae decrease 3 magnitudes in 30 days, and then fade at a rate of 1/70 magnitude per day. Because Type I supernovae possesses a similar intrinsic brightness, the distance of their parent galaxy gets revealed by a supernova's apparent magnitude.

A Type I supernova's spectrum demonstrates that a mass equivalent to our Sun's mass is ejected at speeds reaching 7,500 miles per second. The ejected mass contains about 10 percent hydrogen. In all probability the star, prior to the supernova event, possessed some 10 times the Sun's mass. It is believed that such massive stars evolve over less than 100 million years before they become unstable and erupt.

Our galaxy witnessed supernova events in 185, 1006, 1054, 1181, 1572, and 1604. The event of 1054 left remnants that we now see as the famous Crab Nebula (Fig. 11-8). The Veil Nebula in Cygnus is also the filamentry remains of a supernova. In the Milky Way these events are expected on an average of every 30 to 50 years.

Observing Novae and Supernovae

One of the outstanding thrills in amateur astronomy is the discovery of a nova or supernova. The opportunities for discovery are better in novae hunting than in comet hunting, and the hours are much more agreeable. Anytime the Milky Way is visible you will be in an excellent position to start your search.

Every year 12 or more stars in our galaxy alone blast off their outer shells in the act of going nova, and in so doing go through great changes in magnitude. Where no stars were formerly observed, now one is seen.

Identifying a nova or supernova requires a good knowledge of the heavens, especially those constellations in the Milky Way region. Aquila, Sagittarius, Scorpius, Auriga, Gemini, and Perseus have all proved to be the haunts of nova action.

For the binocularist, nova-hunting will not be much impeded by haziness, light clouding, and the Moon past quarter and headed for full. Bright novae have shown

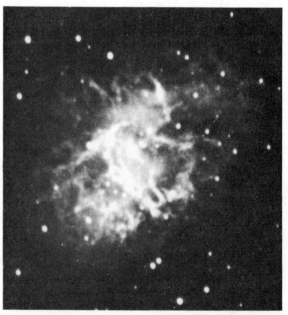

Fig. 11-8. M1, the Crab Nebula, a supernova remnant in Taurus (Courtesy Dr. Jack Marling and Lumicon).

themselves under such poor conditions. Beware! Watch out for the major and minor planets—those bright stars not on an atlas might move over a day's period and show themselves to be solar system objects.

Research on novae and supernovae provides us with much valuable astrophysical knowledge on the evolution of stars. Because novae and supernovae appear without warning, it is highly important that amateur nova hunters search the skies for these cosmic happenings. If these stars were not found by amateurs, professional observatories would lose valuable time in monitoring the full record of these events.

Rising to maximum brightness within hours, a nova might increase 15 to 20 magnitudes. Seldom will the binocularist witness these sudden brightenings as they occur. The nova's maximum light is there to be seen for only a short time. After the brightest part of the event subsides, the nova can quickly be lost in the starfield, especially in such regions as the Milky Way. Most nova discoveries are by accident; however you can up your chances for novae discovery by planning your hunt. Novae occurring in our galaxy, or *galactic novae* as they are known, show up more often in the rich cloud regions of the Milky Way. Because of the vast amount of stars in these regions, detecting these novae is difficult, yet not wholly impossible. Regular novae, occuring in distant galaxies, are too dim to be detected by even 6-inch battleship glasses. However, supernovae, those titanic cosmic blasts, are occasionally observed by the binocularist despite the fact that they are happening in a galaxy millions of light years away. Most supernovae are beyond the magnitude limits of 6-inch apertures. At 12 and 13 magnitudes—likely the brightest seen in distant galaxies—supernovae provide a solid test for the binocularist's eyes. Your best chance of spotting a supernova is to look for them in spiral galaxies. But beware—a supernova might rattle our galaxy at anytime!

To start a regular schedule of nova hunting, you should concentrate on just a few areas of the star-rich Milky Way galaxy. Anywhere from three to five areas will do; plan to spend at least 20 minutes on each. You might spend less time after you have a good handle on those areas.

After choosing your area of the Milky Way for searching out novae, you should get out your star atlas charts and draw your binoculars' field of view. With this drawing you will find it easier to spot any latecomers to the starfield. One of those latecomers just might be a nova.

A fine time to go nova-searching, especially if you are using smaller binoculars like 7 × 50s or 10 × 50s, is just after twilight.

Chapter 12

The Deep Sky

In the deep sky, many objects can be observed with binoculars. In particular, globular clusters, galactic clusters, nebulae, and galaxies are visible.

GLOBULAR CLUSTERS

Globular clusters, those densely packed balls of blazing suns, are found in a halo around the center of our Galaxy (Fig. 12-1). Generally made of old stars, globulars contain between 100 thousand and 10 million stars. In our Milky Way Galaxy over 125 of these clusters are known to exist, and their average diameter is held to be 100 light years across. Omega Centauri and 47 Tucanae, two extremely brilliant globulars, achieve naked-eye visibility for those observers living in the southern United States. For those in midnorthern latitudes, M13, the Great Globular in Hercules (Fig. 12-2), offers a stunning example at the threshold of naked-eye observing.

Globulars gather around the center of our Galaxy, where almost half of the globular population finds itself in the constellations Sagittarius and Scorpius. From the globular distribution in our Galaxy, Harlow Shapley figured the actual size of the Milky Way system and deduced the Sun's position on the Galaxy's edge. Examples of similar globular distribution have been found in

the Andromeda Galaxy and in Virgo's M104, the Sombrero Galaxy (Fig. 12-3). Unlike galactic clusters, which dwell in a galaxy's spiral arms, the globulars lie at fair distances from the galaxy's plane.

Being among the oldest inhabitants of any galaxy, some globulars are believed to be 13 billion years old. Globulars show evidence of containing population II stars such as RR Lyrae variables. Held to be the initial parts of a galaxy to form, globulars are thought to orbit the galaxy's center on elliptical paths similar to comets' orbits around the Sun. Globulars, not connected to any galaxies, have been seen in our Local Group.

OPEN, OR GALACTIC, CLUSTERS

Open, or galactic, clusters are shapeless, loosely packed star clusters found in the spiral arms of a galaxy (Fig. 12-4). These clusters contain youthful population I stars. The Hyades and the Pleiades (Fig. 12-5) are fine examples of open clusters.

Close to 1,000 open clusters are known, yet as many as 18,000 might exist in the galaxy. Some 150 of the nearest examples of these clusters are concentrated in the plane of our Galaxy and are some 10,000 light years from us. Most galactic clusters contain nearly 100 stars

Fig. 12-1. M3, a globular cluster in Canes Venatici; photographed with a Kitt Peak 4-meter reflector (Courtesy National Optical Astronomy Observatories).

and have diameters some 10 light years across.

Because open-cluster stars are formed almost simultaneously, astronomers can learn the different rates at which stars of differing masses evolve. Open clusters have greatly contributed to our knowledge of stellar evolution.

NEBULAE

Cloudlike, *nebulae* are areas of dust and gas in a galaxy. Dark nebulae appear like holes in the Milky Way and are cold clouds of dust and gas that absorb light from the stars behind them. The Coalsack Nebula is a fine example of the dark nebulae. Bright nebulae are dust and gas clouds illuminated by stars (Fig. 12-6).

M-42, the Great Orion Nebula, is an example of an emission nebula. *Emission nebulae* are those whose gas is excited to fluorescence by the ultraviolet light of nearby stars. In 1864 Sir William Huggins discovered emission lines in the spectrum of M42, the brightest of all emission nebulae. Some wavelengths of light from emission nebulae were recognized as coming from hydrogen. Other wavelengths were not recognized immediately and were ascribed to a new element called "nebulium." Eventually nebulium was discovered to be oxygen.

Emission nebulae come in three varieties: *planetary nebulae*, with their faint disks resembling a planet (Fig. 12-7); *loops*, which are supernova remnants; *diffuse nebulae*, with their irregular shapes illuminated by newborn stars. M42 is an example of the last type.

Reflection nebulae are bright clouds of dust that shine by the reflected light of a nearby star and demonstrate the same spectrum as the star. Because dust tends to scatter starlight and because blue light tends to scatter more than red, the reflection nebula will appear bluer than its illuminating star. The nebulosity around Merope in the Pleiades cluster was the first reflection nebula recognized

Fig. 12-2. M13, The Great Globular Cluster in Hercules; photographed with a 10-inch reflector (Photograph by Lee C. Coombs).

Fig. 12-3. M104, The Sombrero Galaxy in Virgo. Globular clusters have been resolved in M104. This photograph was taken with a Kitt Peak 4-meter reflector (Courtesy National Optical Astronomy Observatories).

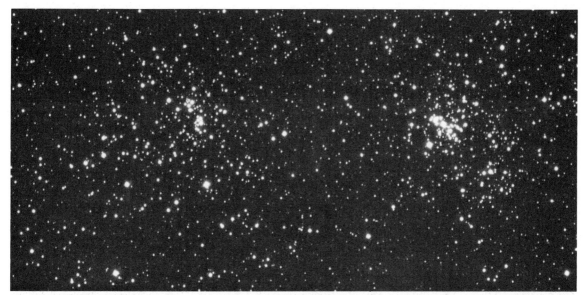

Fig. 12-4. The Double Cluster in Perseus; photographed by Case Western Reserve University with a Kitt Peak Schmidt Camera. A popular binocular open cluster (Courtesy National Optical Astronomy Observatories).

Fig. 12-5. M45, The Pleiades open cluster in Taurus; photographed with an 8-inch reflector (Photograph by Dr. Steve Simmerman).

141

Fig. 12-6. M8, The Lagoon Nebula in Ursa Major; photographed with an 8-inch reflector (Photograph by Dr. Steve Simmerman).

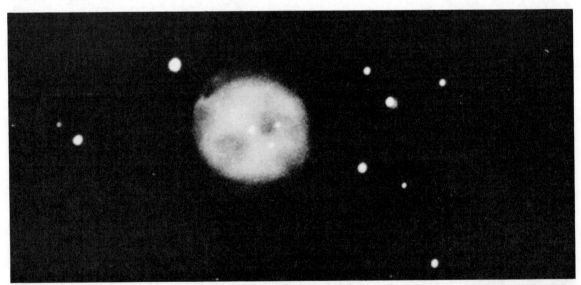

Fig. 12-7. M97, The Owl Nebula in Ursa Major; photographed with a Meade 10-inch Schmidt-Cassegrain (Courtesy Meade Instruments Corporation).

as such, and was observed by Vesto Slipher in 1913.

GALAXIES

Appearing as fuzzy patches of light in binoculars and small telescopes, *galaxies* are systems of billions of stars bound together by their own gravity (Fig. 12-8). Originally thought to reside within our own Milky Way, these deep-sky objects were called *extragalactic nebulae*.

Three basic types of galaxies are found in the universe. *Spiral galaxies*, such as our own Milky Way, possess a bright central region or nucleus and a huge spherical halo composed of old population II stars with a disk of younger stars, dust, and gas surrounding the central region (Fig. 12-9). The disk generally has a diameter of 100,000 light years, yet is only 2,000 light years thick, with its matter concentrated into two spiral arms moving outward from opposing sides of the nucleus. Some of these star systems possess a barred central region with spiral arms beginning at the ends of the bar. The stars and gas clouds in the disk rotate around the galactic nu-

cleus in nearly circular orbits, similar to the planets' movement around the Sun. The total galactic mass can be computed from the star's velocities. A spiral galaxy (Fig. 12-10) is generally believed to be 100 billion times as massive as our Sun. Because our Sun is a typical star, spiral galaxies are likely to hold some 100 billion stars.

Lacking spiral arms, *elliptical galaxies* show themselves as oval systems of old population II stars with no dust or gas clouds. These systems have shapes ranging from circular (EO) galaxies, to flattened ovals three times as long as they are broad (E6). Flatter star systems show a lens shape and are classified SO because their form is in an intermediate stage between elliptical and spiral.

About 1 million solar masses in size, the smallest elliptical galaxies are not much larger than globular clusters. The more massive ellipticals (cD) are supergiants and are believed 100 times heavier than our own Milky Way. Possessing spheres about 300,000 light years across, these elliptical galaxies are easily the most massive star systems known.

Smaller than spirals, *irregular galaxies* contain both

Fig. 12-8. NGC 7331, a spiral galaxy in Pegasus; photographed with a Canada-France-Hawaii 144-inch reflector on Mauna Kea (Photograph by Canada-France-Hawaii Telescope Corporation).

143

Fig. 12-9.M94, a spiral galaxy (Sb) in Canes Venatici; photographed with a Kitt Peak 4-meter reflector (Courtesy National Optical Astronomy Observatories).

Fig. 12-10. NGC 4565, a spiral galaxy (Sb) seen edge on in Coma Berenices; photographed with a Kitt Peak 2.1-meter reflector (Courtesy National Optical Astronomy Observatories).

old and young stars, yet lack any normal structure. Achieving naked-eye visibility in the Southern Hemisphere, the Magellanic Clouds are a form between irregular and barred spiral. The Magellanic Clouds orbit our own Milky Way. Irregular galaxies often give the appearance of having been disturbed by some explosive event.

Seyfert, or N, galaxies have small, bright nuclei. Brilliant at both infrared and radio wavelengths, the nuclei appear to be the sites of extremely violent explosions. A good many massive elliptical galaxies have extended regions of radio emission on both sides, and are thus called *radio galaxies*.

The structure of a galaxy is believed to be determined during its initial formation. Likely, no evolutionary sequence exists from spiral to elliptical and vice versa. Galactic formation theories tend to hold that stars formed during the gravitational collapse of the *protogalaxy*, a giant hydrogen gas cloud. The protogalaxy slowly rotated, then collapsed into a near spherical shape. The remaining, extremely dense, gas quickly formed stars, thus creating an elliptical galaxy lacking gas and having aged stars. When a faster-rotating protogalaxy collapses, just some of the gas falls to the center, where the gas rapidly con-

denses into stars. The remaining gas creates a rotating disk that slowly condenses. A sizable amount of gas and young stars are left over. Forming arms that give the galaxy a spiral appearance, the disk is unstable. Irregular galaxies also appear to have their origins in a rapidly rotating gas cloud.

The majority of galaxies are located in clusters bound together by gravitation (Fig. 12-11). The Local Group, some 30 members strong, includes our own Milky Way and the Andromeda Galaxy. Some clusters are known to support as many as 1,000 members. A fair number of these clusters take on a spherical form and often have a supergiant (cD) elliptical galaxy in their center. Supergiant elliptical galaxies have nearly the same intrinsic brightness. A cluster's apparent brightness is an excellent indication of its relative distance.

Even though clusters of galaxies orbit a common gravitational center, their actual motions in the sky are not large enough to be seen directly. Measurement, based on the Doppler effect in their light, shows a cluster's orbital velocity. From these facts astronomers are able to know how much mass the average galaxy needs in order for the cluster to be gravitationally bound. Because the

Fig. 12-11. M66 (lower left), M65 (top), and NGC 3628 (left) are all spiral galaxies in Leo and are part of the Virgo Cluster of Galaxies; photographed with a 144-inch Canada-France-Hawaii reflector at Mauna Kea (Photograph by permission of Canada-France-Hawaii Telescope Corporation).

Fig. 12-12. M31, The Great Andromeda Galaxy; photographed with a 12-inch f/5 Astromak (Photograph by Jim Riffle).

total is 10 to 100 times greater than usually anticipated in galaxies, a large amount of invisible mass is suspected.

Some galaxies, like M31 in Andromeda (Fig. 12-12), have individual stars that can be observed and thus can tell us much about the galaxy's distance. The measured brightness of these cepheid variable stars permits astronomers to figure M31's distance to 2.2 million light years, making it our nearest neighbor.

The closest galaxy cluster to the Local Group is the Virgo Cluster, which resides in the constellation Virgo. Being on the threshold of resolution, several stars in the Virgo Cluster indicate the cluster is 65 million light years away. The distance of even remoter galaxies can be gauged from the apparent magnitude of the extremely luminous Type I supernovae. Always having the same intrinsic maximum brightness, these exploding stars might outshine their home galaxy for several days.

A galaxy's distance is directly proportional to the redshift in its spectrum. The redshift appears to be the result of a Doppler effect caused by galaxies receding as the universe expands. This redshift-distance connection is named *Hubble's law* after its discoverer, Edwin Hubble, an American astronomer.

OBSERVING DEEP-SKY OBJECTS

Deep-sky objects offer some of the most attractive and satisfying views in the heavens. Composed of globular clusters, open clusters, nebulae, and galaxies, the deep-sky objects are best observed under extremely dark and transparent skies close to the new moon.

Globular clusters (Fig. 12-13), although they are unique and curious in binoculars, are never resolved at low power and will appear as nebulous, hazy disks or

146

Fig. 12-13. M15, a globular cluster in Pegasus; photographed with Canada-France-Hawaii 144-inch reflector at Mauna Kea (Photograph by permission of Laird Thompson and Canada-France-Hawaii Telescope Corporation).

spheres. Once you have viewed one in binoculars you will have an easier time locating others. Truly, globulars best show themselves in telescopes with apertures of 6 inches and up. Globulars require resolution to be appreciated.

Of the deep-sky objects, globulars are least in evidence. Most of these balls of stars concentrate themselves toward the Milky Way's center, although many globulars are scattered throughout our Galaxy. If you reside in the northern latitudes, you will find 29 globulars in Messier's famous list of deep-sky objects. M13, the Great Globular Cluster in Hercules, offers one of the better examples. It is the brightest globular cluster for those binocularists residing in northern latitudes. If you live in the southern latitudes, you will find a treat in Omega Centauri, which is near the Southern Cross. Other fine examples of globulars are 47 Tucanae near the Small Magellanic Cloud, M3 in Canes Venatici, M22 in Sagittarius (Fig. 12-14), and M4 in Scorpius.

A pair of binoculars is the preferred instrument for searching out and enjoying some of the larger and brighter open clusters (often called galactic, or loose, clusters). Appealing to our aesthetic sensibilities, these sparkling jewel boxes of the heavens offer to many observers some of the most breathtaking views in the heavens (Fig. 12-15). Fine examples of these loose groupings of stars are the Double Cluster in the northern portion of Perseus, the Praesepe Cluster in Cancer (M44), the Pleiades, the Hyades in Taurus, M7 in Scorpius, and M41 in Canis Major.

Some open clusters are extremely spread out and may contain hundreds if not thousands of stars (Fig. 12-16). In binoculars some of the remoter clusters will appear as fuzzy, unresolved patches.

Exceedingly dark and transparent skies are a must for the majority of nebulae (Fig. 12-17). Hazy and cloud-like in binoculars, the diffuse and reflection variety of

Fig. 12-14. M22, a globular cluster in Sagittarius; photographed by John Stiles with a 12 1/2-inch reflector (Courtesy Optical Guidance Systems).

Fig. 12-15. M37, an open cluster in Auriga; photographed with a 10-inch reflector (Photograph by Lee C. Coombs).

Fig. 12-16. M67, an open cluster in Cancer; photographed with a Kitt Peak 4-meter reflector (Courtesy National Optical Astronomy Observatories).

Fig. 12-17. M16, The Eagle Nebula in Serpens; photographed with a 10-inch reflector (Photograph by Dr. Steve Simmerman).

Fig. 12-18. NGC 7293, The Helix Nebula in Sagittarius; photographed with a Kitt Peak 4-meter reflector (Courtesy National Optical Observatories).

these deep-sky objects will appear gray and lacking in color, although I have heard owners of larger-aperture binoculars maintain that they have seen an emerald green cast to M42 in Orion. The largest and brightest planetary nebulae exhibit some tint to the keen of eye; however, even the largest of these disklike objects are extremely difficult to observe in binoculars because of the planetary's lack of size. These objects are really for the amateur armed with a telescope.

The binocularist residing in northern latitudes will have a host of nebulae from which to choose in the Messier list and will find many of them challenging because of their faintness. Southern Hemisphere observers, fear not—you have excellent nebulae to view. The Eta Carinae Nebula is a true marvel.

Some of these wondrous Messier-list nebulae are M42, the Great Nebula in Orion, a binocular must; M8, the Lagoon Nebula in Sagittarius; and M20, the Trifid

Nebula (Fig. 12-19), also in Sagittarius. Another excellent site is in Cygnus, where the North American Nebula dwells (Fig. 12-20).

Dark nebulae, or *absorption nebulae* as they are sometimes called, are only visually detected by their contrast to other nebulae or by their blocking of stars. The Coalsack in Crux is an outstanding example.

Perhaps the most disappointing binocular deep-sky objects, and yet the most inspiring, are galaxies. The majority of them are seen as faint nebulous blurs. Like nebulae, most galaxies can only be glimpsed under dark-sky conditions far from urban-light pollution. Only a few look like galaxies under the best conditions. Some hints of dust lanes can be seen in M31, the Great Andromeda Galaxy, with 80mm binoculars and up. The awe I spoke of comes from the fact that when you look at these objects, you will be peering back in time. Existing beyond (far beyond) our Milky Way, galaxies are many millions

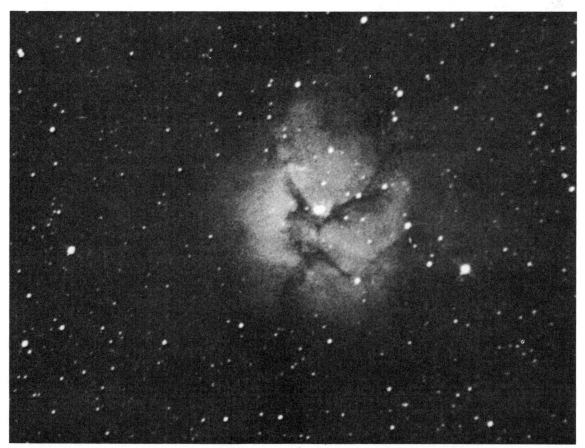

Fig. 12-19. M20, The Trifid Nebula in Sagittarius; photographed with a 10-inch reflector (Photograph by Dr. Steve Simmerman).

of light years distant. M31, a relative neighbor and one of the closest galaxies, is 2.2 million light years away. The light you view from this galaxy will have started on its cosmic journey 2.2 million years ago.

Few galaxies have shape in binoculars. When you see them, generally you are viewing the brighter nuclear portion. The Messier list offers some of the most rewarding galaxies for northern latitude observers. In the southern latitudes, the Small Magellanic Clouds are fine objects.

When you are viewing galaxies (Fig. 12-21), or for that matter any dim deep-sky object, you should employ *averted vision*; that is, direct your gaze at one part of the field while paying attention elsewhere. Slight side-to-side movements of the binoculars might demonstrate the faint contrast between the deep-sky object and the dark sky.

A catalog of binocular deep-sky objects is found in

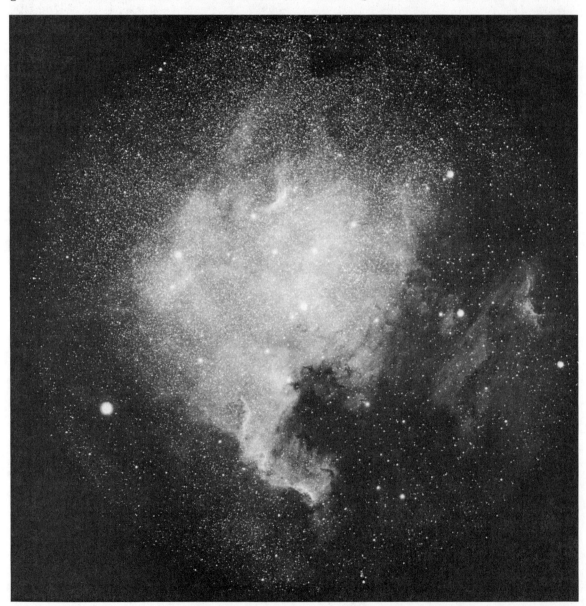

Fig. 12-20. NGC 7000, The North American Nebula in Cygnus; photographed with a 12-inch f/5 Astromak (Photograph by Jim Riffle).

152

Fig. 12-21. NGC 891, an edge-on spiral galaxy in Andromeda; photographed with a 14-inch Schmidt-Cassegrain by Ron Potter and Dr. Jack Marling (Courtesy Dr. Jack Marling and Lumicon).

Appendix A. Two outstanding deep-sky watchers organizations you might wish to contact are:

Alan Goldstien
NDSOS National Coordinator
National Deep-Sky Observers Society
3430 Bryan Way
Louisville, KY 40220

Mr. E.G. Moore
Publications Officer
Webb Society
1, Hillside Villas, Station Rd.
Pluckley, Kent. TN27 OQX
England

Chapter 13

Binocular Astrophotography

A binocular is a potential telephoto lens. With 7×50 binoculars (having 350mm telephoto lens) or a larger instrument (Fig. 13-1), astrophotographs can be attempted. Because most binocular pictures will not be taken with a clock-driven mount, lunar photographs appear to be the best starting point. Do not expect the sharpness or crispness of photographs taken with a telescope; binocular pictures are mostly for fun.

In order to take astrophotographs with your binoculars, you will need to have a firm mounting for the binoculars, either one homemade with wood or metal or a manufactured mounting such as the Edmund Scientific binocular mount. A 35mm SLR camera is recommended. Your mount, if homemade, must simply hold the camera and binoculars together and keep them rigid during picture taking (Fig. 13-2). A flat board or metal plate will do the trick. Hose clamps can be added to further stabilize both binoculars and camera. Ingenuity will be required in making the binocular-camera mount stable and vibration-proof.

Once your binoculars and camera are firmly mounted, bring your camera lens level with the eyepiece. Now you can begin your daylight testing by setting the camera at infinity and opening the camera lens to its widest stop. Next, jacking the camera up and holding it in place with

metal or wood blocks, place the binocular eyepiece to the front of the camera lens. They shouldn't touch, but only come close. Then focus the binocular diopter until the viewfinder image is crisp. The viewfinder should be filled as much as possible with the binocular's image. Try to make the alignment sharp.

It will prove difficult to keep the alignment between the camera and binoculars vibration-free during testing. You will need that previously mentioned mount. Is the image sharp? If so, take a test shot.

Many cameras with through-the-lens exposure meters will adjust to the problems binoculars will introduce. Some cameras will not. Those that don't will force you to calculate. Multiply your camera lens' focal length by the power of your binoculars. For example if you have a 35mm camera lens and a $10 \times$ binocular, the result will be 350mm. Divide the 350mm figure by the front lens' diameter of the camera. (350 divided by 35 equals 10.) This will give you the f/stop you will employ; in this case 10. Likely your camera's nearest f/stop will be f/11.

Next take your reading and adjust your shutter speed as if your camera was stopped to f/11. Employ a cable release to avoid jarring the camera during the test. If you are taking color pictures during the test, take three exposures, varying each by a factor of 4. If you are taking

Fig. 13-1. An Orion 10 × 70 connected to an Olympus OM-1 SLR (Photograph by Dan Stosuy).

Fig. 13-2. A breadboarded camera and binocular (Drawing by Anne Sheppard).

Fig. 13-3. Circumpolar star trails (Photograph by Dr. Steve Simmerman).

a color picture at 1/160 second, then also take one at 1/40 second, and one at 1/640 second. If you are using black-and-white film, which allows a wider variance, you may vary exposures by a factor of 8; for example: 1/20, 1/160, and 1/1280.

After each test shot you will likely be forced to realign your binoculars and camera. The camera must be balanced on whatever mount you employ.

To take long-exposure pictures of stars and planets, you will need a clock-driven equatorial mount, which is expensive and not really designed to support binoculars. However, you can take Moon photographs without a drive or equatorial mount. Short exposures won't hurt because our sister in space won't show that much movement at low power. The Moon's image will be small when taken through binoculars, but if the image is crisp it can be enlarged.

With lunar photography you'll have to experiment with exposures. Take notes. I've seen some surprisingly decent pictures taken with only a 10×50 binocular and

with a 20×80. The best film for this kind of photography would have a high ASA number, possess fine grain, have high contrast, and be panchromatic. I'd recommend Kodak's Plus-X, a good black-and-white film.

A binocular-and-camera setup can be used on bright comets, the star trails of circumpolar stars, meteors, and short exposures of constellations. You will need a dark sky for these projects. Simply aim your camera-binocular setup at the object and open the shutter for whatever time is required to make an exposure.

Exposure times for various objects follow:

Bright comets—5 minutes.
Meteors—30 minutes.
Circumpolar stars—60 minutes or less, depending on sky (Fig. 13-3).
Constellations—1 to 3 minutes.

When you are photographing a constellation's brighter stars, try a 6- to 11-second exposure with Kodak Tri-X film. Short exposures will cut down on star trailing.

Fine circumpolar star trail pictures may be taken with 13- to 40-minute exposures of the area around Polaris. Buildings and tree lines add to the beauty of these photographs.

Meteor showers are excellent subjects for the binocular-camera setup. Aim your camera at the meteor shower radiant and make a 30-minute exposure on fast black-and-white films. Likely you'll capture one or two meteors. Beware of the background skylight . It can wash out meteors appearing early on your photographs.

When you are undertaking photography with a binocular-camera setup, be certain to focus on the stars. If you don't, they might fail to come out sharp in the photographs. Good luck!

Chapter 14

The Story
of Lee Cain's
Mammoth Binoculars

Lee Cain, a well-known and highly innovative telescope maker from Houston, Texas, designed and built the world's largest binoculars, a 17 1/2-inch monster (Fig. 14-1). An outgrowth of his previously designed 13 incher, the 17 1/2-inch mammoth employs a Newtonian mirror system instead of the more normal lens system.

The Newtonian reflecting telescope (Fig. 14-2) uses a main parabolic mirror or objective mirror, which reflects and converges incoming light rays. A second, smaller mirror near the telescope's far end intercepts the reflected light and diverts it at a right angle to an eyepiece, which forms an image for the observer. After successfully rebuilding his first 13-inch binoculars, Lee constructed his mammoth 17 1/2 incher employing a truss structure design with a secondary module that fit inside a primary module, much like Chinese boxes.

Lee's binoculars are built for the faint stuff of the deep sky: galaxies, globular clusters, and nebulae. The Cain binoculars provide a sense of reality—a windowlike effect on the universe. With Lee's giant, the faint and unfamiliar celestial images no longer compete for the brain's attention against the visual noise of an unused eye, such as the afterimages, the floaters, and retinal blood flow. With the 17 1/2 incher the identical celestial imagery in both eyes reinforce each other, while the defects of the individual eyes can be differentiated and eliminated by the brain. Faint extended objects stand out. The brain, according to Lee Cain, works synergistically with the giant binoculars to form a brighter and better resolved "brain image" than it would with a monocular telescope of the same aperture.

The Cain mammoth not only supplies brighter and more colorful and detailed views of deep-sky objects, it makes them appear more realistic as a result of our habituation to dual-eye seeing. Many of us feel odd when we peer through a single eye. Giant binoculars like the 17 1/2 incher produce a windowlike effect when we are looking at the heavens, instead of a single eyepiece effect.

The Lagoon Nebula appears bright and extensive and its central lane exhibits sharp detail in the Cain mammoth. Dark nebulae stand out as dark patches against a faint background of stars. The view has been likened to a highly detailed Schmidt camera photograph. Omega Centauri appears as a terrifically radiant multitude of individual stars, with little of the boiling and rippling associated with large-aperture monocular telescopes. The famed Veil Nebula is brilliant, showing faint nebulosity between its loops. The filamentary structure of the Veil's clouds are amazingly sharp and detailed. Emission nebulae in general offer a nongrainy and milklike trans-

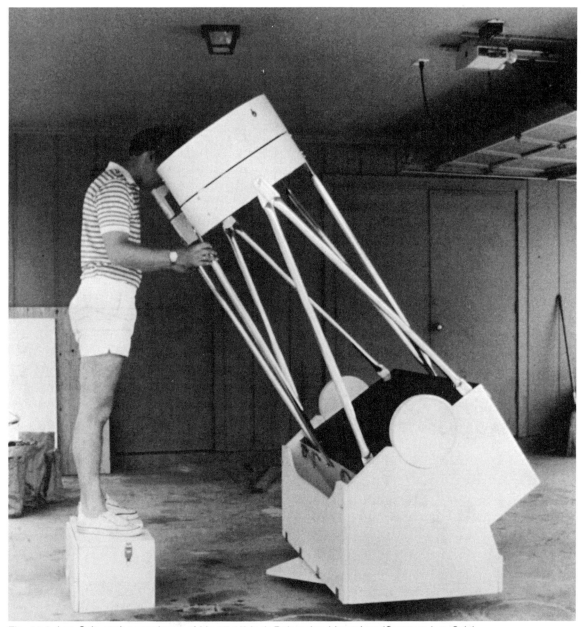

Fig. 14-1. Lee Cain at the eyepieces of his 17 1/2-inch Dobsonian binoculars (Courtesy Lee Cain).

parency not captured by photographs.

Lee Cain's binoculars are mechanically a simple side-by-side, dual Dobsonian telescope possessing altitude/azimuth bearings made of rubber casters, instead of Teflon pads which are more traditional to Dobsonian telescopes. Because the 17 1/2 incher is so heavy, the pressure re-

quirements for moving a Teflon system in azimuth would be great and the binoculars' truss design would produce flexure and an unmerging of images. Lee believed steel wheels and an adjustable friction pad might have served better.

The Cain mammoth has a typical Dobsonian rocker

159

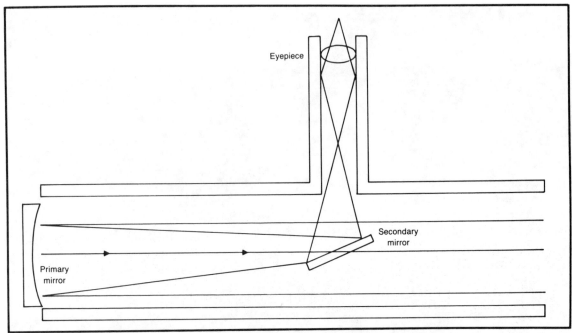

Fig. 14-2. A diagram of a Newtonian reflector (Drawing by Anne Sheppard).

Fig. 14-3. The 17 1/2-inch mammoth binoculars broken down and ready to travel (Courtesy Lee Cain).

box (Fig. 14-3), yet this one can fold flat and fits well in a station wagon. Taking at least two people to set up the binoculars within 15 minutes, the 17 1/2 incher is based on "hardware store technology" and can be built with only hand tools. The rocker box and mirror holders are made of exterior-grade A/C plywood, glued and screwed with durable Formica exterior surfaces. The Formica bolsters the woodwork, especially when it is attached with a hard-drying glue rather than contact cement.

The primary mirrors are a matched set made by Coulter Optical Company, a specialist in thin-mirror Dobsonian technology. Lee stated that the figure on the 17 1/2 incher's mirrors produced almost identical focal lengths. For constructing binoculars, the mirrors' focal lengths should not differ by more than 1/2 percent. If the mirrors' focal length fails to adhere to this 1/2 percent, the images reflected back to the eye will have unequal magnification. Stars would appear double at the field's edge.

The primary mirrors are mounted in a customized Dobsonian sling system. These slings possess dual joints and are suspended from pivots slightly aft of the mirrors' centers of thickness to prevent the mirrors from pressuring the triangular flotation pads even when viewing is done at very low altitude. Permanently mounted, the mirrors each have three flotation pads glued to their backs at three contact points. The mirrors are spot-glued to their slings. No soft materials, such as felt or leather, are used in the mirror supports so that adjustments are made as accurately as possible. Accuracy is most important with such sizable binoculars. An adjusting screw with ultra-fine threads was employed with precision in mind. Glued at their vertices to the mirror's back, the three pads form a nine-point flotation system.

The binoculars' eyepiece tube end is constructed of 20-inch diameter, 3/8-inch wall Sonotube, a heavy-duty cardboard usually employed as a form for concrete pillars. Each barrel possesses a double wall for added strength. Beginning with identical Sonotube pieces, Lee slit the side of one and glued it inside the other. Later all holes were sealed and oil-based paints were used to make the cardboard surfaces water resistant.

Lee Cain believes that interocular adjustment is not critical. His experiences showed him that most observers used his binoculars without having to alter the eyepiece spacing. The proper spacing can first be attempted with small hand-held binoculars. Interocular adjustment on the 17 1/2 incher was provided by having the forward sections on the secondary module counterrotate on Teflon pads. If you observe a dark field, the proper spacing will not be obvious. Use a bright object or the Milky Way when you are making the interocular adjustment.

The 17 1/2 incher's secondary and tertiary mirrors were vacuum overcoated with silver. This coating is about 98 percent reflective, which is superior to standard aluminum coating with its 88 percent reflectivity. Lee maintains the efficiency of each three-mirror system is about 84 percent, a 16 percent gain over using aluminum coatings throughout.

Each binocular tube is collimated using a spot on the axis of the primary mirror. The secondaries and tertiaries are not routinely adjusted. The observer peers through the two focusing tubes with the eyepieces removed, then adjusts the mirrors until they are all merged as if he looked through a single Newtonian system. The 17 1/2 incher maintains collimation fairly well when broken down and then reassembled. The binoculars only require a final fine merging of the star images for each observing session. When the mirrors reach thermal equilibrium, there is generally no need to recollimate at low magnifications, although with higher power a few tweakings will do the job.

The Cain mammoth stands tall when it is aimed at the zenith, so the observer will require a step stool, which may also serve as a diaphragm board to protect the primary mirrors. Further the step stool can be a Velcro platform on which accessories can be stored for transport.

Lee Cain, who built the 17 1/2 incher in about two months, working several hours a night and a half or full day on weekends, offers these following tips on Giant Dobsonian binocular construction:

☆ Mount your optical elements securely to avoid the loss of collimation when you are transporting the instrument. Fast focal-length systems used in low-power RFT style require less critical collimation.
☆ Woodwork should be rigid. A fast focal-length system helps. If the scope is short enough, it might not need to be broken down for transport.
☆ Make certain fine adjustment of mirrors is available for merging images (Fig. 14-4).
☆ Unless the structural design is extremely rigid and has a fine adjustment, the upper magnification limit is about 150x.
☆ Because of interocular adjustment, field rotation can be tricky in many mammoth Dobsonian binocular designs. Test your ideas before starting construction. In each binocular, the axis of light from the tertiary mirror to the eyepiece must be parallel to the axis from the primary to the secondary mirror. If it is not, the images will be rotationally displaced.
☆ The Cain design cannot be applied to primaries

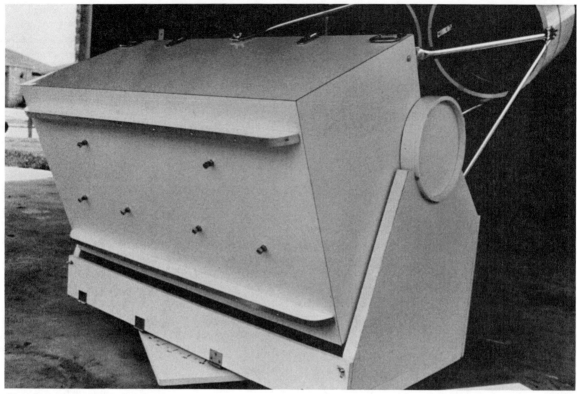

Fig. 14-4. The primary mirror adjustment screws on the rear of the 17 1/2-inch binoculars (Courtesy Lee Cain).

smaller than 8 inches unless you plan to use an over-sized secondary mirror. Perhaps a Barlow lens or a positive transfer lens might solve this problem.

If you have any specific construction questions about mammoth binocular construction contact:

Lee Cain
16206 Grassy Creek
Houston, TX 77082

Large thin mirror optics can be obtained from:

Coulter Optical Co.
P.O. Box K
Idyllwild, CA 92349

Enterprise Optics
P.O. Box 413
Placentia, CA 92670

Chapter 15

The Astronomy Club

For me almost half the pleasure of amateur astronomy comes from the opportunity to affiliate with others who enjoy the same hobby. An astronomy club offers the chance to share observations and discoveries and to find new friendships based on an interest in the heavens. I must enjoy affiliation to some large degree because I am the vice-president of the nation's oldest chartered astronomical society and a member of another club some 30 miles away. I am also a member of the American Association of Variable Star Observers, the Association of Lunar and Planetary Observers, and the Astronomical League.

How do you go about finding an astronomy club in your area? Look in the "Local Events" section of your weekend newspaper. Call your local observatory or planetarium if one is around. Often the heads of local college astronomy departments know the whereabouts of amateur groups. The "Astromart" section of *Astronomy* magazine often provides club announcements. You also might find out about club activity in your area by writing a letter to the Astronomical League, which is an umbrella organization for the many astronomical clubs and societies across the United States. Contact the Astronomical League by writing:

The Reflector
Tom Martinez, Editor
1208 Somerset Ct.
Blue Springs, MO 64015

If no astronomical clubs exist in your area, you might wish to start a club. In order to start one you will want to attract potential members to your first meetings. The best way to approach new members is through the media. *Astronomy* magazine allows free announcements in "Astromart," and your local newspaper often has free event listings. Write them, describing briefly the address of the meeting place, the time, and the name of your group (this can be decided later by group concensus). Stress that this meeting is both free and open to the public. When you write the media use a typewriter and double-space your copy. Give your telephone number for additional information. Let the newspapers know about your initial meeting at least 2 weeks ahead of time. Also contact the science departments of local high schools and the astronomy departments of area colleges and universities.

Aside from the pleasures of friendship and affiliation, clubs also offer entertainment and educational enrichment. These last two items come about through having speakers and showing movies and slides. Open participation at meetings by all members is encouraged.

Where should the club meet? This depends on the club's size. The two local clubs, in which I hold membership, range between 110 and 75 members. One club uses a meeting room at a local educational institution for a nominal fee, and at the other club we use a room in a borough hall. I've heard of really small clubs gathering at people's homes. If your group becomes large you might have to find a large room. Contact borough halls, colleges, high schools, recreational centers, and the like about using one of their rooms. Tell them what kind of club you have and how many group members you possess. Your group's treasurer would become responsible for making the monthly or yearly payment on the room. Someone else, perhaps a volunteer, would handle the room cleanup after the meeting. Often the rooms may be had for no charge or a small deposit as a public service.

When you are forming a club, certain framework problems must be considered. Meetings might be hampered by having too few rules or too many. The best policy is to quickly cover your business first prior to the main program (speaker, movie, etc.). Keep the membership involved in as many ways as possible because if they are not, they are likely to lose interest. Meet at the same time each week or month so people will know when to come.

Even though arguments can be very interesting, keep them to a minimum. Your club's president will gavel the meeting. Let it be known that speaking out of turn and interrupting will not be tolerated. Conversations outside the flow of the meeting are also taboo since they will detract from whoever is speaking.

Your officers should make it a point to help newcomers feel at home. Introducing them informally to others helps.

Plan to have guest speakers. Area professional astronomers, noted amateurs, authors, telescope makers, NASA people, A.A.V.S.O and ALPO recorders, and university teachers all make good guest speakers. Slide shows and movies can be had. Your own membership likely has its share of astrophotographers. Movies can be rented from various outlets or borrowed from colleges and libraries. A good meeting is much more than dry business.

Attempt to arrange star parties and outings to local astronomical facilities. Perhaps you live in an area where some university possesses a large-aperture telescope. Maybe you reside in an area where astronomical optical manufacturing goes on. These places make for interesting trips. Star parties are a great draw. Members love to see and examine other members' telescopes and equipment, as well as get out together under dark skies.

Be aware of astronomy days and astronomy weeks. Perhaps your club can bring displays and presentations to the local planetarium or shopping mall. This is an excellent way to introduce your hobby to others and perhaps find new members. Picnics and softball games can be arranged. Messier marathon nights are good shots at bringing out your membership. On certain nights during the year the constellations are well placed so that all the Messier objects may be seen. Meteor showers during a favorable Moon are also good for drawing your membership to an outing. Committees should be formed to plan these events so more club members are involved.

Don't forget the club's observatory (Fig. 15-1). If your treasury is strong and you have some land under dark skies, your organization should have an observatory. Revenue for such a project can be brought in from dues, donations, and swap meets, and some of the equipment construction can be done by your own membership.

Observing sections can be formed within your club. These sections are formed around a particular area of observational astronomy such as comets, the Sun, planets, deep-sky objects, meteors, variable stars, sky transparency, and double stars. Members of these sections can be active in research and have membership in the A.A.V.S.O., ALPO, or some other fine national amateur organization.

Each observing section should be run by a recorder who will report at the meetings on that section's progress. Keep those progress reports to no more than 10 minutes, unless some special event has occurred. The section recorders will recruit and organize those club members whose interests reside in the section's sphere of observation. At every meeting, or at least once a month, the recorders will speak to the club about their section's activities and any key upcoming events. The recorder will keep records of his section and submit observations to organizations such as the A.A.V.S.O. and ALPO.

The club's regular program might take this shape:

☆ The president will open the meeting and briefly outline what will take place.
☆ The secretary will read the minutes of the previous meeting. This part can be dispensed with if the minutes are covered in the newsletter.
☆ The president will list upcoming events and introduce section recorders.
☆ Reports will be given by section recorders.
☆ Mention any unresolved business from the last meeting.
☆ Speak about possible future activities and have mem-

Fig. 15-1. A club observatory (Photograph by Dr. Steve Simmerman).

bers talk about any newsworthy astronomical items.
☆ The guest speaker, movie, slide-show, or show-and-tell session is next.
☆ Discussion, questions, and answers follow.
☆ Announcement of next meeting date and program is made.
☆ The president adjourns the meeting.
☆ After the meeting provide a time for coffee, informal gathering, parking-lot observation, or to go out for pizza or hamburgers.

Any group of 20 or more should consider having a newsletter. The newsletter might contain the meeting notice, something about the coming guest speaker, perhaps a meeting minutes capsule, mention of past or upcoming astronomical events, and maybe even a list of astronom-ical gear that members would wish to sell or trade. The newsletter can be mimeographed or photocopied. Dues should cover postage. The newsletter editor can be anyone in the club.

Generally it takes four elected officers to run the club. The officers are:

☆ The president, who presides over meetings, organizes programs, and acts as a bridge to the media.
☆ The vice president, who will preside over the meetings in the president's absence and assist the president in organizing.
☆ The secretary, who records meeting minutes, answers club correspondence, also might work as the club's publicity agent.

165

☆ The treasurer, who accounts for the club's finances and collects dues.

The officers will meet to discuss and plan club outings.

Money must be collected to pay for postage, newsletters, and perhaps the club's meeting space. Dues might also pay for observatory construction. Dues should be moderate, except for memberships that include a subscription to one of the astronomical magazines. Sky and Telescope offers its subscription at a discount to clubs.

Once-a-year collection is easiest on the treasurer. Monthly dues can be a problem to chase down so it is best to avoid that situation. All club money should be banked to accrue interest.

Publicity for your club can be generated by your president and your newsletter editor. An astronomy club can never have enough publicity. Make sure your meetings are listed in the weekend sections of your area newspapers. These listings are free. At least once a year make use of the free "Astromart" section in *Astronomy* magazine, which is a great way to reach new astronomy enthusiasts. Often television and radio offer free public interest spots.

Keep your media release brief and to the point. Use a typewriter and double-space your copy and be sure to give your club's name and telephone number. Also inform the media about coming star parties, meteor showers, solar and lunar eclipses, and new comets. Make certain your information is accurate.

Appendix A

Catalog of Binocular Deep-Sky Objects

ANDROMEDA

Northern constellation found by locating a trio of bright stars in the Northeast corner of Pegasus' Great Square. A mid- and late-autumn constellation.

M31. The Great Galaxy in Andromeda (Fig. A-1). Magnitude: 4. An easy object for Northern-Latitude, naked-eye observations under dark skies. 1 degree west of Nu Androm. Length 5.2 degrees, width 1.1 degrees. 2.2 million light years away. Bright core with large extensions; appears like a dim oval glow to the naked eye. Contains more than 300 billion stars. Diameter over 150,000 light years. Larger than our Milky Way. Member of the local group. Interesting neighbors easily viewed in 11 × 80s—M32 and NGC 205 (small elliptical galaxies). M31 has large spiral arms. This galaxy will show hints of dust lanes in 80mm and up binoculars. One of the outstanding binocular objects—a must!

M32. Magnitude: 8.7. South of M31's core. An elliptical galaxy. Appears oval in binoculars. 2000 light years in diameter. Bright center.

NGC 205. Magnitude: 10.8. M31's companion. An elliptical galaxy.

NGC 7662. Magnitude: 8.5. Planetary nebula. Bright blue-green disk that appears as a starlike nebulosity in large-aperture binoculars. 32″ × 28″.

NGC 752. Large open cluster of bright stars. Good binocular object. Magnitude: 8.9-10. 70 odd, scattered stars.

NGC 7686. Galactic cluster of 10 to 12 stars. Magnitude: 8-13. Just visible in 7 × 50s.

Star 56. Double star. Magnitudes: 5.8 and 6.1.

R Andromeda. Variable. 409 days. Magnitude range: 5.8-14.9.

ANTILA

The Airpump Constellation rests near the southern section of the Milky Way. Contains no stars brighter than fourth magnitude. Best seen in February. Possesses a lot of dim galaxies beyond the range of battleship glasses.

NGC 2997. Galaxy, Sc type. Magnitude: 11. A blur in 11 × 80s.

Zeta Antila. Binocular double star. Magnitudes: 6 and 6.

APUS

The Bird of Paradise Constellation is a small triangle of fourth magnitude stars close to the South Celestial Pole.

NGC 6101. Magnitude: 10. Globular cluster. Dim spherical haze best seen under darkest skies and with

Fig. A-1. The nucleus of M31, The Great Galaxy in Andromeda; photographed with the Canada-France-Hawaii 144-inch reflector at Mauna Kea (Photograph by Canada-France-Hawaii Telescope Corporation).

large-aperture binoculars.

Sigma Apus. Binocular double star. Magnitudes: 4.8 and 5.2.

AQUARIUS

The Water Bearer is a constellation in the zodiac and lies between the bright southern star Fomalhaut and the constellation Pegasus. Large in size. Contains dim stars. Best seen in August.

Tau Aquarius. Binocular double star. Magnitudes: 5 and 6.

M2. Magnitude: 6. Globular cluster. Large and bright. 50,000 light years away. Bright core. Easy to see.

M72. Magnitude: 8.6. Small globular cluster. Oval and dim with a brighter side. Hazy.

M73. Small triangle of stars. Not a true loose cluster.

NGC 7009. Magnitude: 8. Planetary nebula. The Saturn Nebula. Blue-green disk.

NGC 7293. Magnitude: 6.5. Planetary nebula. The Helical Nebula. Faint and fit only for larger binoculars. Looks like a large, circular, nebulous patch.

S Aquarius. Variable star. 278 days. Magnitude range: 7.6-15.

X Aquarius. Variable star. 311 days. Magnitude range: 7.5-14.8.

RY Aquarius. Variable star. 2 days. Magnitude range: 8.8-10.1.

AQUILA

Best seen in mid-July, this constellation is the home of Altair and resides in a star-rich portion of the Milky Way. Wonderful in binoculars. The star Altair is the southern corner of the Summer Triangle.

Epsilon Aquila. Binocular double star. Magnitudes: 4 and 3 (yellow and white).

Star 57. Binocular double star. Magnitudes: 5.8 and 6.5.

NGC 6709. Magnitude: 8. Open cluster of 40 stars.

NGC 6756. Magnitude: 10.5. Open cluster of 25 or so stars.

NGC 6760. Magnitude: 11. Globular cluster. Small and ultradim.

NGC 6790. Magnitude: 11.5. Planetary nebula. A real test for large glasses.

NGC 6803. Magnitude: 11. Planetary nebula. Dim patch in 100mm glasses.

B 143. Dark nebula in Milky Way. 1 1/2 degrees West of Gamma Aquilae.

ARA

The Altar lies just south of Scorpius in the Milky Way. This small constellation is home for many fine open clusters and is best seen in June.

Kappa Ara. Binocular double star. Magnitudes: 5.3 and 9.7. Hard for 11×80s.

NGC 6215. Magnitude: 11.2. Galaxy, SB type.

NGC 6221. Magnitude: 11.4. Galaxy, SB type.

NGC 6300. Magnitude: 11.4. Galaxy, SB type.

NGC 6204. Magnitude: 11. Galactic cluster. Needs 11×80 and up under darkest skies.

NGC 6397. Magnitude: 7. Globular cluster. Fairly bright, misty patch. Likely nearest globular to our solar system.

NGC 6193. Magnitude: 6. Galactic cluster of 30 stars. Easy for 7×50s.

NGC 6208. Magnitude: 9-12. Galactic cluster of about 50 stars.

NGC 6250. Magnitude: 8-12. Galactic cluster of 15 stars.

NGC 6362. Magnitude: 8. Globular cluster. Curious nebulous patch.

NGC 6352. Magnitude: 9. Globular cluster. Somewhat difficult in small binoculars.

NGC 6188. Irregular nebula. Very difficult for large binoculars.

ARIES

The Ram rests in the zodiac South of Andromeda. Alpha, Beta, and Gamma create a bright triplet. Not much here except for double stars. An October constellation.

Lambda Aries. Binocular double star. Magnitudes: 4.9 and 7.7.

Star 14. Binocular triple star. Magnitudes: 5.1, 7.7, and 8.7.

R Aries. Variable star. 187 days. Magnitude range: 7.4-13.7.

T Aries. Variable star. 322 days. Magnitude range: 7.5-11.3.

AURIGA

The Charioteer. A mid-December constellation with the Milky Way passing through it. Capella, a star like our Sun, shines brightest here. Home of several curious open clusters. Wonderful Milky Way fields.

M36. Magnitude: 9. Open cluster. 60 stars mostly concentrated in the center. Wide range of magnitude. 4,100 light years away.

M37. Magnitude: 9. Galactic cluster of 150 stars—well concentrated in the middle. Appears nebulous in binoculars.

M38. Magnitude: 8. Open cluster of 100 stars looking like sparkling powder. Almost square in shape. Fantastic!

NGC 1857. Magnitude: 8. Galactic cluster. Ordinary.

NGC 1907. Magnitude: 10. Galactic cluster of 40 stars. Somewhat faint.

NGC 2281. Magnitude: 7. Galactic cluster of 30 stars or so.

NGC 1778. Magnitude: 10. Open cluster of 10 stars.

E Auriga. Dark eclipsing variable. 27.1 years. Magnitude range: 3-4.

UU Auriga. Variable star. 300 days. Magnitude range: 5.1-6.8.

BOOTES

The Herdsman, a late-April constellation. Lies a fair distance from the Milky Way. The fourth brightest star in the heavens, Arcturus (orange in color), is this constellation's major star. Having many faint galaxies, Bootes is not far from Ursa Major.

Mu Bootes. Binocular double star (Alkalurops). Magnitudes: 4.5 and 6.7.

Iota Bootes. Binocular double star. Magnitudes: 4.9 and 7.5. Yellow primary.

NGC 5466. Magnitude: 9. Globular cluster. Faint.

NGC 5248. Magnitude: 11. Galaxy, Sc type. Very difficult to see.

CAELUM

The Chisel Constellation is extremely small and best viewed in late November. West of Columba. Nothing of interest for the binocularist.

CAMELOPARDALIS

The Giraffe is a large constellation close to the North Celestial Pole and is centered between Cassiopeia and Ursa Major. Brightest stars are fourth magnitude.

Beta Camelopardalis. Binocular double star. Magnitudes: 4.2 and 8.8. Yellow primary. Test for 11×80s.

NGC 1502. Magnitude: 8. Galactic cluster of 25 stars.

NGC 1961. Magnitude: 11.6. Galaxy, Sb type.

NGC 2146. Magnitude: 11.6. Galaxy, Sb, peculiar type.

NGC 2403. Magnitude: 8.8. Galaxy, large Sc-type spiral. Member of the local group. Pale blotch.

NGC 2655. Magnitude: 11.6. Galaxy, Sa type.

CANCER

The Crab Constellation, sitting between Leo and Gemini in the zodiac. Consists of five fourth magnitude stars.

Iota Cancer. Binocular double star. Magnitudes: 4.2 and 6.6 (yellow primary and blue companion). Good in 11×80s.

M44. Praesepe (Latin for manger). Also called the Beehive. Magnitudes: 4-5. Galactic cluster. Outstanding in a binocular. 350 scattered stars some 500 light years away. Visible to the naked eye. 1 degree across.

M67. Magnitude: 10. Galactic cluster of scattered bright and faint stars. Misty spot in 11×80s. Stars are gold, rust, orange, and yellow. 2,500 light years away.

NGC 2775. Magnitude: 11.5. Galaxy, Sa type.

R Cancer. Variable star. 362 days. Magnitude range: 6.2-11.8.

S Cancer. Variable star. 9.4 days. Magnitude range: 8.4-11.1.

CANES VENATICI

Marked by a trio of naked-eye stars, the Hunting Dog Constellation sits below the handle end of the Big Dipper. Canes Venatici dwells in a large concentration of galaxies that sweep southward past Ursa Major to Virgo. A few of these galaxies make excellent binocular subjects. A February constellation.

M3. Magnitude: 6. Globular cluster. Some stars to the eleventh magnitude. Looks like a spherical nebulosity in 7×50s. A cloudy disk. Bright in 11×80s and above. First globular where a periodic variable was discovered.

M63. Magnitude: 9.8. Spiral galaxy. Appears as a pale, elongated blur. 35 million light years away. Brighter toward the center.

M94. Magnitude: 8.9. Spiral galaxy of 250 billion suns. 14 million light years away. Cometlike in binoculars with a brilliant center.

M51. Magnitude: 8.7. Face-on spiral known as the Whirlpool Galaxy (Fig. A-2). 3 degrees Southwest of the last star in the handle of Ursa Major. The first galaxy to have its spiral nature observed. Made of 160 billion suns, this fine deep-sky object looks like two galaxies or two nebulous blotches of light. Don't miss it!

M106. Magnitude: 9. Spiral galaxy. Looks like smudge of light. Tight arms with fat central knot. 14 million light years away. Source of radio emission.

NGC 4111. Magnitude: 11.6. E7, edge-on galaxy. Difficult to see.

NGC 4151. Magnitude: 11.2. Sb or S/pec. galaxy. A test for 11×80s.

NGC 4214. Magnitude: 10.5. Irregular galaxy.

NGC 4242. Magnitude: 11.5. S-type galaxy.

NGC 4244. Magnitude: 10.7. Sb-type galaxy. Difficult to see.

NGC 4395. Magnitude: 11. S-type galaxy.

NGC 4449. Magnitude: 10.5. Irregular galaxy.

NGC 4490. Magnitude: 10.1. Spiral galaxy, twin armed. Glimpsed in 10×70s.

NGC 4618. Magnitude: 11.2. Sc/pec. galaxy.

NGC 4631. Magnitude: 9.7. Spiral, edge-on galaxy. Hazy and indistinct.

NGC 4656. Magnitude: 11.0. Sb-type galaxy.

NGC 5195. Magnitude: 11.0. Irregular galaxy connected to M51.

CANIS MAJOR

The Greater Dog Constellation is best seen in early January. Bright, this constellation lies Southeast of Orion and is close to the richest sector of the Milky Way. Home of Sirius, the brightest star, Canis Major possesses four second magnitude stars.

M41. Magnitude: 7. Galactic cluster. 4 degrees South of Sirius. Large and bright toward the center. Looks somewhat powdery in binoculars. 2400 light years away. Low altitude for viewers in the middle Northern Latitude. Some orange stars.

NGC 2362. Magnitudes: 7.5 to 13. Galactic cluster of 40 stars.

NGC 2374. Galactic cluster of scattered bright stars.

NGC 2360. Open cluster. Faint. Magnitudes: 9-12.

A Canis Major. Sirius. The brightest star in the sky.

Fig. A-2. M51, The Whirlpool Galaxy in Canes Venatici. This face-on spiral galaxy was photographed with the Kitt Peak 4-meter reflector (Courtesy National Optical Astronomy Observatories).

R Canis Major. Variable star. 1.1 days. Magnitude range: 6.0-6.6. Short period.

CANIS MINOR

The Lesser Dog Constellation is best viewed in mid January. Bright yellow Procyon marks this constellation East of Orion. Not much here to observe.

14 Canis Minor. A triple star. Magnitudes: 5.5, 8, and 9. Needs $10\times$ or up to observe.

CAPRICORNUS

The Goat, an early-August constellation, sits in the zodiac South of Aquarius. A Capricornus is a yellow, naked-eye double with magnitudes of 3.7 and 4.5. Not much here to observe.

M30. Magnitude: 8. Globular cluster appearing like nebulous sphere. One of the brighter globulars. 40,000 light years away.

Lambda Capricornus. Binocular double star. Magnitudes: 3.5 and 4.2.

Delta Capricornus. Binocular double star. Magnitudes: 5.5 and 9.0.

Beta Capricornus. Binocular double star. Magnitudes: 6.0 and 3.1.

CARINA

The Keel Constellation can be seen in late January in the Southern Hemisphere. Home of Canopus, the second brightest star in the heavens, the keel lies far Southeast of Orion and Canis Major in the southern Milky Way. Carina leads the Southern Cross around the pole.

NGC 2516. Open cluster of 100 stars. Magnitudes: 7-13.

NGC 2808. Magnitude: 6. Globular appearing blotchy and nebulous.

NGC 3114. Galactic cluster of 100 stars. Magnitudes: 9-13. Wonderful!

I 2581. Magnitude: 5. Open cluster of 35 stars.

NGC 3293. Open cluster. Magnitudes: 6-13.

I 2602. Magnitude: 5. Open cluster of 30 stars.

NGC 3532. Magnitude: 8. Irregular galactic cluster of 150 stars.

NGC 3572. Galactic cluster of 40 stars. Magnitudes: 7-14.

NGC 3590. Magnitude: 9. Galactic cluster of 25 stars.

NGC 3372. Keyhole Nebula near Eta Carina. Diffuse nebulosity. Irregular. A must for all binocularists!

Eta Carina. Novalike, irregular variable star in NGC 3372.

CASSIOPEIA

The wife of Cepheus is best viewed in mid October. Shaped like an **M** or **W**, this distinctive northern constellation is not far from Polaris and rests in a rich section of the Milky Way.

Beta Cassiopeia. Binocular double star. Magnitudes: 7 and 7.

NGC 129. Magnitude: 9. Galactic cluster of 50 stars.

NGC 133. Magnitude: 10. Galactic cluster of 40 stars.

NGC 225. Magnitude: 9. Galactic cluster of 20 scattered stars.

NGC 436. Magnitude: 10. Galactic cluster of 40 stars.

NGC 457. Magnitude: 8. Open cluster of 100 stars. Lovely.

NGC 559. Magnitude: 10. Galactic cluster of 50 stars.

M103. Magnitude: 8. Galactic cluster of 40 stars. Very large field. Some of the stars form an arrowhead shape. 8,000 light years away.

NGC 637. Magnitude: 10. Open cluster of 20 stars.

NGC 663. Galactic cluster of 80 stars. Magnitudes: 7-9. Subtle blotch.

Mel 15. Magnitude: 7. Open cluster of 20 stars with some nebulosity.

M52. Magnitude: 9. Galactic cluster of 200 stars (Fig. A-3). Ultra rich, compressed in the center. 7,000 light years away.

NGC 7789. Magnitude: 10. Galactic cluster of 900 stars. Hazy patch.

NGC 7788. Magnitude: 10. Galactic cluster of 10 stars.

NGC 278. Magnitude: 11.6. Galaxy, Sc type.

NGC 7635. Bubble Nebula. Nebulosity around magnitude-8.5 star.

NGC 281. Diffuse nebula around magnitude-8.5 star.

CENTAURUS

The Centaur Constellation is best seen at the end of March and rests in the southern portion of the Milky Way. Alpha Centaurus is the closest naked-eye star.

Delta Centaurus. Binocular double star. Magnitudes: 4.8 and 2.9.

NGC 5139. Magnitude: 4. Globular cluster. Omega Centauri. Terrific! Likely the best naked-eye globular for viewers in the southern United States.

NGC 5286. Magnitude: 9. Globular cluster. Dim in binoculars.

NGC 3680. Magnitude: 10. Open cluster of 25 stars.

NGC 3766. Magnitude: 8. Galactic cluster of 60 stars.

NGC 3909. Magnitude: 9. Open cluster. Scattered field.

NGC 4852. Magnitude: 10. Open cluster of 40 stars.

NGC 5281. Magnitude: 10. Open cluster of 20 stars.

NGC 5460. Magnitude: 8. Galactic cluster of 25 stars.

NGC 5617. Magnitude: 8. Galactic cluster of 50 stars.

NGC 5662. Magnitude: 9. Open cluster of 30 stars.

NGC 4945. Magnitude: 9.2. Spiral galaxy with loose structure.

NGC 4976. Magnitude: 11.6. Galaxy, E4 type.

NGC 5102. Magnitude: 10.8. Galaxy, SO type.

NGC 5128. Magnitude: 7.2. Peculiar galaxy.

NGC 5253. Magnitude: 10.8. Odd elliptical galaxy.

NGC 3918. Magnitude: 8. Planetary nebula. Faint.

NGC 5367. Magnitude: 10. Diffuse nebula. Difficult to see.

CEPHEUS

A late-September constellation that reaches almost to the North Celestial Pole. Close to the Milky Way, Cepheus' southern region offers some fine sights. Only a few bright stars assist in this constellation's identification.

Delta Cepheus. Binocular double star. Magnitudes: 3.6-4.3 (variable) and 5.3. The variable has a period of 5.37 days. Interesting.

NGC 7235. Magnitude: 10. Galactic cluster of 25 stars. Irregular.

NGC 7380. Magnitude: 9. Galactic cluster of 20 stars. Some nebulosity.

NGC 7510. Magnitude: 10. Galactic cluster of 30 stars. Irregular.

NGC 6946. Magnitude: 11.1. Spiral galaxy.

NGC 7023. Magnitude: 7.2. Diffuse nebula. Curious object.

CETUS

The Whale Constellation is best observed in mid October. Because of its proximity to the ecliptic, planets are sometimes found here. Cetus has few bright stars. It is located near Taurus and Aquarius.

Alpha Cetus. Binocular double star. Magnitudes: 2.5 (yellow) and 5.5.

Fig. A-3. M52, an open cluster in Cassiopeia; photographed with a 10-inch reflector (Photograph by Lee C. Coombs).

M77. Magnitude: 10. Seyfert galaxy, some 60 million light years away. Irregular shape with three distinct sets of spiral arms. Strong radio source. Hazy blotch.

NGC 157. Magnitude: 11.1. Sc galaxy.

NGC 247. Magnitude: 10.7. Sc galaxy.

NGC 584. Magnitude: 11.5. E4 galaxy.

NGC 908. Magnitude: 11.1. Sc galaxy.

NGC 936. Magnitude: 11.3. SBa galaxy.

NGC 1087. Magnitude: 11.2. Sc galaxy.

NGC 246. Magnitude: 8.5. Planetary nebula. Similar to Ring Nebula. Large with low surface brightness.

CHAMAELEON

The Chameleon Constellation, best viewed in late February, contains five fourth-magnitude stars. It is a small group and resides close to the South Celestial Pole.

Delta Chamaeleon. Binocular double star. Magnitudes: 4.6 and 5.5.

R Chamaeleon. Variable star. 334 days. Magnitude range: 7.5-14.

CIRCINUS

The Compasses Constellation is best viewed in late April and early May in the Milky Way close to Centaurus.

NGC 5715. Magnitude: 11. Galactic cluster of 30 stars. Difficult to see.

COLUMBA

The Dove is best seen in mid December. Not a whole lot here for binocular viewers. Found south of Lepus and marked by a small triangle of stars (alpha, beta, and epsilon).

NGC 1851. Magnitude: 7. Globular cluster. Nebulous blur.

NGC 1792. Magnitude: 10.7. Galaxy, Sc type.

NGC 1808. Magnitude: 11.2. Galaxy, SB type.

COMA BERENICES

Berenice's hair is a March-April constellation. Large cluster of faint stars to the North of Virgo. Home of a great many galaxies.

Star 12. Binocular double star. Magnitudes: 4.8 and 8.3.

Star 17. Binocular double star. Magnitudes: 6.7 and 5.4.

M53. Magnitude: 8. Globular cluster. Irregularly round and brighter in the center. 60,000 light years away. 60 light years across. Contains twelfth-magnitude stars.

M98. Magnitude: 9.7. Galaxy, SB type with bright nucleus. 37 million light years away. Large and very extended.

M99. Magnitude: 10.4. Face-on spiral galaxy. Round and gradually brighter in the center.

M100. Magnitude: 10.4. Galaxy, Sc type spiral. Mottled and bright nucleus. Face-on. Faint, large, and round.

M85. Magnitude: 8.9. Elliptical galaxy with bright core.

M88. Magnitude: 9. Elongated spiral galaxy that is very large, bright, and extended. 40 million light years away.

M64. Magnitude: 8.6. Galaxy, Sa type. Irregular shape and bright, yet small. Called the Black Eye Galaxy. 12 million light years away. Uneven brightness.

NGC 4251. Magnitude: 11.3. Galaxy, Sa type.

NGC 4274. Magnitude: 11.5. Galaxy, Sb type.

NGC 4278. Magnitude: 11.4. Galaxy, E1 type.

NGC 4314. Magnitude: 11.6. Galaxy, SBa type.

NGC 4450. Magnitude: 11.1. Galaxy, Sb type.

NGC 4477. Magnitude: 11.6. Galaxy, SBa type.

NGC 4494. Magnitude: 10.9. Galaxy, E1 type.

NGC 4548. Magnitude: 10.9. Galaxy, SBb.

NGC 4559. Magnitude: 10.5. Galaxy, Sc type, multiarmed spiral.

NGC 4565. Magnitude: 10.5. Galaxy, Sb type.

NGC 4651. Magnitude: 11.4. Galaxy, Sc type.

NGC 4725. Magnitude: 10.5. Galaxy, SBb type.

NGC 5053. Magnitude: 10.5. Globular cluster. Faint companion of M53.

CORONA AUSTRALIS

The Southern Crown is a late-June constellation. South of Sagittarius, Corona Australis is made out by its curve of faint stars.

Kappa Australis. Binocular double star. Magnitudes: 6 and 6.5.

NGC 6496. Magnitude: 10. Globular cluster. Dim.

NGC 6541. Magnitude: 6. Globular cluster. Bright, easily seen.

CORONA BOREALIS

The Northern Crown, a mid-May constellation, lies East of Epsilon Bootis. It is seen as a semicircle of stars. Nothing here save for low-magnitude cluster of galaxies.

Nu Borealis. Binocular double star. Magnitudes: 4.8 and 5.0.

CORVUS

The Crow, a late-March constellation, is identified by its trapezoid configuration. Corvus is small and south of Virgo.

NGC 4027. Magnitude: 11.6. Sc/peculiar galaxy.

NGC 4038. Magnitude: 11.0. S?/peculiar galaxy. The Ring-Tail Galaxy.

CRATER

The Cup, a mid-March constellation, has little to show the binocularist. It contains a trapezium of fourth-magnitude stars.

NGC 3887. Magnitude: 11.6. Sc-type galaxy.

CRUX

The Cross is a constellation seen the end of March. It rests in the Milky Way close to the South Celestial Pole. Clearly marked by its crucifix shape, it is home to the Coalsack Nebula, a dark nebula.

Alpha Crux. Binocular double star. Magnitudes: 1.6 and 5.1.

Gamma Crux. Binocular double star. Magnitudes: 1.5 and 6.5.

Beta Crux. Binocular double star. Magnitudes: 1.5 and 11.

NGC 4755. Magnitude: 6. Open cluster of 50 stars. The Jewel Box.

NGC 4609. Magnitude: 10. Open cluster of 20 stars.

NGC 4439. Magnitude: 11. Open cluster of 15 stars.

CYGNUS

The Swan, or the Northern Cross, is a constellation visible in late July-early August. A glitter of stars, Cygnus sits in a magnificent region of the Milky Way (Fig. A-4). Binocular clusters abound. There are interesting dark nebulae near Alpha and Gamma. Star clouds by the droves.

Beta Cygnus. Binocular double star. Magnitudes: 3.09 (yellow) and 5.11 (blue). Albireo is one of the most popular doubles in the heavens and a good test for $11 \times$ and up binoculars.

Star 16. Binocular double star. Magnitudes: 6.4 and 6.3 (yellow).

Omicron Cygnus. Binocular triple star. Magnitudes: 4 (yellow), 5 (blue), and 6.9.

Gamma Cygnus. Binocular double star. Magnitudes: 2.2 and 9.5.

M29. Magnitude: 7. Open cluster. Triangular shape, with brighter stars forming a small dipper. 7,200 light years away.

M39. Magnitude: 5.4. Galactic cluster of 25 stars. Attractive. 900 light years away.

NGC 6811. Magnitude: 9. Open cluster of 50 stars.

NGC 6819. Magnitude: 10. Open cluster of 150 stars. Difficult to see.

NGC 6866. Magnitude: 8. Open cluster of 50 stars.

NGC 6910. Magnitude: 6.5. Open cluster of 40 stars.

NGC 7082. Magnitude: 10. Open cluster.

NGC 7039. Magnitude: 9. Open cluster. Small group.

NGC 7086. Magnitude: 9. Open cluster of 50 stars.

NGC 7127. Magnitude: 10. Open cluster of 10 stars.

NGC 7128. Magnitude: 9. Open cluster.

NGC 6826. Magnitude: 8.8. Planetary.

NGC 7027. Magnitude: 9. Planetary. Blue-green.

NGC 7000. The North America Nebula. Glow is larger than the Moon. Difficult to see except under the darkest skies.

NGC 6960. The Veil Nebula. Loop shaped, filamentary structure (Fig. A-5). Glow is difficult, 11×80s and above.

I 5067. The Pelican Nebula. Irregular shape and close to 56 Cygni. Curious.

Chi Cygnus. Variable star. 407 days. Magnitude range: 3.3-14.2.

R Cygnus. Variable star. 426 days. Magnitude range: 6.1-14.2.

U Cygnus. Variable star. 130 days. Magnitude range: 6.8-8.9.

Z Cygnus. Variable star. 263 days. Magnitude range: 7.4-14.7.

RT Cygnus. Variable star. 190 days. Magnitude range: 6.4-12.7.

DELPHINUS

The Dolphin is a constellation visible in late July-early August. It sits on the Milky Way's southern border. Close to Aquila, Delphinus is marked by its five main stars.

NGC 6891. Magnitude: 10. Planetary. Difficult to see.

NGC 6934. Magnitude: 9. Globular cluster.

DORADO

The Swordfish is a mid-December constellation which

Fig. A-4. The Milky Way in Cygnus; photographed with a 50mm f/1.4 lens (Photograph by Lee C. Coombs).

Fig. A-5. NGC 6960, The Great Cygnus Loop, a nebula in Cygnus; photographed with a 10-inch reflector (Photograph by Lee C. Coombs).

contains the Greater Magellanic Cloud. It is located at the far South.

LMC. Large Magellanic Cloud. A highly visible, irregular galaxy. Contains the Loop Nebula. Is only 200,000 light years away.

NGC 1549. Magnitude: 11. Galaxy, E1 type.

NGC 1533. Magnitude: 10.2. Galaxy, SO type.

NGC 1566. Magnitude: 10.5. Galaxy, Sb type.

NGC 1672. Magnitude: 11.4. Galaxy, SBb type.

NGC 1714. Magnitude: 10. Planetary.

NGC 1936. Magnitude: 11. Galactic cluster in LMC.

R Dorado. Variable star. 360 days. Magnitude range: 5.7-6.8.

NGC 2070. The Tarantula Nebula. A diffuse nebula in LMC and the largest diffuse nebula. Surrounds Star 30.

DRACO

The Dragon, best viewed in mid-May, is a large constellation that wraps itself around the North Celestial Pole. Located by finding two bright star pairs between Beta Ursa Minor and Vega.

NGC 3147. Magnitude: 11.3. Galaxy, Sb type.

NGC 4125. Magnitude: 11.1. Galaxy, E5/SO type.

NGC 4236. Magnitude: 10.7. Galaxy, SB type.

NGC 5907. Magnitude: 11.0. Galaxy, Sb type.

NGC 6503. Magnitude: 11.0. Galaxy, Sb type.

NGC 6543. Magnitude: 8.6. Planetary nebula with a bluish disk.

Nu Draco. Binocular double star. Magnitudes: 4.9 and 4.9.

Omicron Draco. Binocular double star. Magnitudes: 7.9 and 4.9.

Psi Draco. Binocular double star. Magnitudes: 4.9 and 6.1.

Star 39. Binocular double star. Magnitudes: 5 and 7.

Star 16, 17. Binocular double star. Magnitudes: 5.2 and 5.6.

EQUULEUS

The Little Horse is a tiny, mid-August constellation on the East side of Delphinus. Nothing much here for the binocularist.

Gamma Equuleus. Binocular double star. Magnitudes: 4.5 and 6.0.

ERIDANUS

The River Constellation is best viewed in mid-November.

West of Orion, Eridanus stretches South toward bright Achernar.

Omicron^2. Binocular double star. Magnitudes: 4.5 and 9.7 (yellow). Best viewed in 11×80s and up.

NGC 1084. Magnitude: 11.1. Galaxy, Sc type.

NGC 1187. Magnitude: 11.3. Galaxy, SBc type.

NGC 1232. Magnitude: 10.7. Galaxy, Sc type.

NGC 1291. Magnitude: 10.2. Galaxy, SB type.

NGC 1300. Magnitude: 11.3. Galaxy, SBb type.

NGC 1332. Magnitude: 11.2. Galaxy, E7/SO type.

NGC 1395. Magnitude: 11.3. Galaxy, E3 type.

NGC 1407. Magnitude: 11.4. Galaxy, EO type.

NGC 1637. Magnitude: 11.4. Galaxy, Sc/Pec.

NGC 1535. Magnitude: 9. Planetary nebula. Pale blue.

FORNAX

The Furnace, an October constellation, resides South of Cetus and Eridanus. It offers only a handful of faint galaxies for the binocularist.

NGC 1097. Magnitude: 10.6. Galaxy, SBb type.

NGC 1302. Magnitude: 11.4. Galaxy, SBa type.

NGC 1316. Magnitude: 10.1. Galaxy, SOp type.

NGC 1344. Magnitude: 11.6. Galaxy, E5 type.

NGC 1365. Magnitude: 11.2. Galaxy, SB type.

NGC 1380. Magnitude: 11.4. Galaxy, E7/SO type.

NGC 1398. Magnitude: 10.7. Galaxy, SBb type.

NGC 1399. Magnitude: 10.9. Galaxy, EO type.

NGC 1404. Magnitude: 11.5. Galaxy, E1 type.

GEMINI

The Twins Constellation, famous for its two brightest stars, Castor and Pollux. Located to the Northeast of Orion. This early-January constellation offers its share of fine binocular viewing.

NGC 2129. Magnitude: 8. Open cluster of 50 stars.

NGC 2158. Magnitude: 11. Galactic cluster of 150 stars near M35. Very faint and 16,000 light years away.

M35. Magnitude: 5.5. Open cluster of 120 stars (Fig. A-6). 2200 light years away. Splendid sight.

I 444. Nebulosity around magnitude-7 star (12 Gemini). Faint.

NGC 2266. Magnitude: 11. Open cluster. Difficult to see.

NGC 2304. Magnitude: 10. Galactic cluster of 20 stars.

NGC 2392. Magnitude: 8. Planetary nebula. Blue disk, faint. The Eskimo Nebula. 3,000 light years away.

NGC 2420. Magnitude: 10. Open cluster of 30 stars. Hard to see.

Fig. A-6. M35, an open cluster in Gemini and the ultracompact open cluster NGC 2158; photographed with a 10-inch reflector (Photograph by Lee C. Coombs).

R Gemini. Variable star. 369 days. Magnitude range: 6-14.

S Gemini. Variable star. 293 days. Magnitude range: 8.2-14.7.

T Gemini. Variable star. 287 days. Magnitude range: 8-15.

V Gemini. Variable star. 275 days. Magnitude range: 7.8-14.9.

GRUS

The Crane is a September constellation resting South of the star Fomalhaut in Pisces Austrinus. Little here to entertain.

I 1459. Magnitude: 11.3. Galaxy, E3 type.

NGC 7552. Magnitude: 11.6. Galaxy, SBa type.

HERCULES

This is a mid-June constellation that is large and difficult to see. Possessing no stars brighter than third magnitude, Hercules sits between Corona Borealis and Vega.

M13. Magnitude: 5.7. Globular cluster. Naked-eye and fine object for Northern-Latitude observers. Misty sphere. Largest and brightest globular in the northern skies. 25,000 light years away. 170 light years in diameter.

NGC 6210. Magnitude: 9.7. Planetary nebula. Bluish disk.

NGC 6229. Magnitude: 8.7. Globular cluster.

M92. Magnitude: 6.5. Globular cluster. Bright nucleus. Very bright and large. 28,000 light years away.

Kappa Hercules. Double star. Magnitudes: 5.3 (yellow) and 6.5 (bronze).

Gamma Hercules. Double star. Magnitudes: 3.8 and 9.8.

S Hercules. Variable star. 307 days. Magnitude range: 6.4-13.8.

T Hercules. Variable star. 165 days. Magnitude range: 6.8-13.9.

U Hercules. Variable star. 406 days. Magnitude range: 6.5-13.4.

HOROLOGIUM

The Clock is a mid-November constellation far to the South. Nothing much of interest here for the binocularist.

NGC 1261. Magnitude: 8. Globular cluster. Dim stars.

NGC 1433. Magnitude: 11.4. Galaxy, SBa type.

HYDRA

The Water Monster, a mid-March constellation, rests North of the equator between Canis Minor and Leo and extends South toward Scorpius. This constellation is the largest and longest in the sky.

R Hydra. Variable star. 388 days. Magnitude range: 3-11.

U Hydra. Variable star. 450 days. Magnitude range: 4.5-6.

M48. Magnitude: 5.5. Open cluster of 50 stars. Large, rich, bright, and attractive. Almost circular. Compressed in the center.

NGC 3109. Magnitude: 11.2. Irregular galaxy.

NGC 3242. Magnitude: 8.9. Planetary nebula. Blue disk.

NGC 3585. Magnitude: 11.3. Galaxy, E5/E6 type.

NGC 3621. Magnitude: 10.6. Galaxy, Sc/Sd type.

NGC 3923. Magnitude: 11.1. Galaxy, E4 type.

M68. Magnitude: 8. Globular cluster. Large, rich, and irregularly round with many RR Lyrae variables.

M83. Magnitude: 8. Galaxy, Sc type, bright, large, and face-on. 10 million light years away. Has abnormal frequency of supernova events.

HYDRUS

The Water Snake, a late-October constellation, is a smaller version of Hydra and resides near the South Pole. Nothing much here for the binocularist.

INDUS

The Indian is a mid-August constellation in the mid-South. Nothing much here.

LACERTA

The Lizard is a late-August constellation between Andromeda and Cygnus. Excellent starfields in the Milky Way.

NGC 7209. Magnitude: 9. Open cluster of 50 stars.

NGC 7243. Magnitude: 8. Open cluster of 40 stars.

LEO

The Lion is a zodiacal constellation best viewed in late February. Leo is home to a large number of galaxies. Its brightest star, Regulus, is slightly North of the ecliptic.

Star 93. Binocular double star. Magnitudes: 4.5 and 8.6.

Tau Leo. Binocular double star. Magnitudes: 5.2 and 8.1.

Alpha Leo. Binocular double star. Magnitudes: 1.3 and 7.6. Regulus.

R Leo. Variable star. 312 days. Magnitude range: 4.4-11.3.

M95. Magnitude: 11. Barred spiral galaxy, SBb type. Bright, large, and round gray patch. Brighter toward the nucleus. 25 million light years away.

M96. Magnitude: 10.2. Galaxy, Sb spiral type. Brilliant and large. Nucleus bright. Curious.

M65. Magnitude: 10.3. Galaxy, Sa type. Bright, large, and extended.

M66. Magnitude: 9.7. Galaxy, Sb type with bright nucleus.

M105. Magnitude: 10.6. Galaxy, E1 type. Very bright and round with bright center. Has soft, hazy texture. Difficult to see.

NGC 2903. Magnitude: 9.7. Galaxy, Sb/Sc type.

NGC 3227. Magnitude: 11.6. Galaxy, Sa/Sb type.

NGC 3377. Magnitude: 11.4. Galaxy, E5 type.

NGC 3384. Magnitude: 11. Galaxy, E7/SO type.

NGC 3412. Magnitude: 11.6. Galaxy, E5/SO type.

NGC 3489. Magnitude: 11.3. Galaxy, E6/SO type.

NGC 3521. Magnitude: 10.2. Galaxy, Sb type.

NGC 3607. Magnitude: 11.2. Galaxy, E1/SO type.

NGC 3626. Magnitude: 11.4. Galaxy, Sb/SO type.

NGC 3810. Magnitude: 11.5. Galaxy, Sc type.

LEO MINOR

The Lesser Lion Constellation lies North of Leo and is a small March constellation, offering little for the binocularist.

NGC 3294. Magnitude: 11.6. Galaxy, Sc type.

NGC 3344. Magnitude: 11. Galaxy, Sc type.

NGC 3486. Magnitude: 11.2. Galaxy, Sc type.

NGC 3504. Magnitude: 11.6. Galaxy, Sb type.

LEPUS

The Hare is a mid-December constellation resting South of Orion. Lepus is found by locating its trapezium of stars.

M79. Magnitude: 8.4. Globular cluster. Hazy and compressed. 54,000 light years away.

R Lepus. Variable star. 432 days. Magnitude range: 5.5-10-5. The Crimson Star.

Gamma Lepus. Binocular double star. Magnitudes: 6.4 and 3.8.

LIBRA

The Balance is a mid-May constellation found between Scorpius and Virgo. Not much here.

Alpha Libra. Binocular double star. Magnitudes: 2.7 and 6.

Delta Libra. Eclipsing variable. Magnitude range: 4.9-6. 2 to 3 days.

NGC 5897. Magnitude: 10. Globular cluster. Difficult to see.

LUPUS

The Wolf is a mid-May constellation on the western border of the Milky Way South of Scorpius.

Eta Lupus. Binocular double star. Magnitudes: 3.6 and 9.3.

NGC 5822. Magnitude: 9. Open cluster.

NGC 5986. Magnitude: 8. Globular cluster. Soft glow.

NGC 5593. Magnitude: 10. Open cluster of 10 stars.

NGC 5643. Magnitude: 11.4. Galaxy, SB type.

NGC 5749. Magnitude: 10. Open cluster of 20 stars.

NGC 5824. Magnitude: 9.5. Globular cluster.

NGC 5882. Magnitude: 10.5. Planetary nebula.

NGC 5927. Magnitude: 9. Globular cluster. Hazy soft glow in $11 \times 80s$.

R Lupus. Variable star. 236 days. Magnitude range: 9.4-14.

LYNX

The Lynx is a mid-January northern constellation between Auriga and Ursa Major. Nothing much here.

NGC 2683. Magnitude: 10.6. Galaxy, Sb type.

LYRA

The Lyre, an early-July constellation containing bright Vega, rests in the Milky Way in an area of attractive starfields. It is just about directly overhead if you live in the Northern Latitudes.

Epsilon Lyra. Binocular double star. Magnitudes: 4.5 and 4.68. Known as the Double-double, this pair can be split into four components in telescopes 3 inches and up.

Zeta Lyra. Binocular double star. Magnitudes: 4.29 and 5.87.

Beta Lyra. Binocular double star. Magnitudes: 3.3-4.2 (variable) and 8.6.

Theta Lyra. Binocular double star. Magnitudes: 4.5 and 9.2.

R Lyra. Variable star. 46 days. Magnitude range: 3.8-5.

W Lyra. Variable star. 196 days. Magnitude range: 7.3-13.

M56. Magnitude: 8. Globular cluster between Gamma and Beta. 40,000 light years away. Large, bright, and irregularly round. Looks like a glowing comet.

M57. Magnitude: 9. Planetary nebula. The Ring Nebula. Gray with a greenish tinge.

NGC 6791. Magnitude: 11. Open cluster of 300 stars. Faint, very difficult to see.

MENSA

The Table Constellation, close to the South Pole, is dim. Best seen in late December, Mensa contains a small part of the Great Magellanic Cloud. Nothing much here.

U Mensa. Variable star. 410 days. Magnitude range: 7-10. Semiregular.

NGC 2058. Diffuse nebula. Part of the Great Magellanic Cloud.

MICROSCOPIUM

The Microscope, an early-August constellation, lies East of Sagittarius and South of Capricornus. Dim stars. Nothing for the binocularist.

MONOCEROS

The Unicorn, an early-January constellation, rests in the Milky Way East of Orion. An exciting area!

NGC 2232. Magnitudes: 6-8. Open cluster. Scattered and bright.

NGC 2244. Magnitude: 5.5. Open cluster of 15 stars. Super!

M50. Magnitude: 6. Open cluster of 100 stars. Rich, large, and compressed. 3,000 light years away.

NGC 2215. Magnitude: 11. Open cluster of 25 stars.

NGC 2237. Diffuse nebulosity surrounding NGC 2244. The Rosette Nebula. Formless aura of gray light.

NGC 2251. Magnitude: 10. Open cluster of 25 stars.

NGC 2261. Magnitude: 10. Hubble's Variable Nebula. Illuminated by R Mon. This nebula changes in luminosity.

NGC 2264. Magnitude: 6. Open cluster of 20 stars. Surrounding nebulosity called the Cone Nebula. Curious.

NGC 2301. Magnitude: 6. Open cluster of 60 stars.

NGC 2324. Magnitude: 11. Open cluster of 50 stars.

NGC 2343. Magnitude: 10. Open cluster of 15 stars.

NGC 2353. Magnitude: 10. Open cluster of 20 stars.

NGC 2506. Magnitude: 11. Open cluster of 75 stars.

MUSCA

The Fly is a late-March constellation near Crux in the Milky Way.

NGC 4833. Magnitude: 8.5. Globular cluster.

NGC 4372. Magnitude: 8. Globular cluster. Hard.

NGC 4815. Magnitude: 10. Open cluster of 40 stars.

NORMA

The Square is a mid-May constellation South of Scorpius in a rich area of the Milky Way.

NGC 6067. Magnitude: 10. Open cluster. Difficult to see.

NGC 6087. Magnitude: 7. Open cluster of 40 stars. Contains S Norma, a curious variable star.

S Norma. Variable star (a cepheid variable). 9.75 days. Magnitude range: 6.1-6.8.

NGC 6031. Magnitude: 11. Open cluster of 10 stars.

OCTANS

The Octant, best seen in August, dwells close to the South Pole and can be seen anytime of the year by observers in the Southern Latitudes. Sigma Octans sits only 1 degree from the South Celestial Pole. Very little here for the binocularist.

R Octans. Variable star. 405 days. Magnitude range: 6.6-13.

OPHIUCHUS

The Serpent Bearer is North of Scorpius and is best viewed in mid June. Ophiuchus' southern section resides in a star-rich part of the southern Milky Way.

Star 53. Binocular double star. Magnitudes: 5.8 and 8.5.

Star 67. Binocular double star. Magnitudes: 3.9 and 8.5.

R Ophiuchus. Variable star. 302 days. Magnitude range: 6.2-14.4.

Chi Ophiuchus. Variable star. Irregular. Magnitude range: 4.2-5.

RS Ophiuchus. Variable star. Irregular. Magnitude range: 4.3-12.3.

Star 66. Variable star. Flare star. Magnitude range: 3-5.

X Ophiuchus. Variable star. 335 days. Magnitude range: 5.9-9.2.

M107. Magnitude: 9. Globular cluster. Dim, large, and fairly compressed. 10,000 light years away.

M12. Magnitude: 8. Globular cluster. 16,000 light years away. Bright and oddly round. Brighter toward the center.

M10. Magnitude: 7. Globular cluster. 16,000 light years away. Bright and round.

NGC 6633. Magnitude: 5. Open cluster of 65 stars.

M19. Magnitude: 7. Globular cluster. Bright, large, and oblate. 20,000 light years away. Compressed.

NGC 6235. Magnitude: 10. Globular cluster.

NGC 6284. Magnitude: 10. Globular cluster.

NGC 6287. Magnitude: 10. Globular cluster.

NGC 6293. Magnitude: 8. Globular cluster.

NGC 6304. Magnitude: 9. Globular cluster.

NGC 6316. Magnitude: 10. Globular cluster.

M9. Magnitude: 8. Globular cluster. Bright, oval, and nebulous.

NGC 6342. Magnitude: 11. Globular cluster.

NGC 6355. Magnitude: 10. Globular cluster.

NGC 6356. Magnitude: 8.5. Globular cluster.

H15. Magnitude: 9. Open cluster of 15 stars.

NGC 6401. Magnitude: 11. Globular cluster.

M14. Magnitude: 9. Globular cluster. Brighter toward the center. 23,000 light years away.

I 4665. Magnitude: 6. Open cluster of 20 stars.

NGC 6572. Magnitude: 9. Planetary nebula. Blue-green tint.

ORION

The Hunter, best seen in mid-December, ranks as one of the best and brightest constellations in the heavens. Home of M42, the Great Orion Nebula, this constellation resides along the western border of the Milky Way. Orion is right on the celestial equator.

Delta Orion. Binocular double star. Magnitudes: 2.5 and 6.6.

Zeta Orion. Area of dim nebulosity around this star (Fig. A-7). The Horsehead Nebula is here. For "mammoth" binoculars.

Theta Orion. Binocular double star. Telescopic quadruple star. Magnitudes: 3.8 and 6.5. The Trapezium. In M42, the Great Nebula.

U Orion. Variable star. 374 days. Magnitude range: 5.3-12.6.

S Orion. Variable star. 416 days. Magnitude range: 7.5-13.5.

M42. Magnitude: 5. Diffuse nebula. The Great Orion Nebula. Hazy, bright patch with filaments. Contains Theta Orion. The most spectacular nebula—a

binocular must! In the belt of Orion. A naked-eye birthplace of stars.

NGC 1981. Magnitude: 8. Open cluster of 10 stars.

M43. Detached from M42. Looks like a faint, soft, glowing comet.

M78. Magnitude: 8. Diffuse nebula. Irregular.

H.V. 28. Faint nebulosity. Part of M42.

NGC 2169. Magnitude: 8. Open cluster of 20 stars.

NGC 2194. Magnitude: 9. Open cluster of 100 stars.

PAVO

The Peacock, best viewed in mid-July, is small and far South. Not much to offer.

Y Pavo. Variable star. 233 days. Magnitude range: 5.7-8.5.

NGC 6752. Magnitude: 7. Globular cluster. Huge.

NGC 6744. Magnitude: 10.6. Galaxy, SBc type.

PEGASUS

An August-September constellation, Pegasus is easily found by its Great Square—Alpheraz, Algenib, Markab, and Scheat—which is west of Andromeda.

R Pegasus. Variable star. 378 days. Magnitude range: 6.9-13.8.

Beta Pegasus. Variable star with irregular period of about 35 days. Magnitude range: 2.4-2.9.

T Pegasus. Variable star. 373 days. Magnitude range: 8.7-15.4.

W Pegasus. Variable star. 344 days. Magnitude range: 7.9-13.0.

Epsilon Pegasus. Binocular double star. Magnitudes: 2.5 and 8.5.

Z Pegasus. Variable star. 325 days. Magnitude range: 7.7-13.

P Pegasus. Binocular double star. Magnitudes: 4.5 and 6.

RS Pegasus. Variable star. 412 days. Magnitudes: 8.2-14.6.

M15. Magnitude: 6.5. Globular cluster. Bright and large. 40,000 light years away. Somewhat nebulous.

NGC 7217. Magnitude: 11.3. Galaxy, Sb type.

NGC 7331. Magnitude: 10.4. Galaxy, Sb type.

NGC 7772. Magnitude: 11. Open cluster of 7 stars. Difficult to see.

PERSEUS

Dwelling in the Milky Way's rich starfields, Perseus is an early-November constellation surrounded by An-

Fig. A-7. The region around Zeta Orionis contains The Horsehead Nebula and the nebulosity NGC 2024. These are targets for Cainian mammoth binoculars; photographed with a 12-inch f/5 Astromak (Photograph by Jim Riffle).

dromeda, Auriga, and Cassiopeia.

Star 57. Binocular double star. Magnitudes: 6.8 (yellow) and 6.1.

B Perseus. Variable star (Algol-the Demon star). 2.8 days. Magnitude range: 2.0-3.3. This eclipsing variable is curious! A must!

R Perseus. Variable star. 210 days. Magnitude range: 8.1-14.8.

U Perseus. Variable star. 321 days. Magnitude range: 7.4-12.3.

M34. Magnitude: 6. Open cluster of 80 stars. Compressed, large, and bright. 1,400 light years away. Attractive.

M76. Magnitude: 11. Planetary nebula. Little Dumbell. A difficult nebulous blur. 3,400 light years away.

NGC 869. Magnitude: 7. Open cluster. Part of the Double Cluster. 400 stars. Beautiful. A binocular must.

NGC 884. Magnitude: 7. Open cluster. Part of the Double Cluster. 300 stars. Highly pleasing to the eye.

NGC 957. Magnitude: 11. Open cluster of 40 stars. Difficult to see.

NGC 1023. Magnitude: 11. Galaxy, E7/Pec. type.

NGC 1220. Magnitude: 11. Open cluster of 25 stars. Hard to see.

NGC 1245. Magnitude: 9. Open cluster of 100 stars, misty patch.

NGC 1342. Magnitude: 9. Open cluster of 50 stars, scattered.

I 351. Magnitude: 11. Planetary nebula. Difficult to see.

NGC 1513. Magnitude: 9. Open cluster of 40 stars.

NGC 1528. Magnitude: 6. Open cluster of 80 stars.

NGC 1499. California Nebula, a diffuse nebula (Fig. A-8). Barely discernible in battleship binoculars.

Fig. A-8. NGC 1499, The California Nebula, an emission nebula in Perseus; photographed with a 12-inch f/5 Astromak (Photograph by Jim Riffle).

Hazy. You need dark and clear skies for this one.

PHOENIX

An early-October constellation in the mid-South, Phoenix rests between Eridanus and Grus. Nothing much here.

Zeta Phoenix. Variable star. 1.67 days (eclipsing binary). Magnitude range: 3.9-4.4.

PICTOR

The Painter, a mid-December constellation, lies near the bright star Canopus. Nothing here for the binocularist.

PISCES

The Fishes, a late-September constellation in the zodiac, is large, is not particularly bright, and resides South of Andromeda and the Square of Pegasus.

Psi Pisces. Binocular double star. Magnitudes: 4.9 and 5.

Kappa Pisces. Binocular double star. Magnitudes: 5 and 6.

M74. Magnitude: 11. Galaxy, Sc type. Face-on spiral looking much like a globular cluster or hazy patch. 20 million light years away.

NGC 488. Magnitude: 11.2. Galaxy, Sb type.

R Pisces. Variable star. 344 days. Magnitude range: 7.1-14.8.

S Pisces. Variable star. 405 days. Magnitude range: 8.2-15.3.

T Pisces. Variable star. 260 days. Magnitude range: 9.2-12.3. Recurrent nova.

Y Pisces. Variable star. 3.7 days. Magnitude range: 9-12.

PISCES AUSTRINUS

The Southern Fish, best viewed in late August, is a mid-southern constellation distinguished by 1.2 magnitude Fomalhaut. Nothing here for the binocularist.

PUPPIS

The Poop, a mid-southern constellation, is best seen in early January. It can be found to the East of Canis Major.

Kappa Puppis. Binocular double star. Magnitudes: 4.5 and 4.6 (both yellow).

L² Puppis. Variable star. 140 days. Magnitude range: 3.4-6.2.

M46. Magnitude: 8. Open cluster of 150 stars. Rich and circular cloud 54,000 light years away. Contains NGC 2438.

M93. Magnitude: 8. Open cluster of 50 stars. Bright. 3,400 light years away.

M47. Magnitude: 5. Open cluster of 25 stars. 1 1/2 degrees West of M46. Bright. 1,780 light years away.

NGC 2298. Magnitude: 10. Globular cluster.

NGC 2421. Magnitude: 11. Open cluster of 60 stars. Difficult to see.

Mel 71. Magnitude: 10. Open cluster of 65 stars. Hard to see.

NGC 2439. Magnitude: 9. Open cluster of 50 stars.

NGC 2438. Magnitude: 11. Planetary nebula in M46. Difficult to see.

NGC 2477. Magnitude: 11. Open cluster of 300 stars. Hazy.

H2. Magnitude: 11. Open cluster of 20 stars.

NGC 2489. Magnitude: 11. Open cluster of 35 stars.

NGC 2509. Magnitude: 10. Open cluster of 40 stars.

NGC 2527. Magnitude: 11. Open cluster of 40 stars.

NGC 2539. Magnitude: 11. Open cluster of 100 stars.

NGC 2546. Magnitude: 9. Open cluster of 50 stars.

NGC 2567. Magnitude: 11. Open cluster of 50 stars.

NGC 2571. Magnitude: 9. Open cluster of 25 stars.

NGC 2587. Magnitude: 9. Open cluster of 30 stars.

NGC 2467. Nebulosity surrounding Magnitude-8 star. Hazy glow.

PYXIS

The Compass, an early-February constellation, is in the southern skies East of Puppis.

NGC 2613. Magnitude: 10.9. Galaxy, Sb type, almost edge-on.

NGC 2627. Magnitude: 11. Open cluster of 70 stars.

S Pyxis. Variable star. 207 days. Magnitude range: 8.1-13.

T Pyxis. Variable star. Recurrent nova. Magnitude range: 7-14.5.

V Pyxis. Variable star. 70 days. Magnitude range: 8.5-11.

RETICULUM

The Net, a mid-November constellation, is found between Canopus and Achernar. Not much here.

NGC 1313. Magnitude: 10.8. Galaxy, SB type.

NGC 1559. Magnitude: 11.1. Galaxy, SB type.

SAGITTA

The Arrow, a small mid-northern group that is best viewed in mid-July, sits North of Aquila. This is an outstanding section of the Milky Way.

R Sagitta. Variable star. 7 days. Magnitude range: 8.5-10.4.

S Sagitta. Variable star (Cepheid). 8.382 days. Magnitude range: 5.5-6.2.

T Sagitta. Variable star. 165 days. Magnitude range: 8.5-10.

U Sagitta. Variable star. Eclipsing binary. 3.381 days. Magnitude range: 6.4-9.

Epsilon Sagitta. Binocular double star. Magnitudes: 8 (yellow) and 5.7.

Theta Sagitta. Binocular double star. Magnitudes: 7.3 and 6.3.

M71. Magnitude: 9. Globular cluster. Large, faint, compressed, and nebulous. 8,500 light years away.

NGC 6879. Magnitude: 11. Planetary nebula. Difficult to see.

NGC 6886. Magnitude: 11. Planetary nebula. Very hard to see.

I 4997. Magnitude: 11. Planetary nebula. Difficult to see.

H20. Magnitude: 11. Open cluster of 20 stars. Hard to see.

SAGITTARIUS

The Archer, an early-July constellation, resides in the zodiac close to Scorpius and Ophiuchus. Near our Galaxy's center, Sagittarius (Fig. A-9) offers some of the finest viewing in the heavens. King of the mid-South constellations. You could spend a lifetime observing here!

X Sagittarius. Variable star (Cepheid). 7 days. Magnitude range: 4.8-5.6.

W Sagittarius. Variable star (Cepheid). 7.6 days. Magnitude range: 4.8-5.8.

RR Sagittarius. Variable star. 334 days. Magnitude range: 5.6-14.

M20. Diffuse nebula. Magnitude: 9. The Triffid. Large and bright. Shines by the light of a double star. 2,200 light years away.

M23. Magnitude: 7. Open cluster of 100 stars. Large and rich. 4,500 light years away. Super!

M8. Magnitude: 5. Diffuse nebula. The Lagoon. Glowing nebulous patch—can be seen naked-eye. Large with irregular shape. 3,000 light years away. Magnificent.

M17. Magnitude: 6. Diffuse nebula (Fig. A-10). The Omega Nebula. Sometimes called the Swan. In an open cluster. Large, bright, and irregular.

M18. Magnitude: 8. Open cluster of 12 stars . 6,000 light years away. Small.

M24. Magnitude: 11.4. Open cluster of 50 stars. In a brilliant Milky Way starfield. Wonderful. Very compressed.

M25. Magnitude: 6. Open cluster of 50 stars. 2,000 light years away. Compressed.

M28. Magnitude: 8. Globular cluster. Very bright, large, and round. 15,000 light years away.

M22. Magnitude: 6. Globular cluster. Among the finest visual globulars. 10,000 light years away.

M55. Magnitude: 7. Globular cluster. Nebulous patch. 20,000 light years away.

M54. Magnitude: 9. Globular cluster. Bright and round. 50,000 light years away.

M75. Magnitude: 8. Globular cluster. Large, bright glow. 100,000 light years away.

M21. Magnitude: 9. Open cluster of 50 stars. Close to M20. Attractive, rich. 3,000 light years away.

M69. Magnitude: 7.5. Globular cluster. Bright and nebulous.

M70. Magnitude: 8. Globular cluster. 65,000 light years away.

NGC 6822. Magnitude: 11. Irregular galaxy. NGC 6818 in the same field.

NGC 6818. Magnitude: 10. Planetary nebula. Greenish.

NGC 6723. Magnitude: 6. Globular cluster. Bright and round.

NGC 6652. Magnitude: 8.5. Globular cluster.

NGC 6645. Magnitude: 9. Open cluster of 75 stars.

NGC 6642. Magnitude: 8. Globular cluster.

NGC 6638. Magnitude: 9.5. Globular cluster.

NGC 6629. Magnitude: 10.5. Planetary nebula.

NGC 6624. Magnitude: 8.5. Globular cluster.

NGC 6569. Magnitude: 10. Globular cluster.

NGC 6568. Magnitude: 11. Open cluster of 30 stars.

NGC 6558. Magnitude: 11. Globular cluster.

NGC 6553. Magnitude: 10. Globular cluster.

NGC 6546. Magnitude: 11. Open cluster. Scattered.

NGC 6544. Magnitude: 9. Globular cluster.

NGC 6528. Magnitude: 11. Globular cluster.

NGC 6530. Magnitude: 7. Open cluster of 25 stars in M8.

NGC 6522. Magnitude: 10.5. Globular cluster.

NGC 6520. Magnitude: 9. Open cluster of 25 stars.

B86. Dark nebula bordering NGC 6520.

Fig. A-9. The Milky Way in Sagittarius; photographed with a 150mm f/4 lens (Photograph by Lee C. Coombs).

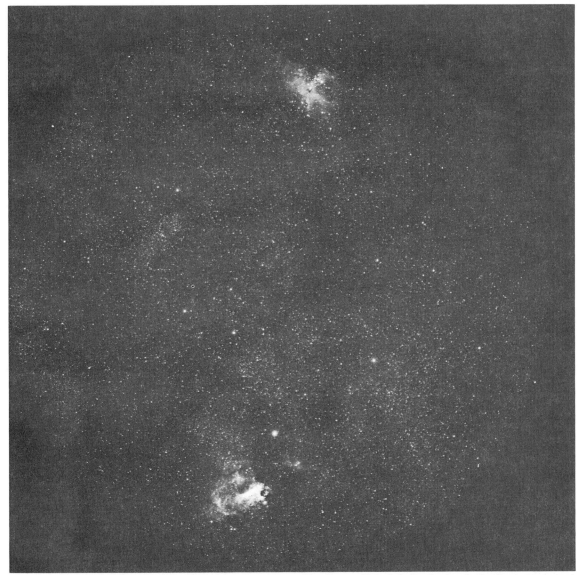

Fig. A-10. M16, The Eagle Nebula in Serpens (top) and M17, The Omega Nebula in Sagittarius (bottom); photographed with a 12-inch f/5 Astromak (Photograph by Jim Riffle).

NGC 6440. Magnitude: 10. Globular cluster. Difficult to see.

SCORPIUS

The Scorpion is a zodiacal constellation best observed in early June. Antares, Scorpius' bright (0.9-magnitude) orange star, immediately attracts your attention to this constellation. The Scorpion's tail hangs low on the horizon and is difficult, if not impossible, to see from some Northern Latitudes. This constellation offers much to the binocularist.

Omega Scorpius. Binocular double star. Magnitudes: 4 and 4.

Nu Scorpius. Binocular double star. Magnitudes: 6.5 and 4.4.

Alpha Scorpius. Antares, a red giant. Variable over 5 years. Magnitude range: 0.9-1.8.

RR Scorpius. Variable star. 279 days. Magnitude range: 5-12.4.

RT Scorpius. Variable star. 449 days. Magnitude range: 7-16.

RV Scorpius. Variable star. 6 days. Magnitude range: 6.6-7.5.

M4. Magnitude: 6.5. Globular cluster (Fig. A-11). 1.3 degrees West of Antares. 10,000 light years away. Circular glow.

M6. Magnitude: 6. Open cluster of 50 stars. Dense, cloudy, magnificent! 2,000 light years away.

M7. Magnitude: 5. Open cluster of 50 stars. Naked-eye, easy to see. 800 light years away.

M80. Magnitude: 8. Globular cluster. Bright nebulous patch. 36,000 light years away.

M62. Magnitude: 6.5. Globular cluster. Irregular outline. Soft and glowing.

NGC 6124. Magnitude: 8. Open cluster of 100 stars.

NGC 6144. Magnitude: 10. Globular cluster. Faint blur.

NGC 6139. Magnitude: 10. Globular cluster. Hard to see.

NGC 6178. Magnitude: 8. Open cluster of 12 stars.

NGC 6192. Magnitude: 11. Open cluster of 75 stars.

NGC 6227. Rich Milky Way starfield.

NGC 6231. Magnitude: 6. Open cluster of 100 stars. A mix of bright and faint stars. Magnificent.

NGC 6242. Magnitude: 8. Open cluster of 45 stars.

NGC 6259. Magnitude: 11. Open cluster of 100 stars. Difficult to see.

NGC 6268. Magnitude: 10. Open cluster of 30 stars.

NGC 6281. Magnitude: 9. Open cluster of 25 stars.

NGC 6388. Magnitude: 7. Globular cluster.

H16. Magnitude: 10. Open cluster of 20 stars.

NGC 6400. Magnitude: 9. Open cluster of 25 stars.

H17. Magnitude: 10. Open cluster of 20 stars.

NGC 6425. Magnitude: 11. Open cluster of 15 stars.

NGC 6441. Magnitude: 8. Globular cluster.

NGC 6451. Magnitude: 10. Open cluster of 50 stars.

NGC 6453. Magnitude: 11. Globular cluster. Near M7.

NGC 6496. Magnitude: 10. Globular cluster.

NGC H18. Magnitude: 10. Open cluster of 80 stars.

NGC 6416. Open cluster of faint stars. Powdery. Difficult to see.

H12. Open cluster of 200 stars. Quite attractive.

NGC 6334. Field of dim nebulosity.

SCULPTOR

The Sculptor, a mid-South constellation best seen in late September, resides South of Aquarius and Cetus and is dim.

NGC 55. Magnitude: 7.8. Galaxy, I or SBp type.

NGC 253. Magnitude: 7. Galaxy, Sc type (Fig. A-12).

NGC 7793. Magnitude: 9.7. Galaxy, Sd type. Large oval galaxy.

NGC 134. Magnitude: 11.4. Galaxy, Sb/Sc type.

NGC 288. Magnitude: 7.2. Globular cluster.

NGC 300. Magnitude: 11.3. Galaxy, Sc/Sd type.

NGC 613. Magnitude: 11.1. Galaxy, SBc type.

R Sculptor. Variable star. 363 days. Magnitude range: 6.1-8.8.

S Sculptor. Variable star. 366 days. Magnitude range: 6.2-13.5.

T Sculptor. Variable star. 201 days. Magnitude range: 8.5-13.5.

SCUTUM

The Shield is best observed in late June and early July and resides in a star-rich portion of the Milky Way. Scutum is tucked between Aquila and Sagittarius. Lots of interesting binocular objects can be found here. Scutum is also a good hunting ground for novae.

R Scutum. Variable star. 140 days. Magnitude range: 4.8-6.5.

S Scutum. Variable star. 148 days. Magnitude range: 7.3-9.

M11. Magnitude: 6. Open cluster of 200 stars (Fig. A-13). The Wild Duck Cluster. Fan-shaped and magnificent. 6,000 light years away.

M26. Magnitude: 9.5. Open cluster of 25 stars. Large, rich, and compressed with a mix of bright and faint stars. 5,000 light years away.

NGC 6682. Milky Way star condensation. Rich star cloud.

NGC 6683. Milky Way star condensation. The Scutum Star Cloud.

NGC 6712. Magnitude: 9. Globular cluster.

NGC 6649. Magnitude: 9. Open cluster of 35 stars.

NGC 6664. Magnitude: 9. Open cluster of 25 stars.

SERPENS

The Serpent is a constellation that is visible in late May-

Fig. A-11. M4, a globular cluster in Scorpius; photographed with a 10-inch reflector (Photograph by Lee C. Coombs).

Fig. A-12. NGC 253, a spiral galaxy (top), and NGC 288, a globular cluster in Sculptor (bottom); photographed with a 12-inch f/5 Astromak (Photograph by Jim Riffle).

early June. It consists of two star groups: Serpens Cauda (the body) and Serpens Caput (the head). Serpens Cauda sits to the East of Ophiuchus and Serpens Caput sits to the West.

R Serpens. Variable star. 357 days. Magnitude range: 5.7-14.

S Serpens. Variable star. 368 days. Magnitude range: 7.7-14.1.

T Serpens. Variable star. 340 days. Magnitude range: 9.1-15.

M5. Magnitude: 6.2. Globular cluster. One of the finest in the heavens. Extremely compressed. 30,000 light years away.

NGC 6535. Magnitude: 11. Globular cluster. Difficult to see.

M16. Magnitude: 6.5. Open cluster with nebulos-

Fig. A-13. M11, a compact open cluster in Scutum; photographed with a 10-inch reflector (Photograph by Lee C. Coombs).

ity. Scattered 100 stars both bright and faint. 7,000 light years away. Highly attractive.

I 4756. Magnitude: 7. Open cluster of 80 stars.

SEXTANS

The Sextant is a faint, late-February constellation South of Leo. Not much here for the binocularist.

S Sextans. Variable star. 261 days. Magnitude range: 8.3-13.

W Sextans. Variable star. 40 days. Magnitude range: 9-10.

NGC 3115. Magnitude: 10. Galaxy, E7/SO type. The Spindle Nebula.

NGC 3166. Magnitude: 11.5. Galaxy, Sa type.

NGC 3169. Magnitude: 11.4. Galaxy, Sb type.

TAURUS

The Bull, a zodiacal constellation best seen in December, can be found North of the celestial equator and is marked by the bright red star Aldebaran (magnitude: 0.8). Taurus is home of the Hyades and Pleiades star clusters.

Phi Taurus. Binocular double star. Magnitudes: 5.1 (yellow) and 8.5.

Tau Taurus. Binocular double star. Magnitudes: 4.3 and 8.6.

Y Taurus. Variable star. 4 days. Magnitude range: 3.5-4.

Lambda Taurus. Variable star. Eclipsing binary. 3.95 days. Magnitude range: 3.4-4.1.

R Taurus. Variable star. 324 days. Magnitude range: 8.1-14.7.

T Taurus. Variable star. Irregular. Magnitude range: 9.4-13.

NGC 1435. Nebulosity surrounding 23 Tauri (Merope) in the Pleiades. Can be detected with 11×80s under excellent conditions.

M45. Ultrabright open cluster. The Pleiades. Small dipper shape with some nebulosity surrounding its stars. Nebulosity can be detected with battleship binoculars under best-sky conditions.

M1. Magnitude: 9. The Crab Nebula. Appears as grayish patch. A supernova remnant. 6,000 light years away.

Hyades. An open cluster of very bright stars at the head of the Bull. V-shaped with close to 200 stars. Easy to locate naked-eye. Aldebaran is not a true member of this cluster.

NGC 1647. Magnitude: 6.5. Open cluster of 25 stars.

NGC 1746. Magnitude: 6. Open cluster of 50 stars.

NGC 1758. Part of the Open cluster, NGC 1746.

NGC 1807. Magnitude: 7.5. Open cluster of 15 stars.

NGC 1817. Magnitude: 8. Open cluster of 50 stars.

TELESCOPIUM

The Telescope stands South of Sagittarius and is best viewed in mid-July. Nothing much here for the binocularist.

Delta Telescopium. Binocular double star. Magnitudes: 5 and 5.

R Telescopium. Variable star. 462 days. Magnitude range: 7.8-14.

U Telescopium. Variable star. 445 days. Magnitude range: 8.8-12.

NGC 6584. Magnitude: 8.5. Globular cluster.

TRIANGULUM

The Triangle, a mid-northern constellation best seen in late October, lies South of Andromeda. Triangulum's three main stars form an elongated triangle.

M33. Magnitude: 6.5. Galaxy, Sc type (Fig. A-14). The Pinwheel Galaxy. Needs dark and highly transparent skies. Appears as glowing patch. Has low surface brightness. A member of the local group. 2.3 million light years away.

NGC 672. Magnitude: 11.6. Galaxy, SBc type.

R Triangulum. Variable star. 462 days. Magnitude range: 7.8-14.

T Triangulum. Variable star. 256 days. Magnitude range: 9.9-12.

U Triangulum. Variable star. 445 days. Magnitude range: 8.8-12.

TRIANGULUM AUSTRALE

The Southern Triangle, best viewed in late May, is a South circumpolar constellation residing in the Milky Way. Some fine starfields.

R Triangulum Australe. Variable star (Cepheid). 3.389 days. Magnitude range: 6-6.8.

S Triangulum Australe. Variable star (Cepheid). 6.323 days. Magnitude range: 6.1-6.7.

W Triangulum Australe. Variable star. 249 days. Magnitude range: 8.1-11.

NGC 6025. Magnitude: 6. Open cluster of 30 stars.

TUCANA

The Toucan is a mid-September constellation flying in

Fig. A-14. M33, a face-on spiral galaxy in Triangulum; photographed with a Canada-France-Hawaii 144-inch reflector at Mauna Kea (Photograph by Canada-France-Hawaii Telescope Corporation).

the far South. Here lies the Small Magellanic Cloud.

Beta Tucana. Binocular double star. Magnitudes: 4.5 and 4.5.

NGC 292. Magnitude: 1.5. Galaxy, irregular type. The Small Magellanic Cloud or Nebecula Minor. A Milky Way satellite galaxy possessing a great many curious open and globular clusters, as well as nebulosities and variables. 200,000 light years away. A binocular must! A large misty cloud easily seen by the naked eye.

NGC 104. Magnitude: 4.5. Globular cluster. 47 Tucanae. Spectacular!

NGC 362. Magnitude: 6. Globular cluster.

S Tucana. Variable star. 241 days. Magnitude range: 8.7-14.

T Tucana. Variable star. 250 days. Magnitude range: 7.7-13.8.

URSA MAJOR

The Great Bear is a mid-March constellation forming a dipperlike pattern in the northern heavens. Also known as the Big Dipper and the Plough, Ursa Major proves a fine hunting ground for dim galaxies. A straight line through Alpha and Beta serves as a pointer to Polaris, the Pole Star.

Zeta Ursa Major. Naked-eye double star (Mizar and Alcor). Magnitudes: 2.3 and 4. A binocular will reveal a magnitude-8 star between them.

R Ursa Major. Variable star. 301 days. Magnitude range: 6.7-13.4.

S Ursa Major. Variable star. 226 days. Magnitude range: 7-12.4.

T Ursa Major. Variable star. 256 days. Magnitude range: 6.6-13.4.

M81. Magnitude: 8. Galaxy, Sa/Sb type. Bright and large, brighter toward nucleus. 7 million light years away.

M82. Magnitude: 9.2. Galaxy, Ip type. Irregular shape in the same field with M81.

M97. Magnitude: 11. Planetary nebula. The Owl Nebula. Difficult to see. Oval, gray shape. A real test for 20× binoculars under the darkest skies.

M101. Magnitude: 9. Galaxy, Sc type (Fig. A-15). Good hunting ground for supernovae. Irregularly round and somewhat large. 15 million light years away.

Fig. A-15. M101, an (Sc) galaxy in Ursa Major; photographed with a Kitt Peak 4-meter reflector (Courtesy National Optical Astronomy Observatories).

NGC 2681. Magnitude: 11.3. Galaxy, SO/Sa type.
NGC 2768. Magnitude: 11.6. Galaxy, E5 type.
NGC 2841. Magnitude: 10.3. Galaxy, Sb type.
NGC 2976. Magnitude: 10.8. Galaxy, Sc/Sd Irr.
NGC 2985. Magnitude: 11.3. Galaxy, Sa/Sb type.
NGC 3079. Magnitude: 11.4. Galaxy, SBb type.
NGC 3077. Magnitude: 11. Galaxy, E2/Ip type.
NGC 3184. Magnitude: 10.5. Galaxy, Sc type.
NGC 3198. Magnitude: 11. Galaxy, Sc type.
NGC 3310. Magnitude: 11. Galaxy, I/Sc type.
NGC 3359. Magnitude: 11. Galaxy, SBc type.
NGC 3556. Magnitude: 10.8. Galaxy, Sc type.
NGC 3610. Magnitude: 11.6. Galaxy, E4 type.
NGC 3631. Magnitude: 11.5. Galaxy, Sc type.
NGC 3726. Magnitude: 11.3. Galaxy, Sc type.
NGC 3893. Magnitude: 11. Galaxy, Sc type.
NGC 3938. Magnitude: 11.2. Galaxy, Sc type.
NGC 3941. Magnitude: 11.3. Galaxy, E3/SO type.
NGC 3949. Magnitude: 11.5. Galaxy, Sb/Sc type.
NGC 3953. Magnitude: 11.1. Galaxy, SBb type.
NGC 3992. Magnitude: 10.9. Galaxy, SBb type.
NGC 3998. Magnitude: 11.6. Galaxy, E2/SO type.
NGC 4036. Magnitude: 11.6. Galaxy, E6/SO type.
NGC 4051. Magnitude: 11.2. Galaxy, Sb/Sc type.
NGC 4088. Magnitude: 11.1. Galaxy, Sb/Sc type.
NGC 4096. Magnitude: 11.5. Galaxy, Sc type.
NGC 4111. Magnitude: 11.6. Galaxy, E7 type.
NGC 5322. Magnitude: 11.3. Galaxy, E2/E3 type.
NGC 5474. Magnitude: 11.5. Galaxy, I/Sc/pec. type.
NGC 5585. Magnitude: 11.6. Galaxy, Sc/Sd type.

URSA MINOR

The Little Bear, best observed in June, is a North circumpolar constellation. Polaris is located here. Not much for the binocularist in this area.

Alpha Ursa Minor. Magnitude: 2. Polaris (the North Star or the Pole Star).
R Ursa Minor. Variable star. 324 days. Magnitude range: 8.7-11.
S Ursa Minor. Variable star. 327 days. Magnitude range: 7.8-15.
T Ursa Minor. Variable star. 314 days. Magnitude range: 8.5-15.

VELA

The Sails Constellation is best viewed in mid-February in the Milky Way, East of Puppis and North of Carina. A few fine starfields here.

S Vela. Variable star. Eclipsing binary. 5.93 days. Magnitude range: 7.7-9.5.
Z Vela. Variable star. 422 days. Magnitude range: 7.9-11.4.
RW Vela. Variable star. 452 days. Magnitude range: 7.8-12.
NGC 2547. Magnitude: 5.5. Open cluster of 50 stars.
NGC 2659. Magnitude: 9.5. Open cluster of 50 stars.
NGC 2660. Magnitude: 11. Open cluster of 25 stars.
I 2395. Magnitude: 6. Open cluster of 16 stars.
NGC 2671. Magnitude: 10. Open cluster of 25 stars.
NGC 2670. Magnitude: 9. Open cluster of 20 stars.
H3. Magnitude: 6. Open cluster of 35 stars.
I 2488. Magnitude: 7. Open cluster of 50 stars.
NGC 2910. Magnitude: 8. Open cluster of 30 stars.
NGC 2925. Magnitude: 8. Open cluster of 30 stars.
NGC 3105. Magnitude: 11. Open cluster of 15 stars.
NGC 3132. Magnitude: 8.2. Planetary nebula. The Eight Burst.
NGC 3201. Magnitude: 8.5. Globular cluster.
NGC 3228. Magnitude: 6.5. Open cluster of 25 stars.

VIRGO

The Virgin, a zodiacal constellation on the celestial equator, is best observed in mid-April. Virgo's most prominent star is the first-magnitude, blue-white Spica. Galaxies abound and many of them are suitable for the binocularist (Fig. A-16). Virgo is between Leo and Libra.

S Virgo. Variable star. 377 days. Magnitude range: 6.3-13.2.
U Virgo. Variable star. 207 days. Magnitude range: 7.5-13.5.
RS Virgo. Variable star. 353 days. Magnitude range: 7-14.4.
SS Virgo. Variable star. 359 days. Magnitude range: 5.9-10.
Tau Virgo. Binocular double star. Magnitudes: 4.3 and 9.6. 10× and up required.
M84. Magnitude: 10.5. Galaxy, E1 type. In the heart of the Virgo cluster. Looks like an unresolved globular. 40 million light years away.
M86. Magnitude: 10.5. Galaxy, E3 type. Pale glow, brighter toward the nucleus. Almost half the distance away from us as M84.

Fig. A-16. The Virgo Cluster of Galaxies; photographed with a 12-inch f/5 Astromak (Photograph by Jim Riffle).

M90. Magnitude: 11.1. Galaxy, Sb type. Difficult to see. Hazy glow. Bright nucleus.

M49. Magnitude: 10.1. Galaxy, E3/E4 type. 70 million light years away. Bright, round, featureless glow.

M59. Magnitude: 11. Galaxy, E3/E4 type. Small, indistinct gray glow that is brighter toward the core. A little over 40 million light years away.

M60. Magnitude: 10. Galaxy, E1/E2 type. Looks like a hazy star. Intrinsic luminosity equals almost 300 million suns.

M61. Magnitude: 10.2. Galaxy, Sc type. Large and fairly bright. Starlike nucleus.

M89. Magnitude: 11. Galaxy, EO type. Small, yet bright. Brighter toward the nucleus.

M58. Magnitude: 10.5. Galaxy, Sb type. Bright, fairly large, and round.

M104. Magnitude: 8.2. Galaxy, Sa/Sb type. Sombrero Galaxy. 37 million light years away. Curious sliver of pale light.

M87. Magnitude: 10.1. Galaxy, E1p type. Bright, round, and featureless. A radio source.

NGC 4030. Magnitude: 11.2. Galaxy, Sb/Sc type.

NGC 4216. Magnitude: 10.9. Galaxy, Sb type.

NGC 4365. Magnitude: 11. Galaxy, E2/E3 type.

NGC 4429. Magnitude: 11.3. Galaxy, SO/Sa type.

NGC 4438. Magnitude: 11. Galaxy, Sa/Pec type.

NGC 4442. Magnitude: 11.6. Galaxy, E5/SO type.

NGC 4473. Magnitude: 11.3. Galaxy, E4/E5 type.

NGC 4517. Magnitude: 11.4. Galaxy, Sc type.

NGC 4526. Magnitude: 10.7. Galaxy, E7/SO type.

NGC 4527. Magnitude: 11.3. Galaxy, Sb/Sc type.

NGC 4535. Magnitude: 10.7. Galaxy, SBc type.

NGC 4536. Magnitude: 11. Galaxy, Sc/SBc type.

NGC 4546. Magnitude: 11.4. Galaxy, E6/SO type.

NGC 4636. Magnitude: 10.8. Galaxy, E1 type.

NGC 4643. Magnitude: 11.6. Galaxy, SBa type.

NGC 4654. Magnitude: 11.2. Galaxy, Sc type.

NGC 4666. Magnitude: 11.4. Galaxy, Sc type.

NGC 4697. Magnitude: 10.5. Galaxy, E5 type.

NGC 4699. Magnitude: 10.3. Galaxy, Sa/Sb type.

NGC 4753. Magnitude: 10.6. Galaxy, Ep/I type.

NGC 4775. Magnitude: 11.6. Galaxy, Sc type.

NGC 4856. Magnitude: 11.4. Galaxy, SBa type.

NGC 4902. Magnitude: 11.6. Galaxy, SBb type.

NGC 4958. Magnitude: 11.5. Galaxy, E6/SO type.

NGC 5068. Magnitude: 11.6. Galaxy, SBc type.

NGC 5363. Magnitude: 11.1. Galaxy, I/Ep type.

NGC 5364. Magnitude: 11.5. Galaxy, Sb type.

NGC 5566. Magnitude: 11.4. Galaxy, SB type.

NGC 5634. Magnitude: 10. Globular cluster.

NGC 5846. Magnitude: 11.5. Galaxy, EO type.

VOLANS

The Flying Fish, a late-July constellation, is far South and dwells between the Large Magellanic Cloud and Carina. Nothing much here.

R Volans. Variable star. 448 days. Magnitude range: 8.7-13.9.

S Volans. Variable star. 396 days. Magnitude range: 7.7-13.8.

T Volans. Variable star. 176 days. Magnitude range: 8.5-12.

VULPECULA

The Fox, best viewed in late July, is a mid-northern constellation residing in the Milky Way. It possesses few bright stars and can be found between Cygnus and Sagitta.

R Vulpecula. Variable star. 137 days. Magnitude range: 7.4-13.7.

S Vulpecula. Variable star. 69 days. Magnitude range: 9.2-10.8.

T Vulpecula. Variable star (cepheid). 4.4356 days. Magnitude range: 5.4-6.1.

M27. Magnitude: 8. Planetary nebula. The Dumbell Nebula. Large, gray glow with greenish tinge. 1,250 light years away.

C399. Naked-eye open cluster. Scattered.

NGC 6800. Magnitude: 10. Open cluster of 25 stars.

NGC 6802. Magnitude: 11. Open cluster of 60 stars. Bar shaped.

NGC 6815. Scattered starfield.

NGC 6823. Magnitude: 10. Open cluster of 30 stars.

NGC 6830. Magnitude: 9. Open cluster of 20 stars.

NGC 6834. Magnitude: 11. Open cluster of 50 stars.

NGC 6885. Magnitude: 6. Open cluster of 35 stars.

NGC 6940. Magnitude: 9. Open cluster of 100 stars.

Appendix B

Binocular Accessories

In addition to binoculars, you might consider purchasing accessories for your night-sky viewing. Some recommendations follow.

TRIPODS

If you own binoculars over $11\times$ you would do well to own a tripod (Fig. B-1). You would need to be a patient gorilla to hold binoculars of $12\times$ to $20\times$. At $20\times$ the stars dance. Even with $10\times$ binoculars, I would recommend a tripod if you plan to split doubles or get a better view of the Moon along its terminator. 10×70s, and especially 11×80s, are not easy to hold steady for more than several minutes.

What might you look for in a tripod suitable for binocular astronomy? Weight for one. A tripod had better weigh at least 8 lbs. if it is not to be blown around in the wind. The more weight the better, yet you want to be able to transport it.

The tripod should have a pan head or binocular mount that is accessible to the zenith so you can look straight overhead without pressing your mouth to the tripod center post. Some video tripods have pan heads that swing out for viewing the zenith. You should keep in mind that most tripods are created for lighter cameras and for terrestrial use. Test the tripod in the store! Can you stand beneath it without getting whiplash? The tripod should stand from 54 inches to 70 inches tall.

Sturdy wooden legs are best for tripods because they will dampen vibrations faster than channel aluminum. If portability is a must, then go with aluminum.

Legs with snap locks had better be as rigid as possible. Keep joints and lock points to a minimum when you are choosing a metal tripod. The more joints, the more flexibility and the worse the dampening of vibration. Make certain your center post is well machined and that guide struts are there for added support.

When you are purchasing a tripod, inspect the movement of the pan head. It must be smooth and not jerky. Watch out on those normal ball-socket arrangements.

Tilt adjustments need to function smoothly with adequate, long, adjustment handles. Horizontal control should also have a substantial handle. A spring-loaded tilt axis is a must so your 80mm binoculars will not fall backward or forward. A pan movement lock must be provided on both sides of the tripod head.

Look for digging points on the base of each tripod leg for added stability. Many of today's heavy-duty video

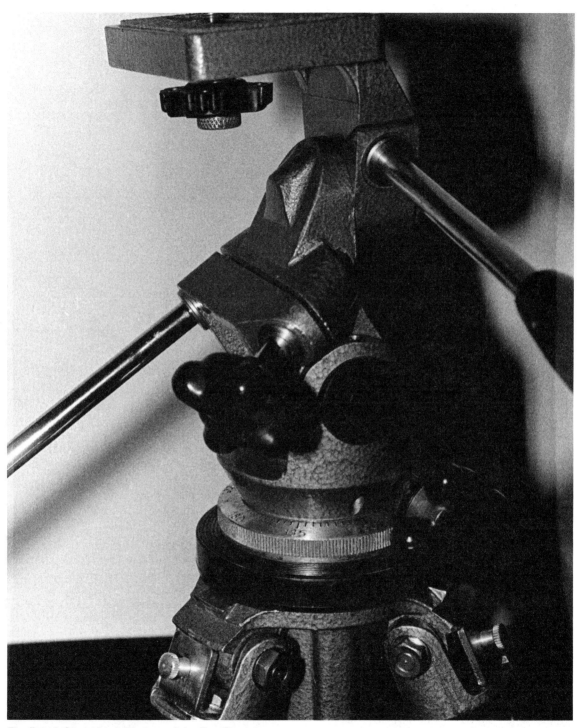

Fig. B-1. A Gitzo tripod (Photograph by Dan Stosuy).

Fig. B-2. Two tripod adapters—the smaller is the typical L adapter (Photograph by Dan Stosuy).

camera tripods work well with giant binoculars. Davis and Sanford, Bogen, Gitso, Slick, Cullmann, and Velbon make excellent tripods. You can find these brands at either your camera store or through astronomical retailers. Also you might want to check out used camera stores and the newspapers for some bargains.

Car window mounts, for binoculars used astronomically, are of little value if you wish to view the zenith.

Many 11 × 80 and 20 × 80 binoculars come supplied with an L piece tripod adapter with a knob for receiving 1/4 × 20 mounting bolts, the standard camera size (Fig. B-2). If your binoculars are not fitted with the L piece adapter, you might wish to purchase a center focus clamp for mounting purposes. Many camera stores carry them.

Tripod cases are more cosmetic than needed. Your tripod and pan head must be sturdy enough to handle travel.

BINOCULAR CASES

Binocular cases (Fig. B-3) are a must unless your instruments are of the rubber-armored variety and have lens covers. Go only for hard cases. Leather is best and it should be padded on the inside and moisture proofed on the outside. Mildew is the great bane of leather cases.

You might have to do the moisture-proofing yourself. Stay away from nylon and thin-walled vinyl because these materials will not properly support your instrument when you travel. One of those most frequent causes for loss of collimation in a pair of binoculars is that it was jarred while in a soft case.

NEBULA FILTERS

Nebula filters, sometimes called *LPRs*, make deep-sky observation of emission nebulae a bit more attainable from urban viewing areas. The nebula filters are generally two glass filters, overcoated with an ultrafine metallic film and threading into 11 × 80 and 20 × 80 binoculars after the eyecups have been unscrewed. These filters can also be purchased to be screwed into the eyepiece threads of regular telescope oculars. A telescope ocular would be used in the mammoth Dobsonian binoculars.

The majority of nebula filters, made for 11 × 80 and 20 × 80 binoculars, include eye shields fitted over the filter to block out ambient light. Nebula filters selectively screen out street lamp light to a degree that serves to enrich the contrast in the viewing image. The Great Orion Nebula, the Ring Nebula, and the Lagoon Nebula are all better seen with binoculars having nebula filters. However, I would recommend that if you own 80mm glasses, you only purchase nebula filters if your glass is 20 ×. Nebulosity is not as much appreciated at 11 ×. Nebula filters are useless on binoculars under 80mm because the smaller glasses do not gather enough light to afford any view.

Nebula filters make light-polluted skies appear darker by rejecting radiation from mercury vapor lamps and from both low- and high-pressure sodium lamps. The filters will also enhance observations in dark-sky locations by cutting down the natural sky glow or the light caused by the air's natural oxygen emissions. The filters transmit the important wavelengths of hydrogen alpha, hydrogen beta, doubly ionized oxygen, and singly ionized nitrogen.

Often these filters can assist the observer in viewing the nebulosity associated with some galactic clusters. The filters help little in observing galaxies, however. A few

amateurs maintain that the nebula filters can be an aid to viewing comets. It has been my experience that these filters will not do a great deal under severely light-polluted skies.

DEW SHIELDS

There are times when you will be out observing and the dew will be heavy. This is when your binocular objectives will mist over and you will require dew shields to continue. Forget about using a dew zapper or a hair dryer because they may fog your lenses permanently by frying the cement or cause the lenses to separate. Lens cement will not hold up under much heat. A simple dew shield can be constructed out of cardboard and held to the binoculars with rubber bands. Have the cardboard tubes extend no further than 3 or 4 inches past the objectives or you will cut off the field.

Fig. B-3. Binocular cases (Photograph by Caroline Meline).

Fig. B-4. A binocular viewer (the Stereoocular) on a Celestron 8-inch Schmidt-Cassegrain telescope (Courtesy Roger W. Tuthill).

FILTERS

Colored, neutral density, and polarizing filters are only useful for terrestrial views or for eyeballing a very bright Moon.

BINOCULAR VIEWERS

Binocular viewers (Fig. B-4) are made for regular monocular telescopes. They seem best adapted for refractors and catadioptric scopes, such as Maksutovs and Schmidt-Cassegrains, with at least 4-inch apertures. The viewers give highly pleasing and relaxing views, even though they cut brightness to each eye by 50 percent. The brain's in-

tegration of the images only recovers about 41 percent of the loss.

Some binocular viewers possess tube heads that rotate 360 degrees for more comfortable observing positions. Interpupilary distance is adjustable in several models and locks once set. The viewer requires two eyepieces of the same make and focal length. Several of these binocular viewers can be employed in reflectors. These particular models have removable Barlow lenses acting as transfer lenses. The Barlows also help to boost the telescope's magnification. Sometimes the dual eyepiece wonder is called a Stereoocular.

Appendix C

The Messier Catalog

A catalog of 109 deep-sky objects such as galaxies, nebulae, globular clusters, and open star clusters was compiled by the French astronomer and comet hunter Charles Messier over a 24-year span, from 1758 to 1782. Messier prepared his list so that he would avoid confusing deep-sky objects with his true love, comets. Messier catalogued 109 celestial subjects appearing blurry and extended in telescopes, by giving them a number preceded by an M; for example, M31, or the Great Andromeda galaxy. Employing a 3 1/2-inch refracter, Messier catalogued the Crab Nebula as his first entry, or M1.

Messier Number	Constellation	Type	Season Best Observed
M1	Taurus	Supernova Remnant	Autumn
M2	Aquarius	Globular Cluster	Autumn
M3	Canes Venatici	Globular Cluster	Summer
M4	Scorpius	Globular Cluster	Summer
M5	Serpens	Globular Cluster	Summer
M6	Scorpius	Open Cluster	Summer
M7	Scorpius	Open Cluster	Summer
M8	Sagittarius	Diffuse Nebula	Summer
M9	Ophiuchus	Globular Cluster	Summer
M10	Ophiuchus	Globular Cluster	Summer
M11	Scutum	Open Cluster	Summer
M12	Ophiuchus	Globular Cluster	Summer

Messier Number	Constellation	Type	Season Best Observed
M13	Hercules	Globular Cluster	Summer
M14	Ophiuchus	Globular Cluster	Summer
M15	Pegasus	Globular Cluster	Autumn
M16	Serpens	Nebula and Open Cluster	Summer
M17	Sagittarius	Nebula and Open Cluster	Summer
M18	Sagittarius	Open Cluster	Summer
M19	Ophiuchus	Globular Cluster	Summer
M20	Sagittarius	Diffuse Nebula	Summer
M21	Sagittarius	Open Cluster	Summer
M22	Sagittarius	Globular Cluster	Summer
M23	Sagittarius	Open Cluster	Summer
M24	Sagittarius	Milky Way Patch	Summer
M25	Sagittarius	Open Cluster	Summer
M26	Scutum	Open Cluster	Summer
M27	Vulpecula	Planetary Nebula	Autumn
M28	Sagittarius	Globular Cluster	Summer
M29	Cygnus	Open Cluster	Autumn
M30	Capricornus	Globular Cluster	Autumn
M31	Andromeda	Galaxy	Autumn
M32	Andromeda	Galaxy	Autumn
M33	Triangulum	Galaxy	Autumn
M34	Perseus	Open Cluster	Winter
M35	Gemini	Open Cluster	Winter
M36	Auriga	Open Cluster	Winter
M37	Auriga	Open Cluster	Winter
M38	Auriga	Open Cluster	Winter
M39	Cygnus	Open Cluster	Autumn
M40	Ursa Major	Double Star	Winter
M41	Canis Major	Open Cluster	Winter
M42	Orion	Diffuse Nebula	Winter
M43	Orion	Diffuse Nebula	Winter
M44	Cancer	Open Cluster	Spring
M45	Taurus	Open Cluster	Winter
M46	Puppis	Open Cluster	Winter
M47	Puppis	Open Cluster	Winter
M48	Hydra	Open Cluster	Spring
M49	Virgo	Galaxy	Spring
M50	Monoceros	Open Cluster	Winter
M51	Canes Venatici	Galaxy	Spring
M52	Cassiopeia	Open Cluster	Autumn
M53	Coma Berenices	Globular Cluster	Spring
M54	Sagittarius	Globular Cluster	Summer
M55	Sagittarius	Globular Cluster	Summer
M56	Lyra	Globular Cluster	Summer
M57	Lyra	Planetary Nebula	Summer
M58	Virgo	Galaxy	Spring
M59	Virgo	Galaxy	Spring

Messier Number	Constellation	Type	Season Best Observed
M60	Virgo	Galaxy	Spring
M61	Virgo	Galaxy	Spring
M62	Ophiuchus	Globular Cluster	Summer
M63	Canes Venatici	Galaxy	Spring
M64	Coma Berenices	Galaxy	Spring
M65	Leo	Galaxy	Spring
M66	Leo	Galaxy	Spring
M67	Cancer	Open Cluster	Spring
M68	Hydra	Globular Cluster	Spring
M69	Sagittarius	Globular Cluster	Summer
M70	Sagittarius	Globular Cluster	Summer
M71	Sagitta	Globular Cluster	Autumn
M72	Aquarius	Globular Cluster	Autumn
M73	Aquarius	Asterism	Autumn
M74	Pisces	Galaxy	Autumn
M75	Sagittarius	Globular Cluster	Summer
M76	Perseus	Planetary Nebula	Winter
M77	Cetus	Galaxy	Winter
M78	Orion	Diffuse Nebula	Winter
M79	Lepus	Globular Cluster	Winter
M80	Scorpius	Globular Cluster	Summer
M81	Ursa Major	Galaxy	Spring
M82	Ursa Major	Galaxy	Spring
M83	Hydra	Galaxy	Spring
M84	Virgo	Galaxy	Spring
M85	Coma Berenices	Galaxy	Spring
M86	Virgo	Galaxy	Spring
M87	Virgo	Galaxy	Spring
M88	Coma Berenices	Galaxy	Spring
M89	Virgo	Galaxy	Spring
M90	Virgo	Galaxy	Spring
M91	Coma Berenices	Galaxy	Spring
M92	Hercules	Globular Cluster	Summer
M93	Puppis	Open Cluster	Autumn
M94	Canes Venatici	Galaxy	Spring
M95	Leo	Galaxy	Spring
M96	Leo	Galaxy	Spring
M97	Ursa Major	Planetary Nebula	Spring
M98	Coma Berenices	Galaxy	Spring
M99	Coma Berenices	Galaxy	Spring
M100	Coma Berenices	Galaxy	Spring
M101	Ursa Major	Galaxy	Spring
M102	Draco	Galaxy	Spring
M103	Cassiopeia	Open Cluster	Autumn
M104	Virgo	Galaxy	Spring
M105	Leo	Galaxy	Spring
M106	Canes Venatici	Galaxy	Spring

Messier Number	Constellation	Type	Season Best Observed
M107	Ophiuchus	Globular Cluster	Summer
M108	Ursa Major	Galaxy	Spring
M109	Ursa Major	Galaxy	Spring
M110	Andromeda	Galaxy	Autumn

Appendix D

Converting to Universal Time

Universal Time or Greenwich Meridian Time is the standard for world time. Highly useful in astronomical record keeping, U.T. does away with time zones and differences in time between observers located around the globe. U.T. is the same everywhere and is measured in 24 hours from midnight to midnight. At midnight on the Greenwich meridian, U.T. is 00 hours 00 minutes, or the start of a new day. The following will help you find the correct U.T. in the United States of America.

Eastern Standard	Central Standard	Mountain Standard	Pacific Standard	Universal Time
2:00 A.M.	1:00 A.M.	12:00 A.M.	11:00 P.M.	07:00
3:00 A.M.	2:00 A.M.	1:00 A.M.	12:00 A.M.	08:00
4:00 A.M.	3:00 A.M.	2:00 A.M.	1:00 A.M.	09:00
5:00 A.M.	4:00 A.M.	3:00 A.M.	2:00 A.M.	10:00
6:00 A.M.	5:00 A.M.	4:00 A.M.	3:00 A.M.	11:00
7:00 A.M.	6:00 A.M.	5:00 A.M.	4:00 A.M.	12:00
8:00 A.M.	7:00 A.M.	6:00 A.M.	5:00 A.M.	13:00
9:00 A.M.	8:00 A.M.	7:00 A.M.	6:00 A.M.	14:00
10:00 A.M.	9:00 A.M.	8:00 A.M.	7:00 A.M.	15:00
11:00 A.M.	10:00 A.M.	9:00 A.M.	8:00 A.M.	16:00
12:00 Noon	11:00 A.M.	10:00 A.M.	9:00 A.M.	17:00
1:00 P.M.	12:00 Noon	11:00 A.M.	10:00 A.M.	18:00
2:00 P.M.	1:00 P.M.	12:00 Noon	11:00 A.M.	19:00
3:00 P.M.	2:00 P.M.	1:00 P.M.	12:00 Noon	20:00
4:00 P.M.	3:00 P.M.	2:00 P.M.	1:00 P.M.	21:00
5:00 P.M.	4:00 P.M.	3:00 P.M.	2:00 P.M.	22:00

Eastern Standard	Central Standard	Mountain Standard	Pacific Standard	Universal Time
6:00 P.M.	5:00 P.M.	4:00 P.M.	3:00 P.M.	23:00
7:00 P.M.	6:00 P.M.	5:00 P.M.	4:00 P.M.	24:00
8:00 P.M.	7:00 P.M.	6:00 P.M.	5:00 P.M.	01:00
9:00 P.M.	8:00 P.M.	7:00 P.M.	6:00 P.M.	02:00
10:00 P.M.	9:00 P.M.	8:00 P.M.	7:00 P.M.	03:00
11:00 P.M.	10:00 P.M.	9:00 P.M.	8:00 P.M.	04:00
12:00	11:00 P.M.	10:00 P.M.	9:00 P.M.	05:00
1:00 A.M.	12:00	11:00 P.M.	10:00 P.M.	06:00

For Daylight Saving Time add 1 hour to Standard time, but U.T. remains the same.

Appendix E

Manufacturers and Importers of Astronomical Binoculars

Bushnell
Division of Bausch & Lomb
2828 E. Foothill Blvd.
Pasadena, CA 91107

Celestron International
P.O. Box 3578
2835 Columbia St.
Torrance, CA 90503

Fujinon Inc.
672 White Plains Rd.
Scarsdale, NY 10583

A. Jaegers
691 Merrick Rd.
P.O. Box G
Lynbrook, NY 11563

Jason/Empire, Inc.
9200 Cody
Overland Park, KS 66214

Kowa Company, Ltd.
Electronics & Optics Division
No. 3,3-chome, Nihonbashi-Honcho, Chuo-ku
Tokyo 103, Japan

Lumicon
2111 Research Dr. #5
Livermore, CA 94550

Meade Instruments Corporation
1675 Toronto Way
Costa Mesa, CA 92626

Milco
Division of I. Miller
35 N. 2nd St.
Philadelphia, PA 19106

Nikon Inc.
623 Stewart Ave.
Garden City, NY 11530

Orion Telescope Center
P.O. Box 1158
Santa Cruz, CA 95061

Parks Optical
270 Easy St.
Simi Valley, CA 93065

Pentax Corporation
35 Inverness Dr. East
Englewood, CO 80112

R.V.R. Optical
P.O. Box 62
Eastchester, NY 10709

Star Flite Instrument Co.
118 Bay 19 St.
Brooklyn, NY 11214

Sky Instruments
P.O. Box F195-105
Blaine,WA 98230

Steiner
Pioneer & Co.
216 Haddon Ave.
Westmont, NJ 08108

Swarovski Optik
Division of Swarovski America Limited
Cranston, RI 02920

Swift Instruments Inc.
925 Dorchest Ave.
Boston, MA 02125

Tasco
P.O. Box 523735
Miami, FL 33152

Roger W. Tuthill, Inc.
11 Tanglewood Lane
Mountainside, NJ 07092

University Optics, Inc.
P.O. Box 1205
2122 East Delhi Rd.
Ann Arbor, MI 48106

Zeiss Optical, Inc.
P.O. Box 2010
Petersburg, VA 23804

Appendix F

Retailers and Mail-Order Houses

RETAILERS: BINOCULARS

Aardvark Optical Company, Inc.
5 Wharf St.
P.O. Box S-11
Portland, ME 04101

Ad-Libs Astronomics
2401 Tee Circle
Suite 106
Norman, OK 73069

Advance Camera
15 West 46th St.
New York, NY 10036

Astro World
5126 Belair Rd.
Baltimore, MD 21206

Berger Bros.
209 Broadway
Amityville, NY 11701

Birding
P.O. Box 5
Amsterdam, NY 12010

California Telescope Company
P.O. Box 1338
Burbank, CA 91507

Cambridge Camera Exchange
7th Ave. and 13th St.
New York, NY 10011

Company Seven
Astro-Optics Division
12002 Dove Circle
Montpelier, MD 20708

Edmund Scientific
101 E. Gloucester Pike
Barrington, NJ 08007

Executive Photo & Supply Corp.
120 W. 31st St.
New York, NY 10001

Garden Camera
135 W. 29th St.
New York, NY 10001

Edwin Hirsh
168 Lakeview Rd.
Tomkins Cove, NY 10986

Lumicon
2111 Research Dr.
Livermore, CA 94550

I. Miller
35 N. 2nd St.
Philadelphia, PA 19106

Mirakel Optical Co., Inc.
331 Mansion St.
West Coxsackie, NY 12192

New England Astro-Optics, Inc.
P.O. Box 834
Simsbury, CT 06070

New York Camera
131 W. 35th St.
New York, NY 10001

Optica b/c Company
Sales/Service Division
4100 MacArthur Blvd.
Oakland, CA 94619

Orion Telescope Center
P.O. Box 1158
Santa Cruz, CA 95061

Pauli's Optical
29 Kingswood Rd.
Danbury, CT 06811

Photo Cine
129 S. 18th
Philadelphia, PA 19103

Quasar Optics
7719 Fleetwood Dr. S.E.
Calgary, Alberta T2H 0X2
Canada

R.V.R. Optical
P.O. Box 62
Eastchester, NY 10709

Scope City
679 Easy St.
Simi Valley, CA 93065

Sierra Peak Observatory and Planetarium
Black Star Canyon Rd.
P.O. Box 402
Atwood, CA 92601

Star Flite Instrument Co.
118 Bay 19 St.
Brooklyn, NY 11214

Startracker
3093 Walnut
Boulder, CO 80301

TBR Optisystems
850 Hudson Ave.
P.O. Box 17129
Rochester, NY 14617

Texas Nautical Repair Co.
3209 Milam
Houston, TX 77006

Roger W. Tuthill, Inc.
11 Tanglewood Lane
Dept. S
Mountainside, NJ 07092

MAIL-ORDER HOUSES:
ATLASES AND ASTRONOMY BOOKS

Herbert A. Luft
69-11 229th St.
P.O. Box 91
Oakland Gardens, NY 11364

Sky Publishing Corporation
49 Bay State Rd.
Cambridge, MA 02238

Willmann—Bell, Inc.
P.O. Box 3125
Richmond, VA 23235

Appendix G

Recommended Binoculars for Astronomy

BAUSCH & LOMB

7 × 50 Discover Standard
10 × 50 Discoverer Standard
7 × 50 Discover Standard Armored Fogproof/ Waterproof

Binolux

7 × 50 CF AT WA.

BUSHNELL

7 × 50 Explorer II
10 × 50 Explorer II
7 × 50 Banner Standard
10 × 50 Banner Standard
7 × 50 Banner Armored Fogproof/Waterproof
7 × 50 Sportview
10 × 50 Sportview
7 × 50 Sportview Camo Armored
10 × 50 Camo Armored

CELESTRON

11 × 80 Giant
20 × 80 Giant

20 × 80 Deluxe
7 × 50 Wide-Angle Nova
10 × 50 High-Power Nova
7 × 50 Waterproof
10 × 50 Waterproof
7 × 50 R Rubberized Classical
7 × 50 Extra Wide Field Classical
10 × 50 Extra Wide Field Classical

FUJINON

25 × 150 Super Giant Right Angle
7 × 50 MT
7 × 50 MTR Rubber Coated
15 × 80 MT
10 × 70 MT
14 × 70 MT

JAEGERS

7 × 50 Dr 1503
7 × 50 Dr 3691
7 × 50 Dr 3223

JASON/EMPIRE

7 × 50 151F Statesman

7 × 50 189F Statesman
10 × 50 191 Statesman
7 × 50 136F Commander
10 × 50 161F Commander
7 × 50 214F
10 × 50 221F
7 × 50 242
10 × 50 243
10 × 50 263
7 × 50 262

KOWA

20 × 80 BL-8A2
20 × 120 BL-12A4
20 × 80 BL-8D
20 × 120 BL-12C5
35 × 150 BL-15D

LUMICON

44 × 250 10″ Cainian Reflecting Binocular

MEADE

11 × 80 Giant Binocular

MILCO

7 × 50 Deluxe

MIRADOR

7 × 50 GNC
10 × 50 GNC

NIKON

15 × 80
20 × 120
10 × 70 IF
7 × 50 Astronomical
7 × 50
7 × 50 rubber coated

ORION

10 × 70
11 × 80

PARKS

11 × 80
15 × 80

20 × 80

PENTAX

7 × 50 ZCF
12 × 50 ZCF
7 × 50 BIF

SKY

10 × 70 ZCF
11 × 80 ZCF

STEINER

15 × 80 Waterproof-armored
7 × 50G
10 × 50G
7 × 50P

SWAROVSKI

10 × 50SL
7 × 50SL
8 × 56SL

SWIFT

7 × 50 Storm King
7 × 50 Armored Storm King
7 × 50 Commodore
10 × 50 Ranger
7 × 50 Armored Sea Hawk
7 × 50 Skipper
7 × 50 Armored Swift Focus
11 × 80 Observer
20 × 80 Satellite

TASCO

10 × 50 450Z
7 × 50 425Z
8 × 56 445BRZ
8 × 56 445Z
7 × 50 328MR
7 × 50 328MW
7 × 50 331R
8 × 56 445BRZ
7 × 50 222RZ
8 × 56 334BCRZ
8 × 56 445CRZ
10 × 50 223CRZ
7 × 50 222CRZ

7×50 222RZLE
10×50 223RZLE
8×56 390RLE
8×56 390BRE
10×50 223Z

TUTHILL

11×80
20×80

UNIVERSITY

11×80
20×80

ZEISS

7×50 B/GA
8×56 B/GA

Appendix H

Drawing the Night Sky

You don't really need an astrographic camera to capture the wonders of the night sky. A pencil or pen will do fine. And you don't require an expensive guiding system because you've come equipped with the best guiding system of them all—your brain and eyes. Comets, open clusters, galaxies, the Moon, nebulae, planetary conjunctions, starfields, and the Sun can all be rendered by sketching what you see through binoculars.

Even if you don't believe you have much artistic ability, you would be surprised at what you are capable of doing with a little pluck and practice. Most deep-sky objects are simple enough affairs (Fig. H-1). Just about anyone can create a glowing smear—even I who must struggle with drawing a straight line.

Before you take your crack at night-sky "art," I'd recommend that you check out the pencil renderings that appear in *Deep Sky* and *Astronomy* magazines. You might also wish to see the drawings in the *Webb Society's Deep-sky Observer's Handbooks* and in Mallas and Kreimer's *The Messier Album*. In these books and magazines you will see outstanding technique in action.

If you are just starting out in drawing the night sky, I would advise you to choose less complex objects that are relatively bright, perhaps M31 in Andromeda or the Pleiades Cluster (M45) in Taurus. Pick a dark, moonless night (you're best off away from urban light pollution) and make certain your eyes are dark-adapted. Give yourself about 20 to 30 minutes of getting aquainted with the night sky before you begin your drawings.

Basic tools follow. You'll need some white lead pencils (light and dark). Stay away from white charcoal, graphite, and wax-based pencils. A blending stump is highly useful in hazing out rough shapes into differing gradations of brightness. Consider purchasing black mat board and cutting it into 5- x -6-inch rectangles or 6-inch diameter circles. The circles will provide you with a binocular eyepiece orientation and help give you a better notion of the field. A large, soft eraser will be of value when you run up against the inevitable errors that befall a midnight artist. A small paintbrush is useful for removing eraser crumbs. Matte-finish spray fixer will seal and protect your sketch, but if you use the fixer, make sure to render your drawings a tad brighter to compensate for the fixer's darkening powers. A small portable table and a dim red light are final musts.

For best results I would recommend that you mount your binoculars so you will keep your object in the field when you turn away to sketch. Drift is minimal in 25 × and under binoculars. If you possess an instrument designed by Lee Cain, so much the better. Giant and mam-

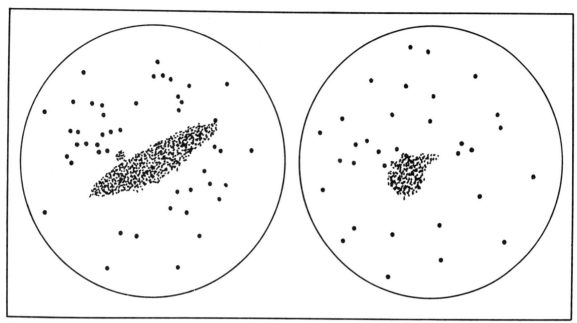

Fig. H-1. Sketches of deep-sky objects: a galaxy (left) and a planetary nebula (right).

moth binoculars will give you fantastic images. Lee Cain has been able to sketch entire fields of galaxies with his 17 1/2 incher.

Take your time and work carefully. It's best to study your object before you put down its brightest stars. Begin with the outer stars then work inward toward the sketch's center. Work lightly at first so you can correct errors. Now add fainter stars. Don't make your stars too large, rather make them points of light. Brighter stars may be slightly larger.

Make a rough sketch of the central object. Shape with your pencil. Observe knots and streaks. If nebulosity is present, smear the object with your finger immediately after it is drawn. Make certain of your position measurements.

When you are starting a drawing note the contrast. Which portions appear brighter? Central and extended areas? Is the alteration in texture gradual or abrupt? Does density alter? Is there any glow? These last few questions apply to galaxies and nebulae. Get a strong mental picture of the starfield and the object's angular size.

Not only can sketching be fun, but it will increase your powers of observation. Employ averted vision on the dim extended objects like galaxies and nebulae. Don't expect perfection. Like any skill, drawing must be learned over time. Count on making mistakes. Later when you're more experienced you can try your hand at white ink. Good luck!

Glossary

aberration—The distortion of a star image by poor optics or bad optical alignment. The star will often fail to be focused down to a point and will appear flared.

absolute magnitude—A standard used to compare the actual luminosity of a star to other stars or celestial bodies.

achromatic lens—A dual-element lens system, often seen in refractor telescopes and binoculars, having a combination of flint and crown elements to cut down chromatic aberration or color fringing.

albedo—The ratio of light received to light reflected.

amplitude—The entire range in magnitude, from minimum to maximum, of light in a celestial body.

aperture—The clear diameter of the objective lens or the primary mirror in a telescope. The larger the aperture, the more light that can be gathered, and generally, the better resolution that can be produced.

aphelion—The point in an orbit when a planet or comet is farthest from the Sun.

asterism—A pattern of stars that may or may not be part of a constellation.

asteroid—A minor planet; neither a major planet nor a moon of a major planet.

astronomical unit—The average distance from the Sun to the Earth; 92,900,000 miles. Abbreviated A.U.

Baily's beads—A phenomenon occurring at the start or conclusion of a total solar eclipse in which the Sun's light shines through the mountains and valleys on the lunar limb or edge.

binary star—Two or more stars that share and orbit the same center of gravity.

black hole—A region having such densely packed mass and, therefore, such great gravitational forces that light can not escape.

bolide—A fireball; a very bright and large meteor.

celestial equator—The great circle in which the extension of our planet's equatorial plane is projected against the celestial sphere.

center focus—The focusing mechanism that appears as a finger wheel between the two barrels of a pair of binoculars.

chromatic aberration—A problem often found in optical systems employing lenses in which light of varying wavelengths fails to be focused at the same distance from the objective lens, resulting in a purple halo or fringe around bright stars or planets.

collimation—In binoculars, the centering of the final image as combined by both eyepieces. In well-colimated binoculars, the images of both eyepieces should appear as a singular image.

coma—A comet's nucleus and surrounding gas cloud. Also an aberration found in short-focus telescopes and binoculars where the star images at the field's edge appear elongated and cometlike.

corona—The Sun's outermost layer, which can be seen as a bright extended halo during an eclipse.

earthshine—Reflected sunlight from the Earth that lights the Moon.

eclipse, lunar—The passage of the Moon into the Earth's shadow.

eclipse, solar—The passage of the Moon's shadow across the Earth.

ecliptic—The Sun's apparent path across our sky during the year. The Moon and planets closely follow this same path.

elongation—Angular distance in longitude (celestial) from the Sun in the sky.

ephemeris—A table listing a solar-system body's orbital elements for a given time, which may be based on magnitude, position on the celestial sphere, or the distance from the Earth or Sun.

Erfle eyepiece—A wide-field eyepiece used in many extra wide field binoculars. The Erfle might possess from five to eight lens elements.

exit pupil—Sometimes called the Ramsden disk or circle, the light disk formed on the eye side of the eyepiece.

field of view—The width, in feet, of viewing area you can see at a distance of 1,000 yards.

fireball—A bolide; a very bright and large meteor.

focal length—The distance between the binocular objective lens and the eyepiece where the light rays converge at a focus.

galaxy—A huge collection of stars, gas, and dust, such as our Milky Way and M31 in Andromeda.

galactic cluster—An open cluster or an irregular star grouping with a common and likely recent origin.

gibbous—Of or relating to a lunar or planetary phase where more than half of the side visible to Earth is illuminated.

globular cluster—Stars grouped in a tight sphere of common origin. Stars in globulars are generally old.

Greenwich Mean Time (GMT)—The standard for time throughout the world, often called universal time; the mean solar time in the time zone centered on the Greenwich meridian or the meridian of 0 degrees longitude passing through Greenwich, England.

individual focus—A binocular focus adjusted for each eye at the eyepiece and used to provide a sturdier construction and moisture-proof conditions within the binoculars.

inferior conjunction—A conjunction in which a planet with an orbit inside the Earth's orbit passes between the Earth and the Sun.

inferior planet—A planet with an orbit inside the Earth's orbit; Mercury and Venus.

Julian day—The number of days since noon on January 1, 4713.

Kellner eyepiece—An ocular, invented by Karl Kellner, having an overcorrected lens pair with its flint component facing the eye. The most common binocular eyepiece.

limb—The edge of the Moon, Sun, or a planet as seen from Earth.

limiting magnitude—A binocular's threshold for discerning a faint star.

luminosity—The absolute brightness of a star, equal to the total energy radiated per second from the star.

magnification—The power of binoculars; the number of times an object appears larger in binoculars.

magnitude, absolute and apparent—The scale of a star's or a celestial body's real (absolute) or apparent brightness. A logarithmic classification of brightness where each change of five magnitudes equals a change by a factor of 100.

maria—The so-called lunar seas; lunar expanses of basaltic lava possessing low albedo.

meridian—The great circle on the Earth's surface at right angles to the equator and passing through the poles.

Messier catalog—A catalog of deep-sky objects such as galaxies, globular and open clusters, and nebulae gathered by Charles Messier in order to avoid confusion in his hunt for comets back in the 1780s.

meteor—A particle entering our atmosphere and creating a streak of light.

meteorite—Any interplanetary debris on the Earth's surface.

neutron stars—A star that has collapsed from extreme gravitation to such a degree that its material has compressed into neutrons.

nova—A star that abruptly increases in brightness and may often become visible for the first time.

objective—The primary mirror or lens of a telescope; one of such in a pair of binoculars. It is this lens or mirror element that gathers the light.

occultation—The passing of a celestial body such as an asteroid, the Moon, or a planet in front of a more remote celestial body such as a star or a solar-system object.

opposition—A situation in which the Moon or a planet is opposite the Sun as viewed from Earth.

orbit—A celestial body's path through space.

penumbra—The halo surrounding a sunspot. It is less bright than the umbra and is often streaked with radiating lines.

perihelion—That point in a solar-system object's orbit when it is closest to the Sun.

perturbation—A nearby mass's gravitational influence on a celestial body that causes the body to alter its orbit.

phase—The area of a solar-system body that is seen illuminated.

photosphere—The Sun's visible surface.

Purkinje effect—The eye's ability to be sensitive to red light after being exposed to it for a short period. A problem for variable star observers, this effect often makes observers record red stars as brighter than others when they actually are not.

quasar—A highly compact object that emits more energy than 100 supergiant galaxies. These quasi-stellar objects are said to be the farthest celestial objects yet known.

radiant—The sky area where meteor showers seem to originate.

red giant—A giant star that has a diameter some 10 to 100 times larger than our Sun. It is much cooler than our Sun and is said to be in its final evolutionary stage.

reflector—A telescope possessing a primary mirror and a secondary mirror, which is smaller and diverts the incoming light from the primary to an eyepiece.

refractor—A telescope having a lens for an objective. Binoculars are a pair of small refractors hinged together.

resolution—The ability of optics to help us discern ultrafine detail; defined by the smallest angle between two points (such as stars) yielding two images clearly not in union.

retrograde motion—The apparent westward motion of a planet or an asteroid when the Earth swings between it and the Sun.

seeing—The steadiness of our atmosphere when viewing celestial objects, said to be caused by convective cells in the Earth's atmosphere.

shower—A group of meteors that enter the Earth's atmosphere in succession and can be tracked back to the same radiant or point of origin.

sidereal time—A time system based on the Earth's true rotation; relative to a fixed point, 23 hours and 56 minutes.

sky glow—The sky lit from reflected artificial night lighting. It is reflected by dust, water vapor, and pollution in the atmosphere.

solstices—Two points on the ecliptic farthest from the celestial equator. The Sun passes these points at midwinter and midsummer.

sunspot—A dark-appearing region on the Sun's photosphere that is made up of the umbra and penumbra, often occurs in groups, is the center of intense magnetic activity, and is somewhat cooler than the rest of the solar photosphere.

supernova—A star that brightens rapidly to an absolute magnitude of over −15, or above 100 times the brightness increase of a nova. It is quite rare.

terminator—The dividing line between the dark and illuminated portions of a moon or planet.

train—The light streak or remaining tail in a meteor's wake.

transit—The passage of an inferior planet across the Sun; the passage of a planetary moon or its shadow across the face of a planet.

umbra—The dark inner part of a sunspot. It is somewhere around 4000 ° C cooler than the Sun's photosphere.

variable star—A star with apparent luminosity or brightness changes over a period of time.

waning—Of or relating to the lunar phase after full or prior to new, when the eastern quarter is illuminated.

waxing—Of or relating to the lunar phase prior to full or after new, when the western quarter is illuminated.

zenith—The point straight overhead that is intersected by the meridian.

zodiac—The 12 constellations through which the Moon, planets, and Sun pass during the year.

References and Recommended Reading

Abell, G.O. *Exploration of the Universe.* Philadelphia: Saunders College Publishing, 1982.

Abetti, G. *The Sun.* London: Faber and Faber, 1955.

Aitken, R.G. *The Binary Stars.* New York: McGraw-Hill, 1935.

Alexander, A.F. O'D *The Planet Saturn.* London: Faber and Faber, 1962.

_____. *The Planet Uranus.* London: Faber and Faber, 1965.

Alter, D. *Pictorial Guide to the Moon.* New York: Crowell, 1979.

Antoniadi, E.M. *The Planet Mercury.* London: Reid, 1974.

Batten, A.H. *Binary and Multiple Star Systems.* Oxford: Pergamon, 1973.

Baxter, W.M. *The Sun and the Amateur Astronomer.* London: Lutterworth, 1963.

Becvar, A. *Skalnate Pleso Atlas of the Heavens.* Cambridge, Mass.: Sky Publishing, 1979.

Bell, Louis. *The Telescope.* New York: Dover, 1981.

Benton, J.L. *The Saturn Handbook.* Savannah: Review, 1975.

Billings, C.M. *History of the Rittenhouse Astronomical Society.* Philadelphia: Rittenhouse Astronomical Society, 1960.

Brandt, J.C., and Chapman, C.R. *Introduction to Comets.* London: Cambridge University Press, 1981.

Bray, R.J., and Loughhead, R.E. *Sunspots.* New York: Dover, 1964.

British Astronomical Association. *Handbook of the British Astronomical Association.* London: British Astronomical Association, 1984.

Brown, S. *All About Telescopes.* Barrington, N.J.: Edmund Scientific, 1981.

Burnham, R. *Burnham's Celestial Handbook.* 3 vols. New York: Dover, 1978.

Cherrington, E.H. *Exploring the Moon through Binoculars and Small Telescopes.* New York: Dover, 1984.

Couteau, P. *Observing Double Stars.* Cambridge, Mass.: MIT Press, 1981.

Dickinson, T.; Costanzo, V.; and Chaple, G.F. *The Edmund Mag 6 Star Atlas.* Barrington, N.J.: Edmund Scientific, 1982.

Firsoff, V.A. *The Solar Planets.* New York: Crane-Russak, 1977.

Gatland, K. *Illustrated Encyclopaedia of Space Technology.* London: Salamander, 1980.

Gehrels, T., ed. *Jupiter.* Tucson: Arizona, 1976.

Glasby, J.S. *The Variable Star Observer's Handbook.* New York: Norton, 1971.

_____. *Variable Stars.* London: Constable, 1968.

Hartmann, W.K. *Astronomy: The Cosmic Journey*. Belmont, Cal.: Wadsworth, 1978.

————. *Moons and Planets*. New York: Bogden and Quigly, 1972.

Hawkins, G.S. *Meteors, Comets, and Meteorites*. New York: McGraw-Hill, 1964.

Howard, N.E. *The Telescope Handbook and Star Atlas*. New York: Crowell, 1975.

Johnson, B.K. *Optics and Optical Instruments*. New York: Dover, 1960.

Jones, G.K., ed. *Webb Society Deep-Sky Observer's Handbook*. Vol. 2-4. Hillside, N.J.: Enslow, 1981.

King, H.C. *The History of the Telescope*. New York: Dover, 1979.

King-Hele, D. *Observing Earth Satellites*. New York: Van Nostrand Reinhold, 1983.

Kuiper, G.P., ed. *The Sun*. Cambridge, Mass.: Harvard University Press, 1959.

Maag, R.C.; Sherlin, J.M.; and Van Zandt, R.P. *Observe and Understand the Sun*. Washington, D.C.: Astronomical League, 1979.

Mallas, J.H., and Kreimer, E. *The Messier Album*. Cambridge, Mass.: Sky Publishing, 1978.

Mayall, M.W. *Manual for Observing Variable Stars*. Cambridge, Mass.: American Association of Variable Star Observers, 1970.

Menzel, D.H., and Pasachoff, J.M. *A Field Guide to the Stars and Planets*. Boston: Houghton Mifflin, 1983.

Middlehurst, B.M., and Kuiper, G.P. *The Moon, Meteorites and Comets*. Chicago: University of Chicago Press, 1963.

Miles, S.H. *Artificial Satellite Observing*. London: Faber and Faber, 1974.

Moore, P.A. *A Guide to Mars*. New York: Macmillan, 1956.

————. *A New Guide to the Moon*. New York: Norton, 1977.

————. *A New Guide to the Planets*. New York: Norton, 1972.

————. *Atlas of the Solar System*. Chicago: Rand McNally, 1983.

————. *Comets*. New York: Scribners, 1976.

Muirden, J. *The Amateur Astronomer's Handbook*. New York: Harper & Row, 1983.

Mullaney, J. *Binoculars*. Barrington, N.J.: Edmund Scientific, 1979.

Naval Personnel, Bureau of. *Optics and Optical Instruments*. New York: Dover, 1969.

Newton, J., and Teece, P. *The Cambridge Deep-Sky Album*. Cambridge, Mass.: Cambridge University Press, 1983.

Noyes, R.W. *The Sun, Our Star*. Cambridge, Mass.: Harvard University Press, 1982.

Pasachoff, J.M. *Contemporary Astronomy*. Philadelphia: Saunders College Publishing, 1981.

Paul, H.E. *Binoculars and All Purpose Telescopes*. New York: Amphoto, 1980.

————. *Outer Space Photography*. New York: Amphoto, 1976.

Peek, B.M. *The Planet Jupiter*. London: Faber and Faber, 1958.

Rackham, T.W. *Astronomical Photography at the Telescope*. London: Faber and Faber, 1972.

Roth, G.D., ed. *Astronomy: A Handbook*. Cambridge, Mass.: Sky Publishing, 1975.

Roth, G.D. *The System of Minor Planets*. London: Faber and Faber, 1963.

Satterthwaite, G.E.; Moore, P.A.; and Inglis, R.G., eds. *Norton's Star Atlas & Reference Handbook*. Cambridge, Mass.: Sky Publishing, 1978.

Schwarzschild, M. *Structure and Evolution of the Stars*. Princeton: Princeton, 1958.

Scovil, C.E., ed. *A.A.V.S.O. Variable Star Atlas*. Cambridge, Mass.: Sky Publishing, 1980.

Sears, D.W. *The Nature and Origin of Meteorites*. London: Oxford, 1978.

Shapley, H. *Galaxies*. Cambridge, Mass.: Harvard University Press, 1961.

————. *Star Clusters*. Cambridge: Harvard University Press, 1930.

Sherrod, P.C. *A Complete Manual of Amateur Astronomy*. Englewood Cliffs, N.J.: Spectrum, 1981.

Sidgwick, J.B. *Amateur Astronomer's Handbook*. London: Faber and Faber, 1958.

————. *Observational Astronomy for Amateurs*. New York: Dover, 1980.

Tirion, W. *Sky Atlas 2000.0*. Cambridge, Mass.: Sky Publishing, 1980.

Turnhill, R. *The Observer's Spaceflight Directory*. London: Warne, 1978.

Index

Edited by Suzanne L. Cheatle